The Straight Scoop

An Expert Guide to Great Community Journalism

By the Staff of
The Hartford Courant

Edited by
Bruce DeSilva
and John Mura

The Hartford Courant
Hartford, Connecticut
1996

BOOK STAFF

Bruce DeSilva
John Mura
Editors

Bill Healy
Copy Editor

Scott Johnson
Designer

Susan Acker
Marketing Manager

THE COURANT

Michael E. Waller
Publisher

David S. Barrett
Editor

Marty Petty
Senior Vice President and General Manager

Clifford I. Teutsch
Managing Editor

G. Claude Albert
Deputy Managing Editor

First Edition
Copyright © 1996 by The Hartford Courant
A Times Mirror Newspaper

Printed by Times Mirror Higher Education Group
Dubuque, Iowa

ISBN 0-9646638-1-3

Library of Congress
Catalog Card Number   96-76109

A NOTE FROM THE PUBLISHER

March 1996

Community reporting can help make newspapers invaluable to today's readers.

Other media may attempt to match our reporting on national and international developments but only newspapers have the ability to provide meaningful coverage — day after day and year after year — of the communities in which we all live.

Newspapers have the expertise and responsibility to report on everything from the schools where you or your neighbors send your children to the local tax rate to the popular new restaurant that opened down the street.

The newspaper should be the best source for interesting, detailed, insightful and authoritative information about your hometown because we are closest to all aspects of community life. Newspapers can make themselves indispensable to readers well into the future if we build upon this strength.

Connecticut is a state where cities and towns have a strong identity. Packed into what is one of the smallest states in the nation, we have 169 municipalities, almost all with their own taxing and zoning authority, police and fire departments and school systems.

As a result of the great interest in local news here, community reporting has been a very important part of The Courant for many years. We now cover more than 60 cities and towns on a regular basis and produce nine editions of a town news section six days a week.

We want to thank the 46 authors of this book for sharing what they've learned about this brand of journalism. We hope this book encourages the growth and development of community reporting and is useful to you, whether you are a student, or a teacher, or a newcomer to journalism or a veteran reporter.

Michael E. Waller
Publisher and CEO
The Hartford Courant

CONTENTS

CONTENTS

INTRODUCTION

By Bruce DeSilva

This is the only book on community reporting we know of that was written entirely by practitioners of the craft. We are the writers and editors of The Hartford Courant, the oldest continuously published newspaper in America, and we have been doing community news longer than anyone else.

The 47 authors of this book nearly all began their journalism careers covering small towns. They have many years of experience in community reporting and together have won most major journalism awards, including the Pulitzer Prize.

The origins of this book

When we began work on this book, our intended audience was our own staff. The Courant is both a metropolitan newspaper and the local newspaper for more than 60 Connecticut cities and towns. We thought the 70 reporters who cover local news for us would benefit if we tapped the community reporting expertise of our 330-member news staff and made it available in one volume.

So we asked experienced reporters and editors throughout the newspaper to tell us what they know about local reporting. Their submissions were so full of insights and practical advice — much of which we had never seen in print before — that we decided it should be available to journalism schools and reporters at other newspapers.

How to use this book

Whether you are a journalism student or a 25-year veteran, this book can make you a better community news reporter.

A student might want to read it cover to cover. We believe no other book on local reporting is as thorough or sophisticated about communities.

A reporter beginning a new beat might turn to the chapters on getting started and then use the rest of the book as a reporting resource, flipping to the chapter on budget coverage, for example, when budget season rolls around, or looking up the chapter on getting information from the military should the need arise.

An experienced reporter will find useful insights about how communities work and unexpected tips on reporting techniques throughout the book. The two editors of this book, with a combined 44 years of local newspaper experience, admit they have learned a great deal from its authors.

A philosophy for local news

This book reflects The Hartford Courant's philosphy that the best community reporting requires more than covering local government and the police. The best local news celebrates the complex lives of readers, from their homes, gardens and workplaces to their churches, shopping malls and schools. As William Allen White once put it, the job is to cover "the sweet, intimate story of life."

So when the news is about government and police, it should be reported as much as possible from the point of view of the consumers of government services and police protection — not from the point of view of the officials.

A stepping stone or a career?

Community reporting can be a stepping stone to other beats or a lifelong vocation. Whichever path you choose, you should treasure your time as a local news reporter. Your community reporting is likely to have a greater effect on readers than anything else you will ever write, no matter where your journalism career may take you.

The aforementioned White, one of the greatest journalists America has produced, was a community journalist — the editor of the Emporia (Kansas) Gazette. His sentiments about local reporting are as valid today as when he wrote these words in 1916:

"When the girl at the glove-counter marries the boy in the wholesale house, the news of their wedding is good for a forty-line wedding notice, and the forty lines in the country paper gives them self-respect. When in due course we know that their baby is a twelve-pounder named Grover or Theodore or Woodrow, we have that neighborly feeling that breeds real democracy. When we read of death in that home we can mourn with them that mourn. . . . Therefore, men and brethren, when you are riding through this vale of tears upon the California Limited, and by chance pick up the little country paper . . . don't throw down the contemptible little rag with the verdict that there is nothing in it. But know this, and know it well; if you could take the clay from your eyes and read the little paper as it is written, you would find all of God's beautiful, sorrowing, struggling, aspiring world in it, and what you saw would make you touch the little paper with reverent hands."

We hope you enjoy this book.

CHAPTER I

The first four weeks: Breaking into a new town

By John Moran, Chris Sheridan, Mike Swift and Paul Marks

Covering a new beat is a lot like entering a dark room: Until you find the light switch, plan on bumping into the furniture for a while.

How you spend your first month is crucial. In this brief time, you have an invaluable opportunity to use ignorance to your advantage, to ask a ton of questions without arousing suspicion. Later, every query will spur a flurry of phone calls among local leaders trying to learn collectively what that reporter is after.

What follows, then, is a brief to-do list for your first four weeks.

1) Read every scrap your paper's written on the community.

Go into the morgue and dig in. Your goal should be to become the most knowledgeable person who ever covered this community. Take notes if you have to. The hours spent here will pay off big time.

2) Drive around.

Open up a street map, put a good tape in the stereo, and take a careful tour.

Drive every road and notice everything. Go ahead, be a snoop. Check out the boundries of the town, especially the dead-end roads and far-flung reaches where nobody goes.

Besides giving you plenty of story ideas, these drives will give you a good idea of how people interact there. Where are rich and poor sections? Who lives there? What schools do their children go to? Where is the landfill? Are some roads paved better than others? Do some parts of town have sewers and others not?

Get a feel for your town. Notice the hotdog stand, the company housing that's boarded up, the small for sale sign in front of a local landmark.

Often, it's the stories right in front of your face that make for the finest reads.

3) Identify the power people and go meet them.

Some will be the usual suspects: elected and appointed officials, committee chairmen, business owners, school principals, clergy. Get these folks to talk about their perceptions of the town. What's important to people there? Why, for example, did they elect you, Mr. Mayor?

One reporter had a favorite question for these early get-acquainted sessions: Who are the 10 most-important people in town? Those lists yielded tidbits he wouldn't otherwise hear for months.

Often, retired local officials and employees still live locally. Seek out the former mayor, the ex-town manager, the last auditor. They can be fertile sources of information.

Some of the best sources are those who don't make the decisions but know how they are made. The quietest person on the council frequently knows best where the bodies are buried.

The goal is to learn quickly who's aligned with whom, so you can go to different factions when you hear things and need to find out the truth.

4) Get everyone's home phone number.

Doing this right away spares you from any inference that you have a particular intention to use the number. It also means you'll have the number when you need it, regardless of what terms you later are on with that person.

One reporter's line: "Lots of times I'm writing a story at 6 or 7 o'clock, and being able to check a fact with you can keep a mistake from getting in the paper." That is humble and respectful, but carries an implication that seems to encourage agreement. Some people even will give you their cellular phone numbers.

5) Spread around your business cards.

Get them made quickly and hand them out to *everyone you meet*. In addition to all the public officials and business owners, make sure anyone even remotely connected with politics gets one.

Leave a couple at the fire station and ambulance bays. Post them on supermarket bulletin boards. Ask gas station owners to post one near the phone in case they hear of a bad wreck or something.

6) Get on every mailing list you can think of.

From ones issued by the historical society and the ambulance association to those sent by school principals and parent groups, you never know when one of these mailings will offer a quick-hit feature or more. Suggest faxing.

7) Find the money.

There are thousands of ways that money flows through a community. All of them establish power relationships. Who are the town's biggest employers, taxpayers? Who are the presidents and directors of the banks? Who are the biggest real estate brokers and contractors? Who gets the most overtime on the town payroll?

Call them, meet them, get their impressions of town and allow them to tell you about their business. Again, these meetings must take place early on your beat, or else you're more likely to be seen as a snoop instead of a friendly face.

8) Spend a shift riding with the police.

Most departments allow reporters to do this. If you cover police, riding with officers can be an invaluable introduction to the politics of the department and the hot spots in any community.

Remember, most cops were born in the town they now patrol. They know it well and most are happy to try to impress you with that knowledge. Bonus points for making the cop one of your regular sources.

9) Seek out union officials.

The heads of the teachers' union, town employee unions, police and fire unions and unions representing workers at large private employers are worth knowing. Not only can they give you the lowdown on any contract negotiations, grievance or strike, but union leaders generally love to expound on the deficiencies of management at their particular institutions.

10) Assemble special reference library.

Nothing saves more time than having information at your fingertips. So spend a little time organizing your own little library of facts. Find the local charter. Get a copy of the local budget.

Get every piece of paper you can, from lists of officials and meeting calendars to plans of development, brochures about business centers and schools, to old annual reports.

Get a list of the top 10 taxpayers from the assessor and a list of the top 10 tax delinquents from the tax collector. Get a listing of all town-owned property from the mayor, first selectman or town planner.

Other important resources are the zoning map (tells you where a town had decided to put its rich people and its less desirables). Get a map that shows where utilities are placed, such as water mains and sewers.

Get census information and town-by-town comparisons from organizations such as regional planning councils, conferences of municipalities, state policy and economic councils, chambers of commerce or the state labor department reports.

Be forewarned that all this won't come easy. Even in this high-tech era, starting a new beat is mostly hard work and shoe leather. But your vision will never be as fresh as it is when you take on a new beat.

For a while, you'll introduce yourself to everyone you meet. For a while, you'll ask directions to everywhere you go. Still, with the right plan of attack, you will quickly be impressing editors — and yourself — with how much you've learned about your beat.

Mike Swift got his start as a stringer covering the town of Harwinton, Conn., for The Courant. He now covers downtown Hartford, regional issues and urban affairs for The Courant. His honors include an Associated Press Sports Editors Award for enterprise reporting.

Chris Sheridan began her journalism career covering junior high basketball games after her jump shot failed to win her a place on the team. She covered education and health care in the Courant's Middletown bureau, where she won The Courant's Gield Award for community reporting. She is now the editorial writer at The Cleveland Plain Dealer.

Paul Marks began his career as education reporter of the News-Register in Wheeling, W.Va. He now covers the towns of Windsor Locks and Bradley International Airport.

John M. Moran, who began his career as a reporter for the Westfield (Mass.) Evening News, is now a member of The Courant's projects desk covering computers, technology and on-line services. He has received an Associated Press award for business coverage.

CHAPTER 2

Documents you need at your fingertips

By Brant Houston

When you begin a new community beat, you should compile a few basic documents for your desk. They will save you a lot of time scratching around for basic information later, and they can help you spot important stories.

Some of these documents can be provided to you by the town. Others you will have to assemble for yourself; but it will be worth the trouble.

Here is what you should get:

▶ A list of top local elected officials, including local state representatives, the local state senator, and the U.S. congressman from your area.

▶ A list of all board and committee members in town.

▶ A copy of bidding procedures. Once you get it, make sure to read it, understand it, and write a summary for yourself of the dollar limits over which the community must bid for services or supplies.

▶ A list of vendors. Most communities now have computerized their purchasing records. Ask the director of that office (purchasing or finance) for the vendor list, preferably in computerized form. It should show from whom services or goods were purchased and how much each vendor has been paid in a year.

▶ A list of property owned by the town.

▶ A list of vehicles owned by the town.

▶ The town's annual budget.

▶ The town's annual report.

▶ Any annual audits of departments or the town.

▶ The town's ethics code.

▶ The chamber of commerce membership list and any reports on the business community. Know who the top private employers are.

▶ Zoning regulations.

▶ Building and fire codes.

▶ Health codes.

▶ A list of five or so comparable communities in the state. Usually, a town has this list already so that it can compare itself favorably when it can.

▶ A list of the powerful and famous in the town government and business and a list of the gadflies who torture them. You can cull this from clips and interviews.

▶ A list of neighborhood and taxpayers' associations.

▶ A phone directory of town agencies and their employees.

▶ A phone directory of employees who work for the agency that supplies water and sewer services.

▶ A list of regional agencies of which your town is a member.

▶ A list (preferably computerized) of all town employees, their titles and their salaries.

▶ A phone directory of state and federal agencies in your area that address local issues.

▶ A list of spokesmen for all of the utilities that serve your town.

Brant Houston worked as a reporter and database editor at The Courant. He now is managing director of the National Institute of Computer-Assisted Reporting, a joint venture of Investigative Reporters and Editors and the University of Missouri School of Journalism.

CHAPTER 3

Reporting on the calendar

By John M. Moran

In this business, no matter how hard you work or how well you prepare, the clock will always be your enemy.

But the calendar, that's another story.

Whether you consider yourself well-organized or haphazard, a few minutes a day gazing at the calendar can bring huge rewards. Consider it a form of self-defense.

I use two calendars: week-at-a-glance and year-at-a-glance. One keeps me focused on the here and now, the other shows me the big picture. Both make the future an integral part of the present.

The year-at-a-glance calendar is especially helpful. (I drew one for myself on a legal pad.) Sketch in the annual milestones: Election Day, campaign finance filing deadlines, major holidays, key community events, anniversaries of news events, changing of the seasons, the opening of school.

When you make friends with the calendar, you see new patterns emerging in your coverage — patterns you can use to outwit the competition and stay ahead of the bureaucrats. You'll also have time to make your coverage interesting and innovative, rather than routine and reactive.

There's nothing quite like scooping the other guy because you planned it. It's a tremendous service to readers, as well, because it informs them of events in time for them to participate.

Why not do it now? Here is a sample calendar to get you started. Feel free to tailor it to your own needs:

Elections

Every year is an election year. In odd-numbered years, local politicians hustle for votes; in even-numbered years, state and federal seats are up for grabs. But don't just mark down Election Day. Call the secretary of the state's office and local party organizations for such things as nomination deadlines, primary dates, campaign finance filing deadlines and party caucuses.

Budgets

Every year is also a budget year. Assembling a budget is an enormously complex undertaking — even in the tiniest towns. Schedule this in detail. Start with early coverage of whether the town will finish the current year with a deficit or surplus. Take a look at how revenue trends are shaping the budget process before it even begins. Then get a detailed listing of the budget process. When do department heads start preparing their requests? When are they due to the mayor's office? When must the mayor present his or her request to the council? What is the schedule of budget hearings? When must the budget be adopted?

Don't forget that this budget cycle applies not only to towns and school boards, but to virtually all institutions, including nonprofit groups, hospitals, even major businesses.

Holidays

For suburban reporters, holidays provide great opportunities to produce high-profile, all-editions stories — if you plan ahead. The usual crush of events slows down a bit over holiday weekends, so a well-researched piece relating to the occasion is a sure winner. It's almost impossible to ignore what I call the "Big Six" holidays: Christmas, New Year's, Memorial Day, Independence Day, Labor Day and Thanksgiving. But you're likely to get even more notice if you pay careful attention to others such as Martin Luther King Day, Kwanzaa, Veterans Day, ethnic religious holidays, etc.

The school year

It's hard for the childless to appreciate how much impact the school calendar has on young families. But believe me, especially with today's single-parent households and two-income families, it's big news if the school board so much as thinks about altering the start of school, school vacations or the end of the school year. And even if those events occur as usual, they present opportunities for covering how everyone from parents, to child-care workers, to police and recreational officials are preparing.

The seasons

Winter, spring, summer and fall. Not much news there, you think. Ah, but there is. Every year is different from the year before. And that's where the news is when it comes to the changing of the seasons. Have cuts in the snow budget resulted in depleted stockpiles of road salt? Is the town leaf collection overwhelmed? Are spring rains likely to undermine a heavily traveled street? A calendar that prompts you to ask these questions in a timely fashion puts you ahead of the competition.

Anniversaries

The anniversaries of major local events are excellent occasions for a look back at what happened and a fresh look at how, if at all, things have changed as a result. Once again, though, the key is having these events on your calendar far enough in advance to plan and execute your coverage. If you realize at 4 p.m. that tomorrow is the 10th anniversary of a horrible triple-homicide on Main Street, you won't produce the story you could have written if you started two weeks ago. Today's electronic news libraries are a boon for skimming through years gone by in search of anniversary stories to cover. An added bonus is that these are great fun to report and write.

John M. Moran, who began his career as a reporter for the Westfield (Mass.) Evening News, is now a member of The Courant's projects desk covering computers, technology and on-line services. He has received an Associated Press award for business coverage.

CHAPTER 4

Getting creative with local news

By Hilary Waldman and Rick Green

It's Monday morning and five long news days loom ahead. Community news, every day. It can become a grind. But it doesn't have to.

The best coverage starts with a question: "What can I tell people about this town that's interesting?"

Repeat this to yourself like a mantra.

Never let the answer be: "Nothing." And almost never let the answer be: "A meeting story."

Instead, ask yourself, what would you care about if you lived in this town? You'll find that if you approach stories creatively, amazing things happen.

Say there's a council meeting tonight, but the agenda is pretty thin. Let's start at town hall and see what we can find.

On the bulletin board of the clerk's office is a stack of legal notices the town published in that tiny print. The type is single-spaced, the language is legalese. Nobody reads those things. But read on.

Hmmm, the town council is proposing an ordinance to limit each home-owner to five cats. Wonder what that's about. You can bet there's some crazy lady who has 50 cats and neighbors have been nagging the town to clean up her property.

DON'T WRITE ABOUT THE ORDINANCE. Find the lady and her neighbors. The town manager or the mayor or the town planner will know the story behind the story. Assign a photographer.

This really happened in Cromwell, Conn., and it turned out the lady was spending her Social Security money to feed the cats. Now you have a story that everyone will read.

Often, stories are right in front of you. Recognizing them is the challenge.

You walk into town hall and you see long lines of people challenging tax bills. Do you do a story about long lines, or do you do a story about why this is occurring this year?

Ask the people in line why they're there. Or try a new perspective. See if you can stand behind the counter with the clerk and see what it feels like to take abuse from angry taxpayers all day.

While you're in town hall, you notice a new brass plaque dedicating the elevator to the memory of Mary Healy. You also noticed a dedication resolution scheduled for passage by the town council tonight. Pretty dull, eh?

But think again. Who was Mary Healy and why would an elevator, of all things, be dedicated to her memory?

You ask around town hall and a pretty good story emerges. Turns out, Mary was an advocate for the handicapped who agitated for the elevator. She had a hard time walking up the steps to the council chamber. She also was hard of hearing, and it's because of her that there are microphones at each of the council desks.

Next, stop by the police station. Don't bury yourself in the blotter. Look around. Open your ears. What are the clerks in the records department talking about?

One day, a reporter walked into the Newington, Conn., Police Department and saw about 20 bicycles standing in the hallway. A junior biker convention? A raid on a bike shop?

Nope. The storage garage for recovered stolen bicycles was overflowing. People were not claiming lost or stolen bikes and now there were so many they had to be kept in the hall.

Sometimes, you will see something 10 times before realizing it may be a story. Take the woman in Bloomfield, Conn., whom a reporter saw day after day digging up shrubbery on public property all over town.

Finally the reporter caught on that this might be a story. Claire Swallow was happy to talk to the reporter, and an amusing story of her one-woman bush-and-shrub recycling campaign took form.

You may not notice the Claire Swallows the first time, or the second time. The trick is being observant. And being willing to get out of the car and ask a few dumb questions.

In another instance, a reporter kept seeing tiny real estate signs around town. After months of seeing them, thinking "isn't that quaint," our reporter realized, hey, there is a story here.

It turns out that there was a minor ruckus between the town and local real estate brokers who were angry about a town ordinance requiring for-sale signs to be 1 foot by 1 foot. Upon investigation, the reporter found out that the ordinance was enacted by skittish town officials worried that too many for-sale signs could spur white flight in the integrated town.

Another example:

Residents of a small neighborhood in Rocky Hill, Conn., were selected to be guinea pigs for a new townwide recycling program. For several weeks they were supposed to rinse their cans and glass containers and put them at the curb. The results of the experiment were to help iron out kinks before the program was initiated townwide.

The reporter decided to find out how the recycling program was working. Instead of asking the recycling coordinator, she took to the street, knocking on doors. How's it going, the neighbors were asked. Are there family fights when someone accidently tosses the cat food can in the garbage instead of the recycling bin? The resulting story was filled with the trials and tribulations of discarding trash. And the reporter got fresh chocolate-chip cookies at one house, and lemonade at another.

In Bloomfield, a new reporter drove past a farm implement museum every day. A farm implement museum? One day he decided to stop in. Well, a local museum usually has been written about 1,000 times, but in this case there was a new story. The Internal Revenue Service was trying to take this guy's home and his museum. A home and museum that Muhammad Ali one visited and which, at one time or another, most prominent local citizens had tried to organize a campaign to save.

He was more than happy to talk — it's just that until that moment, nobody had asked him, "What's new?" The result was a compelling series on an old man who wouldn't listen to anybody — and who lost his home as a result.

The lesson here is to get out of the newsroom. You don't get stories by phone. You don't get stories drinking coffee with your colleagues. Sometimes you do get stories by going to meetings, but not by simply recording what people say at them.

Remember, stories are everywhere. A reporter recently did his own grocery shopping at the Stop & Shop in West Hartford, Conn., and noticed all of the food baggers were Russian immigrants. They were packing the paper bags as though they were packing family heirlooms for a long overseas passage. Maybe there was a story in the trend to hire immigrants rather than teenagers as supermarket baggers.

And if you didn't know it already, this would be pretty good proof that your town was experiencing an influx of immigrants. Now there's a wealth of stories.

Tips:

Don't think boring.

If you think it is boring, it will be. Instead ask, how can I make this interesting? The town is dedicating its new elevator to some woman named Mary Healy? Don't write about the elevator, write about Mary and why the elevator now has a plaque bearing her name.

Make lists.

Of everything. People to call, people you need to meet, places to go, story ideas. When you've called and met all of them, find new ones.

Find new ways to do old stories.

Don't do a year end wrap-up; do a year-end news quiz. If you see a proposed ordinance limiting the number of cats a person can have, you just KNOW some busy-body resident is complaining about the lady with 100 cats. Find the cat lady.

Find a reason to go into one of the schools in your town at least once a week.

Write profiles of principals. Find out who is in charge of curriculum and the new things they are doing. What do teachers earn compared with teachers in nearby towns? And if you're doing something in a classroom, talk to the kids.

Look at meeting agendas carefully at least a day before the board or commission meets. Try to find at least one non-meeting story in there. Many times you can do the story before the meeting. Agenda item: proposal to limit the sale of junk food in school cafeterias. Don't wait for the meetings. Go into the cafeteria at lunch time, talk to kids about what they're eating, call school nutritionists at the state education department. Many parents and others would be shocked to find out that their kids can buy Slim Jims for lunch.

Go to town meetings with a plan.

Pay attention to people who show up. Don't sit at the press table scribbling notes. Sit in the back, wander around the hallway. Talk to people, meet people. Watch people. Cultivate people who you know will befriend you and tell you things. If you are going to do a meeting story, try to write it before the meeting. Read the agenda in advance and see if anything quirky pops out at you.

Find 12 people you can call anytime you don't know what to write about. The local minister, the nursery school director . . . people who are not directly involved in town government.

Check a copy of the town history out of the library.

Plenty of story ideas here. Story is part of hiSTORY's name. If you're writing about a grant to restore the historic Smith-Jones house, don't tell us about the grant; use the grant application papers to tell us about the house in its heyday and why the town wants to spend $350,000 to restore it. If you are new to the town, history gives you perspective.

Shop in local stores, read bulletin boards.

Think about what it is like to live in the town and what you would care about.

Local news doesn't happen in a vacuum. Read The New York Times, The Wall Street Journal and national news magazines. In some ways, your community is a microcosm of the nation. Draw on that. Find the stories. This is local news.

Hilary Waldman began her career covering town meetings for WRKL-AM radio in Rockland County, N.Y., for $12 a story. A former reporter for the Gannett News Service, she covered legislative issues, with a concentration on casinos and Indian gambling, as a member of The Courant's politics desk. She now is the paper's medical writer.

Rick Green got his start as a stringer in San Francisco and Chicago before coming to The Courant to cover a small town. He now covers Hartford schools and school privatization.

CHAPTER 5

Getting religion

By Gerald Renner

Religion illuminates human nature as no other subject I can think of — the high, bright side of altruism and the low, dark side of depravity. You meet Mother Teresas and Elmer Gantrys and, most of all, a lot of people stumbling around between heaven and hell.

Once you get beyond the veneer of scoffing indifference many people feign when asked about religion, you trigger emotional responses that few other questions could. It tells you who people are and what they think is important.

There is some reason more people are in church on Sunday than watch all sports events combined, Super Sunday not excluded. It's incumbent on a responsible newspaper to try to explain why (even if we can't report who's ahead on scoring souls, God or the Devil.)

The only real skills you need are the ones you are supposed to have as a journalist — a nose for news, willingness to probe and ask dumb questions, fairness, balance and respect for others' opinions. The worst motivation of all, which afflicts some religion writers misplaced in the trade, is a messianic complex that you have a missionary role.

It is a mistake to think that covering religion is any different from covering town hall. Like the town hall, the churches are important institutions in your community. They raise money, provide services, set moral standards and help shape attitudes. Just as a good sports writer doesn't write about sports but people who play sports, a good religion writer doesn't write about religion but people in religion — who they are and what they are doing that affects their neighbors.

Getting started

So you are new to a town and you must churn out a story a day and the only thing that seems to be newsworthy is that the grass is turning brown on the village green. What do you do?

Speaking generally, you get to know who is who in the predominant houses of worship and schmooze with them straight off. In most Connecticut towns, for example, that means: Congregational, Catholic and Episcopal.

Pay a visit to that white-spired Congregational church and say hello to the pastor. The Congregational minister is unusually tuned in to the community and is ecumenically minded. He or she can give you pointers about the other churches, not to mention scuttlebutt about what is going on in town. Ask to get on the mailing list for the weekly church bulletin. Ask to attend the next meeting of the clergy association (most towns have one) to meet the other ministers and, possibly, rabbis, if there are any in town.

Also say hello to the Catholic pastor. If you are in Connecticut, it will probably be the biggest church in town, because Catholics account for half the population in the state and for seven out of 10 churchgoers. There may be several Catholic churches, and, if it is a heavily ethnic town, you are likely to find ethnic Catholic churches (Italian, Polish, Lithuanian, Slovak, etc.). With the ethnics you get a bonus, gaining an insight into what might ordinarily be a closed community.

The Episcopal Church is usually also in the middle of community stuff, and, confirming every stereotype you have ever heard about Episcopalians, its membership probably includes some of the town's movers and shakers and the wannabes.

Obviously you should make a personal call on the rabbi if there is a synagogue in town. Ditto if there is a major presence of Lutherans, Baptists, Methodists or others (your reconnaissance among the Big Three will establish that).

The black and Hispanic churches are also special cases and some of the most exciting things going on in the religious community are often centered in those churches. One of the major modern trends is the movement of the historic, middle-class black churches — e.g., Baptist, A.M.E. and A.M.E. Zion — out of the inner city and into the suburbs. Inner-city roles are being picked up by the more Pentecostal black churches. A good basic reference work is "The Black Church in the African American Experience" by C. Eric Lincoln and Lawrence Mamiya. (Duke U. Press, 1990). Be alert, too, for other religions such as Mormons, Muslims, Hindus, Buddhists, etc.

Be sure to let churches and synagogues know about your newspaper's religion page, if it has one, and how to get information printed in it.

What are the stories?

What kinds of stories are you after? The kind you might find on any beat.

Profiles, of people and groups, are always good, and there are probably more characters per square foot of sanctuary in religion than anywhere outside of a Mafia craps shoot.

There are trend stories, such as the decline of denominationalism, how Protestant churches are following the lead of Catholics and having more and more Saturday services and the growth of "non-traditional" religions.

There are money stories, about how much the church needs for maintenance, staff and ministries, and how it goes about raising this money.

There are church anniversaries, which give you a good opportunity to take a look at an important part of the community.

There are stories of redemption, such as the heroin addict who found God and now runs the local teen center.

There are stories about social services, such as the ecumenical soup kitchen or homeless shelter and the stories about the people who use these services and the volunteers who provide them.

There are religious-choice stories such as yuppies with growing families looking for a church home.

There are the church conflicts, when half the congregation gets up in arms because the pastor repainted the Virgin Mary yellow instead of blue, or fired a popular assistant or quit because he or she lost the board's confidence and other of the timeless reasons for church conflicts.

There are also the stories about pastors' hitting on church secretaries or little boys, or the church treasurer making off with the Sunday collection. You don't need to hear a firebell ring to run after them.

Keep an eye on trends. In many areas, the fastest growing churches are the store-front churches, mostly independent and unaffiliated or perhaps members of a Pentecostal denomination such as the Assemblies of God or the Churches of God in Christ. They are too busy surviving to worry about media attention, and generally have an unecumenical outlook on life. They usually do not mingle with the other churches. They do best with the poor, particularly minorities. They may be sensitive and unsophisticated and have such fervor they may try to convert you. But, they like to be noticed and will probably be tickled to cooperate.

(I'm often asked, by those bent on conversion, what religion I am. I usually decline to say, pointing out politely that as a journalist I try to be fair and respectful to all religions.)

And there is the unexpected. In my view, the best religion story of the decade in Connecticut was Connie Neyer's account of how Trinity Episcopal Church in Hartford discovered a century of pigeon droppings in the belfry and bagged it for sale as fertilizer. The story was picked up worldwide.

Watch the calendar

Put out your antennae as the big religious holy days approach. After Genesis, everything else is a follow-up, and we on the religion beat grow stale coming up with ideas. I mean, after the Resurrection, what new can be said about Easter?

The other Christian biggies, for which it is almost mandatory we have a story, are Christmas, perhaps Ash Wednesday, when Lent begins, and Good Friday (when, like clockwork, The Courant has a story about Puerto Ricans carrying a cross around town. Maybe someone can find out if the Slovaks or some other group are as colorful). Then there are Hanukkah, Passover and Rosh Hashana, beginning the high holy days. Get a good idea and, be my guest, write about it on Page 1.

Sometimes projects in religion suggest themselves. Connie Neyer and I teamed up on religious charities' inability to pick up the slack when governments cut back. Valerie Finholm and I looked at the ethics of pulling the life-support plug. Then there were the cult stories, of how Brother Julius exploited his followers for sexual favors and financial gain, and of the deceptive recruiting practices of Fred Lenz, a Stamford mayor's son who became Grand Master Rama.

You won't get many good stories from PR handouts. You have to schmooze. I seldom go anywhere to cover one story that I don't pick up an idea for another.

Resources

What resources do you have?

▶ Your newspaper library. Stories your newspaper has written about religion and specific churches will be filed there.

▶ Reference works. One of the most helpful is a big tome by J. Gordon Melton called "The Encyclopedia of American Religions," which has clear essays on religious families and then lists denominations. A companion volume is Melton's "New Age Encyclopedia." The Courant's news library has a copy, and perhaps your news library does, too.

The "Yearbook of American and Canadian Churches" is an essential compendium published by the National Council of Churches of Christ that covers a wealth of information, including officers, telephone numbers and addresses of churches' national headquarters.

Another helpful resource, also in The Courant's news library, is the annual "Official Catholic Directory." It lists every priest, parish, institution and organization in the United States along with other useful information.

On my desk are various church directories, including state directories for Catholics, Episcopalians and United Church of Christ (listing clergy and churches), "Yearbook of the Evangelical Lutheran Church," "United Methodist Annual Conference Journal," "American Jewish Yearbook," "Deseret Church Almanac" (Mormons), and assorted other volumes — various editions of the Bible, biblical dictionaries, "Encyclopedia of Jewish Concepts," handbooks on Hindus, Buddhists, Muslims, etc.

You should also keep handy a list of key sources and telephone numbers. For example, in Connecticut you might want numbers for the communications directors of the three Catholic dioceses, The Office of Catholic Schools, the Connecticut Conference of the United Church of Christ, Episcopal Diocese of Connecticut, Christian Conference of Connecticut, and Capitol Region Conference of Churches.

And if your newspaper has a beat writer covering religion, as The Courant does, his/her number might be the handiest of all.

Gerald Renner got his start when he convinced the Navy he would make a better editor than a carpenter. A former director of the Religious News Service, he is now The Courant's religion writer. He has been cited by the Religion Newswriters Association and he was part of a team that won The John Hancock Award.

CHAPTER 6

Homing in on housing stories

By William Hathaway

As many as two-thirds of your newspaper's readers own their own homes. Little is more important to them than its value.

But houses are anti-news. No matter how long you watch them, they hardly do anything newsworthy.

Housing, though, will play a part in almost everything you write.

Consider this.

▶ Scholastic performances of school districts affect the desirability of communities, and therefore home values, the major source of middle-class wealth.

▶ Burglaries and violent crimes promote fears that neighborhoods are becoming less desirable.

▶ Every budget approved by the town council is directly related to property taxes and the affordability of housing.

▶ The most devisive problems of race and class become acutely focused around the issue of where people live. The location, type and condition of apartments are key social issues for communities, particularly in urban areas.

So when writing about housing, you're actually writing about residents' sense of community, economic security and the quality of their lives.

Find the patterns

There is no better way to learn about a town than by studying its housing patterns — finding out which sides of the tracks are where.

Every town has these metaphorical tracks. Getting to know where the lines are drawn can be like trying to solve a puzzle; once you have some of the pieces in place, a larger picture will come into focus.

There are several statistical guides that can help.

Local or regional realtor boards usually track home sales and median prices by town and report to members monthly. State agencies usually track housing statistics because they collect taxes on real estate transfers.

In some states, private publications track real estate sales and sell the information to members of the real estate industry.

Use caution when reporting these figures. Remember, the residential real estate market is seasonal, and comparisons should always be made for similar periods. And in small towns, where a half-dozen more sales in a month could be a huge percentage increase, monthly sales data are essentially useless in reflecting trends.

Most statistics use median prices, which reflect the market more accurately than mean average prices, but can also be misleading. For instance, a steep rise in median price may indicate that a lot more rich people are buying homes in town, not that the overall market is heating up.

Stories among the trends

But insight — and good stories — come when you dig beneath the numbers. Are there more homes on the market than a year or two before? Or less? Why?

When the real estate market dropped in Connecticut at the start of the decade, several interlinked things occurred, all of which led to fascinating stories.

For instance, many young couples couldn't sell their condominiums and delayed having children or began raising kids in small housing units. Some people rented their condominiums, worsening a rental housing glut by luring people out of apartments. The result was a domino effect that contributed to the abandonment of rental housing in major cities.

When people move, they frequently have interesting stories to tell: Fear of crime. The economy. Because they want a bigger place and now feel their jobs are safe.

Did they move because of changes in school policies, or because of the guy who keeps those junk cars down the road? Was it the smells from the old sewer plant? Because a spouse lost a job? Are they moving to a better place in town, or leaving the state or country altogether? The answers to all these questions could give you a good local, state or even national story.

One person's reason is an anecdote. A lot of people with similar reasons is a trend.

If you suspect a trend, you might run it by a real estate agent, who may or may not be honest with you. Check it out further by getting the names of buyers and sellers from the land transfer records in your town. Give some of these people a call.

Don't overlook the individual home. Does that old home on the market have some historic significance? There may be an architectural wonder right in your town, which only librarians or history buffs know about.

If it looks interesting, ask about it.

Building permits

Building permits often provide valuable insight into the housing in your town.

But as with sales figures, the best stories come from the information contained in the permits. What types of homes are being built? Are they condominiums, rental apartments, large homes, or homes for first-time buyers? What will they do to the character of the neighborhoods?

Who will live in them? Will they be young people, old people, immigrants, people of color, executives from a firm moving into town? Are they moving from other areas? Why?

Who moves into a town will dictate its character. And a close look at building permits may also tell you who has clout.

Local builders and developers, as befits large taxpayers, often exert considerable influence over local politicians. It isn't unusual, then, for a town to agree to extend city sewer and water lines into areas that builders and developers own. Or city officials may overlook building code violations to give someone a break.

You have probably noticed that sewer plants and affordable housing never get built on the rich side of town. That is one reason why it so important to get different people in your stories.

I remember sitting in a mayor's office, when a small group of condo owners presented him with a petition demanding that the city provide the same services to condo owners that owners of traditional single-family homes receive.

The mayor was polite, but when they left he turned to me and said, "(Expletive deleted) them. They don't vote."

Folks who can help

Here are some people who can help you get started.

▶ The town clerk. He or she usually knows who is doing the building, the buying, and whether those people are friendly with the powers that be.

Town clerks know so much because they oversee land records. Between land records and the assessor's property cards, you can find out who bought a house or land, a description of the property, how much it cost, who provided the mortgage, what the taxes are and whether they have been paid.

▶ Land-use attorneys. They will talk if they get stiffed by builders or feel their clients have been treated unfairly. They also know who is behind developments, which are often limited partnerships that hide the identity of some big players.

Perspective

When you report about any housing issue, be it suburban, rural or urban, try to include historic context.

Many long-time homeowners, for instance, may not realize that they are the beneficiaries of social change and government action — real estate inflation caused by the creation of interstate highways, for example, or large-lot zoning that artificially decreased the housing supply.

But also understand that the neighborhood may be the one area in which residents feel they still have some voice in controlling their surroundings. You should respect that passion; it is the glue that holds communities together.

Don't ignore the poorer sections of a community; they are rich in stories. Even in the most affluent towns, there are the working poor, who because of housing costs face struggles, such as finding day care, finding recreation for children, saving for homes, and dealing with stingy and shabby landlords.

A common housing story is the proposal for an affordable-housing development.

There is a tendency to focus on the irate homeowners who gather at public hearings to protest because the proposed development will lower their property values; increase traffic, etc.

When one of the complainers says, as they always do, "those people don't mow their lawns," make sure you can tell your readers who those people really are. Find someone who might qualify to live in a new development. Maybe it's the guy who fixes the complainer's car, or the secretary in his office.

And never assume that your affordable-housing developer is Mother Teresa. Building and managing housing for the poor is, has been and will be a lucrative enterprise that attracts the politically well-connected.

Know the agencies

Finally, make sure you know the roles of the various agencies involved in housing in your state. For example, in Connecticut, you would need to be familiar with these:

Connecticut Housing Finance Authority — a quasi-public agency, authorized to sell its own bonds and use the proceeds to issue below-market-rate mortgages to low- and moderate-income, first-time buyers. Also grants federal tax credits to people who invest in development of rental housing for low- and moderate-income people.

Department of Housing — a state agency that uses bond money directly for grants and low-interest loans for a variety of different affordable-housing programs. Generally targets lower income populations than does CHFA.

Connecticut Housing Coalition — an advocacy group for nonprofit housing groups that push for affordable-housing initiatives. Good contact for finding housing groups in your towns or background on how programs work.

U.S. Department of Housing and Urban Development — the federal agency in charge of a variety of housing and homeless programs. Funds most housing authority developments and the Section 8 program, which provides tenants with rent subsidies after they pay 30 percent of their income toward rent. HUD aid is usually reserved for very low-income people. However, also provides insurance for developments that have higher-income tenants and mixed use buildings with stores and office space.

Greater Hartford Association of Realtors — does monthly in-depth report on housing market that contains a variety of statistics, including sales numbers and median prices. However, does not include all towns in The Courant's readership area and all sales.

Commercial Record — a publication that tracks real estate statistics statewide, which generally supplies numbers as long as source is attributed.

William Hathaway began his career covering local and college sports for the Longmont (Colo.) Times-Call. He is now the housing and real estate reporter for The Courant. His honors include the National Association of Black Journalists' Award for enterprise reporting.

CHAPTER 7

A piece of the planet:
Local environmental reporting

By Daniel P. Jones

Covering the environment is the best job anyone could have.

You get to talk to some of the weirdest scientists, such as the atmospheric chemist who flies old spy planes through the stratosphere to check on the ozone layer, or the biologist who gives the highway builders headaches because she regularly catches them screwing up streams and wetlands.

You can have fun while learning about what I consider the most important issue of our time.

Best of all, lots of newspaper editors think it's very important, too.

Newspapers weren't always that interested, though. When I was getting out of graduate school in 1984, many of my classmates were amazed that I wasn't planning to cover politics. I told them that politicians soon would be dealing with environmental issues, whether they wanted to or not.

The main reason I wanted to cover the environment was an abiding interest in science and nature — in the world, how it works and how it is being degraded. If you have these same interests, then environmental reporting can be approached like any other type of reporting.

And you can do it as a local news reporter, because you are covering one little piece of the planet.

Getting ready

All you need is some extra background in scientific areas, and knowledge of where to find sources on such subjects as environmental law, hazardous waste, automobile emissions and the like. The best part about doing environmental reporting in the '90s is that there are so many more sources — experts, books, magazines, government reports — than there were when I started doing it.

Some of the types of stories you can easily produce include: pollution and odors from sewer plants; chemical emissions and odors from chemical plants and other factories; low-level radioactive waste storage; pesticide and fertilizer use on farms and wetland damage at highway construction sites or at the sites of home or commercial building construction.

Several sets of laws and regulations make all of these stories possible. An example: Congress in 1986 passed a law — the so-called Community Right-to-Know Act as part of the new Superfund law — that requires manufacturing companies to report annually on their emissions of some 300 chemicals. The reports are filed with the U.S. Environmental Protection Agency and the state environmental agency (in Connecticut, that's the state Department of Environmental Protection) each July 1 for the preceding calendar year. You can ask for them by company or you can get the reports for all of the companies in your town.

Which company is emitting chemicals that eat the ozone layer? Which are emitting chemicals that are suspected of causing birth defects or cancer? These documents will tell you which companies and how much. You should ask the companies what they are doing to reduce their emissions, and ask them to explain exactly how they achieved reductions — if they are claiming them.

In each town or fire district, the town's plans for dealing with chemical emergencies must be kept on file, and you can get these. Ask the town manager or comparable official who holds the job of emergency coordinator to let you see the plans, and you might want to do a story on what the fire and police departments would do in case of an emergency such as leaks from a chemical plant.

Sewer plant operators also must keep track of what's passing through their plants into streams and rivers. In accordance with federal water pollution laws, and with state laws in many states including Connecticut, monthly reports must be submitted to the state. (In Connecticut, that means the Department of Environmental Protection's water management bureau.) And you can see these.

Municipal landfill operators also must report periodically on groundwater contamination, and the dumps are inspected by state environmental officials. The records are available for your inspection.

There is a similar requirement for industries to record the pollution they emit into streams, and you can view these monthly reports at the state environmental agency as well. Federal courts have ruled that when a company reports pollution above a monthly limit, the excess pollution is a violation of law and the state or citizens' groups can sue and win monetary penalties automatically. So these records are quite important; don't over-look them as sources for stories.

I've produced stories using all of the records mentioned above. And in case you're intimidated by names of chemicals or heavy metals, there are plenty of books and experts to guide you in knowing what ailments the substances can cause, and what they are used for in industry. Some of these guides and sources: The Merck Index, a guide to chemicals in indus-try; EPA's Right-to-Know-Act hot line (800-535-0202); and the Chemical Manufacturers Association chemical referral library (800-262-8200). I also have found a handbook published by the National Wildlife Federation to be particularly useful in identifying toxic substances. It's called "Phantom Reductions: Tracking Toxic Trends."

Eyeball it

Once you have the scientific information you need, and you have com-pleted your interviews with experts, environmental officials, business rep-resentatives and, perhaps, representatives of a citizens' group or environ-mental organization, I suggest that you visit the offending sewer plant, chemical plant or town dump. There is no substitute for eyeballing a prob-lem. And I suggest making the visit with someone who knows the area — someone who can tell you, for example, where the polluted wells might be downhill from the dump.

Then interview some of the people who live nearby. Don't skip this part. They might provide just the type of insight or anecdote you need to trans-form your reporting from a list of facts into a real story.

Now for the hard part

Now comes the most difficult task in environmental journalism, but also the most fun and the most rewarding. You've got to make the technical, sci-entific and legal information accessible to anyone who picks up the paper. The way to do it, of course, is to show the people, events, situations, scenes and conflicts that make up your story.

You've got to do this at the very top of your story. Like this:

"If you think the prospect of global warming and rising seas is still a matter of academic debate, you might want to consider what one of the world's largest corporations thinks about it.

Royal Dutch Shell has begun to build its gas-drilling platforms in the North Sea higher off the waves. . . ."

You get the idea. Use telling details and write in conversational language, just as you should in any story.

One of the tricks I've picked up over the years is to translate extremely large figures — such as volumes or weights or total amounts of some item — into equivalents that the reader can visualize.

For example, I once wrote a story about the difficulties of disposing of old tires. In all, 240 million tires are discareded each year in the United States. How do you understand a number that big? It's enough to stretch around the Earth more than four times if placed tread to tread on the equator. When I was working in Denver earlier in my career, covering cleanup plans for the Army's old nerve-gas factory, I was told that an awfully large amount of soil would have to be cleansed of chemical contaminants. I called an architect's office to find out the volume of the most visible building in the Denver skyline. With a simple calculation, I was able to tell readers that the contaminated soil would fill the building 11 times over.

Be creative with such visualizations; use a number of railroad cars or tanker trucks to picture the size of a chemical spill or a mound of garbage. Readers will appreciate your effort to help them understand.

To advocate or not to advocate

Finally, I want to touch on a subject that has become a point of much contention among environmental journalists: whether environmental reporters should be advocates for environmental causes. The issue has been coming up regularly at the professional conferences I've attended in the past few years.

Some renowned environmental journalists, from some of the largest news organizations in the country, openly say that they are advocates for saving the environment and that there is too little time left for the Earth's oceans, forests and other resources for them to argue the point.

They are in the minority, however.

I come down on the side of the majority of environmental journalists, who believe it is dangerous to advocate for causes. Of course, nearly all of us who cover the environment would be lying if we said we did not wish to see clean air, clean rivers and seas, and a safe environment for children not yet born. The difference is that we bring a healthy amount of skepticism into every interview or story, whether we are talking to the head of a corporation accused of pollution or the head of the Sierra Club.

I recall the words of a professor in graduate school who toned down my copy:

"When you're on the side of the angels, there's no need for brickbats."

In other words, let the reader make judgments. Most readers already care about the environment. Give them the facts, as fairly and accurately as possible, and they can decide for themselves.

Daniel P. Jones began his career covering city hall and the police beat for the Linden (N.J.) Leader. He is now the environment writer for The Courant. His honors include the Connecticut Society of Professional Journalists' Stephen A. Collins award for public service.

CHAPTER 8

Nature as news

By Steve Grant

As automobiles replaced horses and electric power replaced beeswax candles, we lost our intimacy with the landscape. The loss gnaws at us. It is as if we've forgotten something, but can't remember what.

Without realizing why, we erect bluebird nesting boxes, swarm through the mountains in summer, and hunger to know more about landscapes and luna moths. The bookstores are ever more stocked with guides to trees, birds and stars.

People are concerned about air pollution and water pollution and want to know about these things. That's been clear for years. But they want something else, too.

They want to understand the rhythms and workings of nature.

It is not that we don't have stories about nature in American newspapers. We carry stories about the scientist who's determined why snakes have forked tongues, stories about the comeback of the bald eagle. We just need more of them.

What kind of stories are we talking about?

Stories that explain what is going on out there.

Some of these stories would fit into a traditional environment beat, but environment reporters have their hands full with hazardous waste, air pollution and water pollution. They seldom get around to writing about whipporwills or ash trees.

We need stories that are grounded in nature, stories in which the focus is not pollution but the plants and animals, rocks and clouds themselves.

Here are some examples.

Pests

Perhaps one September day you'll hear your neighbor complain that the yellow jackets have never been worse. Then, at the office, someone else will say, "The yellow jackets ruined our picnic yesterday." There's a possible story here, maybe a Page 1 story. Call a couple of entomologists in your area and ask them what is going on. It may be that the weather this year has produced a bumper crop of wasps. Include in the story some anecdotes from people whose picnics were ruined, along with the best, most environmentally sensible ways to protect yourself from a yellow jacket sting, and there's the story. Almost. While you have people's attention, explain the life cycle of the insect. It's almost always interesting, and usually can be done in a paragraph or two. Then explain why the weather led to a population boom. It's a painless way for everyone to pick up a natural history lesson, and it often makes for interesting reading.

Endangered species

In every state, some plants and animals face extinction. If someone in your area is trying to save a species, tell the story. How plentiful was this organism? Why did it decline? What must be done to restore it? You may find there is more drama than you expected here. Check whether the factors that caused it to decline are still at work. You will find that no matter how obscure the plant or animal, whether it be a sedge or a sedge wren, somewhere in the United States there is a scientist who is expert on the subject. The local people trying to save the species will know who that person is. Make sure you give people a sense of the organism, its place in the ecosystem, its value.

Weather

Newspapers are forever carrying stories that tell us how many fender benders happened because of some snowstorm in Hartford or Chicago. There's a lot more to the weather. Like the stock market, weather runs in cycles, short term and long term. Ask some government and private meteorologists about it. Maybe your region has settled into the pattern that produces a long, hot summer. Maybe the region seems headed toward a decade of cooler-than-normal weather. These trends have enormous implications for people, crops and nature. If your area is pummeled by a major storm, have the scientists explain the origin of the storm, the factors that went into its creation, the statistical likelihood of its happening again. If your region is enduring a heat wave or cold snap, write about how plants and animals fare under this stress (often pretty well.)

Trees and forests

People care deeply about trees — not just the tree-hugger crowd but your neighbors, even the ones who don't know a white pine from a White Tower. When those pines along the highway die, they'll wonder why; but they won't know whom to ask. (Road salt applied during winter storms is the usual culprit.) Unless your newspaper has a reputation for writing about this kind of thing, readers won't ever call in with the story suggestion. So, if you see something amiss in the woods or along the roadsides, ask your state environmental authorities, or the U.S. Forest Service, or the forestry departments at many of the larger universities. There are many other story possibilities here. Forests worldwide are dynamic, ever-changing, and constantly threatened by alien insects and diseases. When forests of hemlocks or oaks or hickories die, the landscape changes. That's a story.

Geology

Rocks are often overlooked as a source of news. Unchanging as they may seem — un-newsworthy as they may seem — their history is ever evolving. Scientists each year learn more about how our landscapes came to be. Why that river takes the seemingly inexplicable turn it takes may no longer be so inexplicable.

Rivers, lakes and oceans

These places are loaded with life, and news. Fish and shellfish are both sport and food resources. They often are covered from a sportfishing perspective: whether they are biting. They are less often written about from a natural resource perspective, though this vantage point offers many a journalistic twist. To begin with, aquatic creatures are affected by an array of natural and man-induced forces. If you hear people complain that the bluefish aren't biting, or the lobsters have disappeared, or there aren't any mussels left in the river, ask why. For example, bluefish may be suffering from overfishing, pollution or disease. The zebra mussel, accidentally imported from Europe, is undergoing a population explosion in the United States, showing up in new rivers and lakes every month. It is choking out other life and causes enormous damage to utility pipes. These are important stories.

Getting started

These stories won't show up on the city council agenda. To get started, check local colleges and universities. Meet the heads of the biology and botany departments and tell them you're interested in writing about the natural sciences. You'll almost certainly find them delighted by your interest. Ask them to explain what each faculty member is studying. You'll find that one has spent years researching the importance of marsh grass in coastal ecosystems, that another is studying the food preferences of deer, that another is studying the strength of amphibian vocal cords. Much of it will seem esoteric, useless perhaps. Where's the news?

Ask next which faculty members are far along enough with their work to have published papers, drawn conclusions or simply found something interesting. Do any of their findings have practical application? The department heads know these things.

Amphibian vocal cords? A University of Connecticut biologist's research into the energy expended by spring peepers was a national story a few years ago. He determined that each spring night a peeper expends an amount of energy equivalent to running a marathon — all to attract a mate. Understanding how the muscle involved can work that hard could have significant implications for people. The field of sports medicine, for example, is interested.

Next, talk to conservation groups. These are groups such as the Nature Conservancy, which has a chapter in every state. There are many others, some devoted to forest protection, some to land protection in general. Ask them what issues your area faces. They'll know, and they will fill your ear. These groups often know which prized pieces of the landscape are threatened by development.

Contact fishermen and hunters. They know the woods and the water and quickly spot anything amiss. They'll hear if someone wants to build a dam, drain a marsh or develop a marina.

And keep in mind

Here are a few other things to remember.

▶ The landscape is ever changing. Even without the influence of people — and people are part of nature — nature changes.

If people were to leave the planet, forests would mature, collapse and begin again. Mountains would erode and the courses of rivers would be shaped by hurricanes and floods. If a hurricane or a tornado strikes your community, keep in mind that harm to people is not the only story. Forestry scientists can explain what will happen to the woods that were blown down. Others can explain what it means for rivers and marshes.

▶ Be sure to take the story out of the laboratory. If your scientist has done his research in a marsh, report the story from the marsh. Tell the reader what the marsh looks like, feels like and why it matters. If you're writing about striped bass, take us to the bass.

▶ As with all reporting, be as specific as you can without burdening the reader. When you have a story that says the town plans to cut down an old tree for this or that reason, tell us whether it is a sugar maple or boxwood. When a duck and her ducklings stop traffic and it makes for a bright, tell us it's a mallard or a merganser.

▶ Check the credibility of your sources. If you are writing about a discovery by a scientist, ask if it is genuinely new. If the answer is yes, double-check with other experts in the field, preferably from outside your immediate area. Do other scientists dispute these findings? If so, talk to them.

And don't let your editor read the story and have to ask: "Why should anyone care about such and such a frog or tree or rock?" The scientists and the naturalists will have an answer. Make sure it's in the story.

Steve Grant began his career as a local news reporter for the Journal Inquirer of Manchester, Conn. He now writes about nature for The Courant. His first-person accounts of long-distance hiking and canoeing have been instrumental in reviving the 19th-century tradition of adventure journalism.

CHAPTER 9

Making local business your business

By Lou Golden

A town reporter, looking for news, heads straight for town hall. And why not? Municipal boards conduct their business mostly in public, and their decisions affect town residents. Yet many reporters never venture into an area that can have much — if not more — impact on a community as government.

Business.

As employers, companies greatly influence the lives of residents. People spend a great deal of their lives in the workplace, not in sewer commission meetings.

As corporate citizens, companies can greatly influence a community — whether it's by building a shopping center that brings thousands of people to town, by creating hazardous wastes that pollute groundwater or the air, or by donating thousands to restore a landmark building, beautify a park.

And as businesses, companies contribute directly to the well-being of many in a region — workers who receive paychecks, retirees who receive pension benefits, stockholders who receive dividends, and suppliers who receive payments, that they can, in turn, feed into the economic cycle.

In many towns, the power structure involves business people — bankers, real estate agents, merchants — as much as politicians.

But among many reporters there is a wariness, reluctance, even outright fear, of business news. For one thing, the world of business is foreign to many reporters. Few reporters, in college or afterward, are exposed to a corporate environment or business executives. Many don't understand the underlying pressures and motivations of business other than the ill-informed tendency to equate a desire for profits with greed.

Further, the language of business can be dry and technical. Face to face with a buttoned-down corporate type, what reporter wants to admit he or she thinks a "yield curve" is some kind of road sign and a "durable good" is what you try to get on your performance evaluation.

Most executives don't help the situation much. They tend to use colorless, contorted expressions that have all the punch in print of lukewarm oatmeal. While we might say something is horrible, criminal or abominable, a corporate clone might simply describe it as 'inappropriate."

Business people, for their part, sometimes understand journalists as poorly as journalists understand them. Very few understand the newsgathering process or, for that matter, how we make news judgments in the first place.

They've heard horror stories from colleagues who were once "burned" by a reporter. Or they've been unsuccessful in trying to get a "good news" story (a groundbreaking, store opening or trade association award) into the newspaper. Or worse, they've wasted hundreds of dollars on a PR firm that has been unsuccessful in getting that story into the newspaper.

The fact is that reporters and business people usually socialize in different circles and tend not to see each other in realistic terms. This breeds a lack of trust, making many executives suspicious and tightlipped around reporters.

And business people don't have to talk. A politician knows he or she has to talk to the press to reach the electorate. But executives usually let hired mouthpieces talk for them in statements as witty and spontaneous as any developed by a committee of lawyers.

Much of what goes on in the business world goes on in private. Freedom of information laws do not apply.

There are federal Securities and Exchange Commission regulations, but they govern only publicly traded companies (those whose stock is bought and sold by the public). These laws dictate that public companies must disclose how much money they make or lose. They must also announce any occurence — a contract, a grand jury investigation, an illness of a key officer or a lawsuit — that would affect the company "materially" (a word open to myriad interpretations).

Privately owned companies — the majority in America — don't have to say a word about anything.

This, then, is one of the biggest challenges of covering business: getting business people to talk to you. As members of The Courant's business staff will tell you, it's difficult, not impossible. Learn the fundamentals (the language, the issues and the specifics of an industry) and you can gain the trust of sources.

As with any beat, there are ways to get tips and gather information: by checking courts, state and local regulatory agencies, trade and business associations. Here is a list of places to check for information about companies:

The SEC

All public companies must make periodic filings with the Securities and Exchange Commission. These include:

▶ Registration statements. Whenever a company wants permission to sell stock, it must register its plans with the government. The resulting document, known as a registration statement, can be a gold mine of information, including details about how much stock top executives own, projected sales and earnings, outstanding lawsuits and the costs of operations.

▶ 10K filings. These contain similar information to registration statements, but must be filed annually by companies — an update on important information.

▶ 13D filings. If anyone buys more than 5 percent of the stock of a company, he or she must make a filing with the SEC within 10 days. This includes someone who already holds, say, 4 percent and then buys an additional 2 percent, so he or she holds more than 5 percent. Once investors have joined this group of large stockholders, they also have to file a Schedule 13D if they buy more stock or sell some. For reporters, this is a handy way to keep track of whether an investor is trying to gain control of a company.

▶ 8K filings. These, also known as "reporters' best friends," are filed by companies as a way of notifying the SEC — and the public — of any "material" events. Often a company may not put out a release on something, but it will show up in the SEC files as an 8K. This may include such minor bits of information as a change in the fiscal year or such major information as a bankruptcy filing.

To obtain an SEC filing, you can call a service, Disclosure Inc., which will send it to you for a fee, usually $20 to $30. Like many newspapers, The Courant has an account with Disclosure.

The annual report and proxy

Public companies are usually willing to supply you with a copy of their annual reports (usually a glossy, photo-filled book) and their proxy statements, (the reports to shareholders in preparation for annual meetings). In addition to the beautiful photography and slick paper, the annual reports usually give a basic outline of a company's business, its operations and its performance — how much it made or lost, borrowed or lended.

The proxy lists the compensation of the five most highly paid executives of the company. It also gives detailed information on members of the board of directors and their backgrounds.

Court records

Many fascinating details about a company's operations show up in court documents if a company is sued. While the suits themselves may be newsworthy, it's often the depositions and other filings that provide details public relations departments would never release. This includes filings in the state court system and U.S. District Court and U.S. Bankruptcy Court. Find out where the federal courts are located in your state. In Connecticut, they are in New Haven, Hartford and Bridgeport.

Town hall

Public records can tell much about a company. The assessor can tell you about the value of a company's land, buildings and equipment. The tax collector can tell you if the company is delinquent on back taxes, often a sign it is having financial difficulties. The town clerk will know if any liens have been attached on a company's property, another danger sign of problems. And the planning and zoning permits will show if a company is planning to expand — a sign of economic health.

State agencies

Certain agencies can provide valuable information. In Connecticut, for example, companies have to let the state labor department know if they are planning to lay off more than 50 people or transfer more than 50 jobs out of state. And Department of Environmental Protection records can show if a company has been cited for pollution violations. Other agencies regulate specific industries. In Connecticut, for example, they include the Department of Real Estate, the Department of Banking and the

Department of Insurance.

Cultivating sources

Obviously, it's important to cultivate people — not just records. One of the handiest groups is financial analysts. Every major Wall Street firm employs specialists who follow particular publicly traded companies and industries. As a result, they are very good at giving perspective and analysis — and simply explaining the significance of a company's announcement. They're also good at giving background on a particular industry, even if you are doing a story about a private company in that area.

The Nelson's Directory offers a listing of analysts arranged by the company and industry they follow. The Courant has one in its business news department, and your newspaper probably has one, too. If not, try the public library.

Similarly, trade associations can educate reporters quickly about the major issues, companies and controversies in their particular fields. Your news library may have a multi-volume listing of trade associations; The Courant's does.

For strictly local companies, you may find town officials knowledgeable. Similarly, officials of other companies sometimes will provide helpful information about their competitors. But remember, they have a vested interest in boosting themselves at the expense of their competitors.

Mastering the playing field

Now that you know where to get information, are you going to understand it? That's a fear of many reporters approaching a business story. There is no way to adequately cover all business topics in this chapter, but let's clear up a few basics that tend to confuse people new to business.

▶ Profits and revenues are not the same thing. Revenues are the money a company brings in by selling its products and services. Profits are what's left after the company pays its expenses. Thus, a company could have revenues of $10 million and profits of only 50 cents. How? By paying out expenses of $9,999,999.50.

▶ Equity and debt are not the same thing. Equity means ownership; debt is the result of borrowing money. Often equity takes the form of stock. When you buy a share of stock, you buy a piece of the company. As a result, the company shares its profits with you in the form of dividends.

When you buy a bond, on the other hand, you're buying debt — the company (or whomever) is promising to pay you back over a certain period at a specific rate of interest.

▶ Partnerships and corporations are not the same thing. In most partnerships, two or more owners share the assets (what they own) as well as the liabilities (what they owe). Thus, if a partnership is sued, each partner can be liable personally. A corporation, on the other hand, is itself the legal entity that owns and owes. When a corporation is sued, shareholders are not liable personally. It's important to remember that not all companies are corporations.

▶ Bankruptcy and insolvency are not the same thing. When a company owes more than it owns — in other words, if it can't pay its bills — it's insolvent. But it isn't necessarily bankrupt. Bankruptcy simply is protection. If a company owes you money, you could try to seize its assets. But if the company files for bankruptcy, it is protected by the court.

The two most common forms of bankruptcy filings are Chapter 11 and Chapter 7. Under Chapter 11, the company tries to reorganize itself while it works out a plan to pay off its creditors. It stays in business. Under Chapter 7, it ceases operations and sells off its assets to pay creditors. Nearly all insolvent companies file for bankruptcy protection, but a company doesn't have to be insolvent to file.

Another important point: Companies can be forced into bankruptcy court by its creditors, fearful it will go out of business, leaving the unpaid bills. A company can fight it, and some even convince the court that it should not be there. A company fighting being forced into bankruptcy should never be called bankrupt.

Lou Golden, former Courant business editor, began as a reporter for the weekly Bethel (Conn.) Home News. He is now The Courant's vice president of marketing. His experience includes helping found and edit Weekly World News, which scoops The Courant regularly on alien landings and Elvis sightings.

MOST OF LIFE IS NOT GOVERNMENT

CHAPTER 10

We can write it for you retail

By Gregory Seay

Understanding retail

The buying and selling of goods and services keeps families, neighborhoods and communities productive and growing.

The local supermarket, for example, not only sells food but also employs people who use their wages to buy necessities and luxuries. That spending, in turn, provides income for others. Each retailer is a link in a long and vital chain.

The close inspection of one or more of those links provides news: a new store comes to town; an old retailer goes bankrupt; inflation drives prices up or competition drives them down.

Retail touches everyone, and that makes it interesting to readers and important to communities.

Where are the stories?

Retail stories are easy to spot once you start looking for them.

▶ There are seasonal stories, such as sizing up stores and malls on their outlook for the Christmas, the back-to-school and Easter seasons.

▶ There are stories about successes and failures: the new business that is making it big, the old company that has suddenly failed. It's up to you to explain why. And the owners of these businesses can make good profiles.

▶ Many communities have retailers who have succeeded by finding an unusual niche: the pizzeria that will ship a frozen pizza anywhere in the world; the entrepreneur who has turned an old Fotomat film drop into a drive-up "Condom Hut;" the ex-corporate executive who is getting rich building designer birdhouses. They make good features.

▶ How are rival businesses competing for customers? Are they running more sales? Offering more personal service? And what do customers say about why they chose one store over another?

▶ Read signs at construction sites. They often give the name, address and even telephone number of the general contractor or the leasing agent, who can tell you what is being built and who is going to locate there.

▶ Make it a point to ask shopkeepers, "How's business?" Merchants are usually the first to know when their communities are on the verge of an economic rebound or downturn — just by how often the cash register rings.

▶ Often, national trends can quickly be localized. Is that hot new toy big in your town, too? If it is, it's a story. If it's not, that's a story, too.

▶ Check the wires. Retail chains are always expanding or closing stores and distribution centers. If you spot a wire story about a retailer with a presence in your town, call and ask how the announcement might affect your community. Wire stories seldom provide all the details. Sometimes a store-closing in one town will result in an expansion in yours.

▶ Give your curiosity free rein and you will see stories everywhere. When you go to the grocery store, do you wonder why the price of beef or coffee has risen sharply since your last visit? Curious why that restaurant you drive by every day is always packed with diners? Want to know what's going to occupy the new shopping center on the edge of town? Wonder how a new department store will affect rival retailers in town?

Readers wonder about those things, too. Find the answers and you will have stories with reader appeal.

Before the first Wal-Mart opened in Connecticut, for example, The Courant checked with communities that already had Wal-Marts to learn what impact the retail giant had had on communities and its competition.

Getting started

Start with experts. You can find them in the Yellow Pages.

If you want to know why food prices are rocketing upward, call area supermarkets. To find out why several furniture stores are opening in the same area, call not only the new players but the existing competitors.

Get independent assessments as well. Good sources for that are business or retail experts at local colleges. In Connecticut, for example, the University of Connecticut and the University of Hartford have retailing and marketing experts who are helpful. You can find people like them in your area.

Local banks and the telephone companies also usually have staff economists who can provide unbiased retail analysis. And if your newspaper has a marketing department, it may have a lot of data that can be of help in explaining retail trends.

Don't forget trade groups. In Connecticut, for example, there is the Connecticut Retail Merchants Association, as well as associations for car dealers, supermarkets and restaurants. These groups have counterparts at the national level as well. Your news library or your business news department has a directory of industry trade groups.

When you've done enough background work to ask good questions, call the store or business you want to focus on and ask for the owner or manager. Try to talk with the owner first. If it's a chain, ask the manager for the number or location of the home office, and seek out the public relations staff for help.

The same basic approaches works in whatever kind of retail story you're pursuing — a new restaurant, a piece about dueling dry cleaners, etc.

Gregory Seay began his career as a business reporter for The Journal-Record in Oklahoma City. He is now assistant business editor for The Courant. His accomplishments include award-winning coverage of the Texas savings and loan scandal.

Local interest:
How to cover the banks

By Gregory Seay

Behind the carefully cultivated mystique of respectability and trustworthiness, a bank is just a business, albeit a powerful one.

Just as retail stores profit from the purchase and sale of goods, banks profit from the purchase and sale of money. Understand that and you're well on the way to understanding a bank's role in the community.

Banks "buy," or pay interest, to collect deposits from families saving for a rainy day or for retirement.

In turn, they "sell" those deposits to borrowers who use it to buy everything from new homes and automobiles to inventory for the corner hardware store. Borrowers agree to repay the principal, plus interest, within a certain period.

Banks make money in other ways, too. They can charge fees for handling other people's money and they can slap customers with penalties when they mishandle their own money.

The special power banks hold in the life of a community lies in their ability to decide who gets loans and who doesn't. Banks control the capital that lubricates the economic gears of a community.

Know the difference

Banking is often used as a catch-all term to describe a variety of financial institutions.

Banks typically make commercial loans to businesses to buy inventory to stock their shelves, build factories or buy equipment. They also grant loans to consumers to buy such items as cars and boats, or to finance a home remodeling or a college education. Many banks also issue credit cards, yet they rarely issue home-mortgage loans.

But banks aren't the only institutions that accept deposits and make loans.

Savings and loans, also called thrifts, are a type of financial institution whose main role is to collect deposits and loan them to consumers to buy houses and other real estate, and to finance automobile purchases. Unlike banks, savings and loans rarely make business loans.

Credit unions are members-only financial cooperatives that fund mostly auto, home and home-improvement loans. (Your newspaper, for instance, may have a credit union to serve only the paper's employees.) Some also issue credit cards. They, too, rarely grant business loans.

So, if you're working up a story about a spurt of home-buying in your area, the local savings and loan and the local credit unions probably would be better sources of information than the bank.

On the other hand, the bank would be a better source than the other two for a story about whether businesses are borrowing more money when interest rates are falling.

But all three would be ideal sources if you're looking for information about trends in automobile financing or the outlook on the direction interest rates — for loans or deposits — are headed.

Source development

Leaving out for a moment the technical ends of banking (which are probably handled by your newspaper's business desk), the industry can be a rich lode of stories.

Take the economy angle. The local banker is usually a reliable interpreter of the economic vitality of a town or community. The bank president or a senior loan officer almost always knows which businesses are faring well and which are not.

Cultivating bank officers and employees as sources is always a good idea, too. You can use their expertise, along with other sources, to understand what is happening in the local economy.

If you are covering a small community, your readers probably know the top officials of local banks. If the officials are well-respected, their views add credibility to what you write.

Top bankers are easier to find and get to know than many other players in the banking industry. For example, state and federal regulators rarely poke their heads out for the public to see them. Even less visible are bank examiners, the professionals who keep track of healthy and unhealthy banks.

But that doesn't mean you shouldn't try to get to know them. Any bank regulator you can cultivate as a source can help you spot and analyze trends or industry developments.

Trend-spotting

Many good bank stories grow out of interesting observations by you or readers.

▶ You call the bank to refinance your mortgage and find it will be months before it can be done because dozens of customers are in line ahead of you. A story emerges about the flood of refinancings swamping area banks.

▶ You stop at the bank to open a checking account. The bank also offers you a savings account, a mutual fund and even a home equity line of credit. Perhaps a story is in order about how the growing wave of aggressive bank marketing has reached the local bank.

▶ You notice that your supermarket now lets customers pay for groceries with bank cards that make direct withdrawals from their accounts. What do the locals — customers as well as the grocers who aren't equipped to offer the service — think about it?

With the sweeping changes reshaping the financial industry, you can find banking stories almost everywhere you go. The key is to look for the trends that affect consumers.

Bank failures and mergers make for big headlines. But local readers are most interested in how those events affect them. The best stories explain how the new trends might change the way readers do their banking.

Follow the money

When you notice a new development like one of the above, contact a stock analyst who follows the bank for investment purposes or one of the many state and national bank trade organizations. Chances are the analyst or trade group can tell you whether the development is unique to that bank or a trend taking hold throughout the industry.

You might find that the bank with the long wait for refinancings is one of many being flooded with refinance applications because interest rates have hit record lows. That might give you a regional trend piece instead of a local story. More likely, it will provide you with the information you need to give your local story perspective.

The bank that now offers multiple financial products is probably one of many working harder to serve all of a consumer's banking needs to boost business in the accelerating competition for customers.

Analysts and industry experts will help you explain to consumers that the supermarket that accepts bank cards is one of many expanding automated services to make it easier for people to conduct business.

For a story about a local lender who is preparing to offer credit cards, you could call on experts such as the RAM Bankcard newsletter in Washington, D.C., for statistics on the number of Americans with credit cards, the average number of cards each carries, and the average outstanding balance.

Then you're better prepared to interview your bank source in detail about the new strategy, the bank's motivation for introducing it and the way it might be changing future business plans.

Most sources don't mind taking the time to explain complicated topics if you show you've done some homework and made an effort to understand. If you do some research in advance, bankers think twice about trying to snow you.

As with any story, the human side makes it go. Nothing brightens a story about how to apply for a bank loan than talking with a homebuyer or business that has recently been through the exercise.

Better yet, get permission to walk through the process with a bank and its customer. If you work at it, you can usually find a banker and customer who will go along with such an idea.

Happy trails

There are many good banking stories besides consumer pieces.

A financial institution's annual financial report and the financial reports they release four times a year tracks its basic health. Watch for changes income, problem loans and capital, or financial cushion.

The state and federal regulators who monitor banking practices can tell you if a bank has been ordered to improve its financial condition. Regulatory orders become routine during a recession.

Be careful how you report the financial troubles of a bank, savings and loan or credit union. Rarely is the money of depositors at risk. Even when a bank fails, money is usually safe, because most banks carry government deposit insurance. That must be spelled out clearly and high in the story to reassure nervous investors. Never panic depositors unnecessarily; never provoke a run on a bank.

If you have a checking or savings account, you may be familiar with some of the alphabet-soup acronyms that identify the two federal deposit-insurance funds — FDIC (Federal Deposit Insurance Corp., which protects bank and savings and loan deposits) and NCUA (National Credit Union Administration, for credit union deposits). Most institutions are insured by one of these, or in some states they may be insured by state deposit insurance. You can confirm that a bank has insurance by asking the bank officer, a regulator or the deposit insurance funds themselves.

The ins and outs of various deposit insurance funds can be complicated, but understanding the details may be important to your story. Someone at the fund that insures the bank you are writing about should be willing to explain how the insurance works.

Write for the consumer

Financial recovery programs by banks often result in staff eliminations and branch closures. The annual meetings that banks hold for shareholders are often forums for spirited exchanges between stockholders and bank executives.

Bank foreclosures of well-known real estate properties are common in recessions and stories about them are of strong reader interest.

When approaching these or any banking stories, try to write not for the financial industry but for consumers.

Everyone banks, so your stories should have a broad audience.

The people stories

Meanwhile, don't forget to write the human stories. Banks are often a stable source of employment to a number of people — everyone from tellers to cashiers to loan officers.

More than one bank chairman has retired from a local bank where he started right out of high school in the bank's collections department or in the teller cage. Interesting profile material can be found there.

Or, in many one-bank towns, the lender is one of several businesses that underwrite the local pee-wee baseball or soccer league, which is about to send its first group of wide-eyed youngsters to a regional or national championship. The bank paid for the plane fare or supplied the uniforms.

Gregory Seay began his career as a business reporter for The Journal-Record in Oklahoma City. He is now assistant business editor for The Courant. His accomplishments include award-winning coverage of the Texas savings and loan scandal.

CHAPTER 12

Looking out for the local consumer

By Anthony Giorgianni

Town coverage can provide good opportunities for stories that affect consumers.

Those issues can include illegal going-out-of-business sales, advertising violations, wrongdoing in connection with car sales and repairs, supermarket price violations and home repair contractors.

Learn about the consumer laws in your state and the agencies responsible for enforcing them. In Connecticut, for example, many of the consumer laws are enforced by the state Department of Consumer Protection, which has divisions assigned to general fraud, weights and measures, food, the automobile Lemon Law and the licensing or registration of tradespeople, including home improvement contractors, plumbers, electricians and others. Other agencies include the attorney general's office (which files suits and handles antitrust investigations), the banking department, the department of motor vehicles, and the insurance department.

Among the good sources for town-related consumer stories is the town health inspector and inspection records of restaurants and other facilities that serve or prepare food.

The town's building inspector may know about home improvement contractors who are doing substandard work and contractors who are working without the required licenses or registrations. There may be some good human-interest pieces: for example, elderly people who have lost some of their life's savings to fly-by-night contractors.

Health clubs are good businesses to watch because they often go out of business, stranding customers who commonly pay hundreds of dollars for memberships. Health clubs are regulated by the consumer protection department.

When local businesses fail, it is important to check with the appropriate state agency to determine whether consumers are complaining about lost deposits and other problems. The consumer protection department, for example, may have found that a failing health club was accepting membership money up until the morning it closed or that the bridal shop shut down unexpectedly, leaving hundreds of frantic brides wondering about their wedding gowns. Or maybe the car dealership closes, taking with it money that was supposed to be used to provide extended warranties.

Some other things to consider: Local supermarkets' weighing devices, sanitary conditions, unit prices and checkout scanners, all of which are inspected periodically by consumer officials. You can ask to review those inspection reports.

Many states, including Connecticut, have a public charities unit with financial information about charities and other nonprofit groups in your town, including the police and fire unions and others that do fund-raising. If they use a professional fund-raiser — and there's a good chance they do — how much of the money really goes to the charity and how much to the fund-raiser? Sometimes, the figures can be shocking.

If you are writing a piece that involves a local business or business person — particularly if it is a harmless feature story — check out the business' reputation with state officials, the Better Business Bureau and The Courant's clip files. The last thing you want to do is a nice feature on a restaurant, for example, and discover that it's repeatedly been cited for health violations.

Anthony Giorgianni got his start as a local reporter for weekly newspapers on his native Long Island and has also covered small towns for The Hartford Courant. Today, he is the newspaper's consumer affairs reporter.

CHAPTER 13

The world of work

By Andrew Julien and Michael Remez

Americans, more than many other people around the world, define themselves through work. Our jobs determine how we do financially, how we view ourselves, who our friends are and where we live. Look at the workplace from that perspective, and the potential for stories becomes infinite.

A reporter covering a community should be as familiar with the major industries as he or she is with the mayor, the town council and the chief of police.

It is, in the end, the availability and quality of employment that drives a community to prosper or fail. The Connecticut landscape is littered with once-thriving communities that became blighted neighborhoods when the factories closed.

Too often, reporters write off the places where people work as constants that need to be considered only when they shut down, lay off workers or get hit by strikes.

So visit the workplaces in your town. Call first to tell them you are coming. Ask for a tour of the factory, the office, the field. If a local employer puts out a press release on something not all that newsworthy, use it as an excuse to learn more about the company.

Don't stop there, though. Open your ears to what the working people have to say.

Get to know the local union officials. For non-union places, make a habit of asking people about their jobs when you are doing stories about other subjects. People who work together tend to hang out together, so if you are interested in learning about a particular workplace, use one source to get to the next. If a particular place intrigues you, follow that instinct.

Strikes are stories, contracts are stories and layoffs are, obviously, stories.

But there are a lot more stories that fall under the general heading of work.

Many great stories don't meet the traditional definition of news: A person leaves a job he's had for 40 years and finds it hard to fill the time; a woman struggles with the guilt she feels over paying someone else to care for her children while she works. These are universal stories. Well reported and well told, they can reach many readers.

Let your imagination and your ears be your guide.

People like to talk about their jobs, although they are often reluctant to go on the record, for fear of upsetting the boss. This is a real fear. Take people's fears seriously and work with them.

Here are some general areas that might be worth exploring:

The changing workplace

America's workplaces are undergoing a dramatic change. Economic forces are driving many companies to reduce their payrolls. They are laying people off, cutting their wages, redefining jobs to get more out of each worker.

These moves are having a profound effect, leaving many workers more nervous about the future and less certain about the present.

Where can you find the stories about what's happening to these people? Probably not at the office or the factory. But talk to local alcohol abuse counselors or family violence experts. Tension at work often spills into the home. A riveting story about one person can be far more compelling than a story that quotes a bunch of experts talking about what other people are going through. (But call the experts anyway, so you can write with authority about how your one story is part of a trend.)

Discrimination

This is still part of life in the American workplace. Stories of true discrimination can be compelling and enlightening, but the challenge is separating the legitimate claims from the illegitimate.

It has become almost routine for someone who feels wronged by an employer to cry discrimination of one type or another. And there are so many types of discrimination today — race, sex, sexual orientation, religion, physical handicap, age — that just about everyone falls into one protected class or another. Review such claims carefully.

Most states have an administrative mechanism for filing discrimination claims. Aggrieved workers can also go directly to the federal Equal

Employment Opportunity Commission.

The disclosure laws vary from state to state, so check with your local human rights agency. Note: Often a given claim is not public information until there has been a preliminary determination made whether the claim has some validity.

Even if you can't get the documents from the state, lawyers in discrimination cases will often give you a copy because they want some press. Companies don't like negative publicity, and labor lawyers are aware of that. Get to know the lawyers in your community who specialize in labor law. The civil court docket can also be a good place to find these kinds of stories.

Work and family

As more women enter the work force, leaving no parents at home, family issues are quickly becoming a major story in the workplace.

Day-care centers in offices, family-leave programs and even adoption benefits are becoming routine. Many employers are realizing that it is in their interest to help employees juggle the demands of work and family because concerns about children tend to distract workers.

Still, there are many problems in this area. In Connecticut, as in other states, the labor department has investigators whose job it is to check out violations of the family and medical leave act.

These stories often involve an employer's promising a position to a person who takes an unpaid family leave, and then reneging when the worker is ready to return.

This is one of the many areas related to the workplace where a seemingly routine story can become a compelling tale.

Government and regulation

America has laws that govern just about every aspect of the workplace: wages, hours, working conditions, safety and more. These laws are enforced on both the state and federal level.

If someone tells you that working conditions are unsafe at a local factory, the federal Occupational Safety and Health Administration may have conducted an inspection. If an employer is forcing workers to work 60 hours a week without paying overtime, state or federal wage and hour investigators may have a case going. If a worker trying to organize a union has been fired, the National Labor Relations Board may be looking into it.

Most of the work these agencies do is public. The trick is knowing where to start. If you pick up a cop brief about an accident at a local factory, check the company's safety records with OSHA — it could be part of a pattern. If busloads of workers are being "imported" to work at a local farm, call the Immigration and Naturalization Service to see if there is a possibility the employer is using undocumented workers.

Don't stop with the government, though. Go out and talk to workers.

Unions

With only about 15 percent of the American work force belonging to trade unions, the role of unions has declined. But unions are still a major player.

On the national, state and local level they are very active politically. In cities and towns, public-employee unions tend to exert quite a bit of influence, and it's worth exploring the relationship between union leaders and local politicians. If the mayor suddenly decides the police union's demand for a big pay increase is justified, find out if the union is out helping the mayor get re-elected.

Unions can also be tremendously helpful in covering stories about a particular company. Unionized workers tend to be less fearful than non-union workers and will often tell you things the company won't.

Unions also get involved in grievances over potentially interesting issues and might be willing to leak you something good. Don't take the union's word as gospel. Sometimes workers in the union don't agree with union officials.

Organizing drives are always a good thing to look at. Companies generally want to keep unions out, and workers who push for the union sometimes get fired.

Are workers concerned about job safety? Are they struggling to make ends meet because the wages are so low? Be thorough and fair, but don't let the company and the union drag you into simplistic, "he said, she said," coverage. Look for the nuggets. In organizing cases, complaints about illegal behavior — either by unions or employers — are handled by the National Labor Relations Board.

And don't overlook the possibility of union corruption. The U.S. Labor Department requires unions to file records outlining the salaries and perks given to union officials. Most of the investigating is done by the federal government through the Department of Justice and the Department of Labor.

Finding the right balance in labor reporting can be tricky. In a labor dispute, both sides are generally convinced theirs is the only legitimate point of view. The union talks about economic justice, and the company talks about survival. Often there are elements of truth in both positions.

Covering negotiations

When talks are under way, it can be tough to get much information out of either side. That's why it's good to develop sources who will talk off the record or at least verify what you've gotten from other sources. Those sources could include talkative attorneys or rank-and-file workers frustrated with what's been happening.

Again, be careful of accepting any one side's analysis.

If you are covering a strike in your community, try to assess the local impact. What are the costs to the town in extra police protection or people steering clear of a certain area for fear of encountering strikers? What is the effect on local businesses?

Is there a family where one man is out on strike but his brother is crossing the picket line because he desperately needs the work? It happens. And it makes for good stories.

Andrew Julien got his start at an English-language political monthly published in Tel Aviv. He now reports on workplace issues for The Courant, where he formerly had the city police beat. His honors include a Connecticut Society of Professional Journalists award for his labor column.

Michael Remez began as a local news reporter for the Easton (Pa.) Express. A former labor reporter for The Courant, he now works in the newspaper's Washington bureau. His honors include the John Hancock Prize, one of the top awards for business journalism.

CHAPTER 14

Getting around

By Bill Keveney

Transportation is commuters (including us) dodging potholes and praying to avoid traffic jams. It is kids getting safely off a school bus. It is the promise of fast, shiny trains in the age of the automobile.

The issues are everywhere, but it takes thought and imagination to create insightful and/or entertaining stories out of the pedestrian (only a partial pun).

Everybody has to get around, so this is one of the few topics that has almost universal interest. And everyone is an expert. More people are aware of and can understand transportation issues than will ever know the intricacies of the president's economic plan.

Roads and highways

Transportation is more than roads and highways, but it sure pays to look at them, too. Every city or town has a public works and/or transportation department charged with building, repairing and maintaining roads, the latter running the gamut from snowplowing to street sweeping.

Potholes and snowplowing budget overruns are two seasonal events that are worth looking into. It pays, however, to look for different angles, since these topics are written about frequently.

For example, it can be helpful to look at snowplowing budgets when the municipal budget is proposed and approved in the spring, not just after a few snowstorms in the winter. This tells you whether a town is gambling on good weather. Skimping on snowplow budgets can be a sign of difficult economic times.

Potholes, too, deserve attention. Pothole stories can make for fun features, but it might also be useful to check the resurfacing schedule in your city or town. The longer a road hasn't been repaired and paved, the more likely it is to have potholes. Strapped towns often put off such work to save money; they shouldn't be allowed simply to blame bad weather for the resulting problems.

And what about the cost of unrepaired potholes to motorists? Might a check of local garages and tire shops uncover an increase in undercarriage repairs and tire damage?

Check road resurfacing or widening projects, too. They may be conducted either by the town or the state transportation department. In cold-weather states, these generally take place in the spring or summer, and they can mean detoured traffic, traffic jams and/or lost business for area stores.

State and federal money

Much of the money to pay for road expansion or improvements comes from the state and federal governments. Know how their funding programs work.

Connecticut, for example, has two general municipal aid programs affecting road improvments: the Town Aid program and the Local Infrastructure Capital Improvement Program (LOCIP). Money is distributed by formulas based on the number of people and miles of road in a municipality.

Is state money being cut this year? Increased? How is that going to affect roads in your town?

For state roads and interstate highways, the state transportation department makes most of the decisions on improvements, relying to a large extent on federal funds to cover the costs. The federal government usually pays 80 percent of the cost of the approved projects, with the state picking up the other 20 percent.

Is money for these projects increasing or decreasing this year? Which projects in your town might be affected? Which roads that lead to your town are being affected? Are local officials and state legislators from your area pushing to have cut projects restored?

And business will follow

When roads are built or expanded, new businesses are likely to open. This can provide a number of stories, including ones relating to the town's economy, tax base and traffic.

You could also examine commercial zones along major roads, examining why they work or don't work, and how the transportation system can be used to enhance commercial development.

Enforcement

Traffic enforcement is another issue. Some towns make a big deal about it, but others don't. From experience, I know traffic enforcement is a high priority in Manchester, Conn., while in Hartford, it's not a priority because there are so many other things keeping cops busy.

If your local police department appears to have a different practice than surrounding towns, it would be worth a story. Does your town ignore stop sign violations while neighboring towns crack down on them? Why? And what do residents think of that? You might also want to interview officers who have years of experience in traffic control. They might have ideas, or be a story themselves.

In recent years, some cities have been computerizing traffic signals on major thoroughfares to allow for a smoother flow of traffic and also for centralized control in the case of an emergency. This could be something to look at in your town as the practice becomes more common.

Buses

School bus service is an obvious issue. Who provides the service and what is their record for safety? How about their drivers? Requiring school bus monitors has become more common in recent years and groups have been forming in some towns to promote such a measure.

Bus service for commuters also could yield stories. You could ask whether the town has enough commuter and local bus service and whether residents want more or, in some cases, less.

Remember, transportation affects how towns develop. Wealthy towns, for example, often have little transportation, because everyone has a car — and, by not having much mass transit, everyone will always have to have a car. So if you don't have a car, you can't live there. That's how some people want it.

Regional planning

Find out which regional planning agency covers your town and talk to its officials about their transportation plans for the region. For towns near Hartford, for example, the Capitol Region Council of Governments is the regional planning agency.

Under recent federal transportation legislation — the Intermodal Surface Transportation Efficiency Act of 1991, or ISTEA (pronounced in the trade as ICE TEA) — regional planning agencies have a much greater role in determining transportation planning.

For example, regional planning agencies will play a large role in planning and obtaining state funds for bicycle and multipurpose trails. State and federal transportation regulations now require that some funds go toward such projects. Stories on bicycle trails have high readership.

If there are abandoned rail lines in your town, or some other right of way that is not open to regular traffic, chances are that somebody is thinking about making a bicycle trail. Chances are, too, that somebody will oppose that plan.

Riding the rails

Although rail commuting is uncommon in most parts of the country, there are a lot of unused railroad rights of way and unused rail lines around. Commuter rail plans surface every few years around many cities and make for good stories. In Connecticut, for example, the proposed light-rail Griffin Line has been — and will continue to be — the source of many stories. Rail also has been a major issue for years in Wallingford, Conn., where many people have been killed at local rail crossings.

Spotting the trends

Trends are also worth pursuing. How many people ride their bicycles to work — or store them at a commuter lot, before taking the bus to work? Census records can provide answers and organizations dedicated to a particular hobby or pursuit – in this case – cycling, can identify interview subjects.

There are plenty of other possible trends. How many parents drop their children off at day care before driving to work? The census might be able to help again, as can calls to day-care centers themselves, if interview subjects are needed.

How many families in your town have more than two cars, or no car at all. The assessor's records could give you some help with the last question.

Since everybody can relate to transportation matters such as commuting, there's plenty of leeway to do town point-of-view stories. For example, you might write a story about the worst intersection in town or particular traffic trouble for commuters driving from the town you cover. This kind of story allows for anecdotal material and interviews with average Joes, because their opinions count as much as anyone's when it comes to transportation.

Finally, remember the adage that most kids learned in the first grade: Stop, Look and Listen. There are plenty of transportation stories out there waiting to be written; look beyond the obvious and you'll find them.

Bill Keveney got his start covering schools and zoning for the Journal Inquirer of Manchester, Conn. He is now the media reporter for The Courant, covering television and radio issues. He has also served as Hartford City Hall bureau chief and transportation columnist for The Courant.

CHAPTER 15

Telephone, gas & electric

By Susan E. Kinsman

Public utilities provide vital services to customers — you and me, your neighbors, friends and family. If the services change or are interrupted, if the price goes up or down, it affects everyone, and that's a story.

Sometimes, it seems as if it would be easier to translate one of the Dead Sea scrolls than to explain industry jargon so that readers can understand it. But once you dig into utilities, there's no end to the stories.

Public utilities include services essential to public health, such as water supplies and sewers, and services essential to public welfare, such as electric, gas and telephone services. They also include services, such as cable television, that require equipment or delivery systems so costly to build that competition has been limited in the interest of keeping down costs to the public.

Regulatory agencies

Public utilities can be provided by cities and towns or by private, investor-owned companies. In Connecticut, for example, we have both. Private companies in the public utility business usually have a monopoly in their service areas. In return, the amount of money they can earn and the rates they can charge customers are regulated.

Make sure you know what state agencies regulate your utilities, and develop sources in those agencies. In Connecticut, for example, most major utilities are regulated by the state Department of Public Utility Control. A five-member decision-making body within that agency is the Public Utilities Control Authority. Its members are called commissioners.

With cable television companies, it works differently. Local officials grant franchises to cable companies for limited terms, usually five to 10 years. But the rates cable companies charge are not set by the officials.

Under new federal rules, the Federal Communications Commission can set rates for basic cable services. However, rates for premium cable services are not regulated, although that could change in the future.

What are the stories?

Outages

Nothing sends people running to the telephone (if it is working) faster than losing their electricity, gas or telephone service. Each of the utilities has special customer service numbers, listed in the telephone book, to report outages. They also have 24-hour contacts for reporters to be updated on how many people have lost service, what the problem is and when service will be restored. Make sure you know in advance whom to contact about outages for each of the utilities that serve your community.

Rates

Another area is utility rates. People want to know how much more they are going to be charged for service and why. Since most utility companies are large, with thousands of customers in many different cities and towns, a statewide story, (written by the newspaper's utilities beat reporter if it has one) may be the best approach for rate stories.

But there are spinoff stories to be done by reporters covering individual communities. What do local residents think about a proposal to increase rates? Who will be hurt most? Who will be helped? Will companies that consume a lot of energy consider cutting jobs or moving out of state? Would the increase be accompanied by improved services that would help specific groups, such as the elderly or people with disabilities?

Community involvement

Look at any special programs that companies provide. Connecticut utilities, for example, are required to invest substantial sums in conservation and economic development. Are any companies or residents in your area benefiting? If not, why not? This may be a good urban/suburban story if most of the resources are being directed to the suburbs.

What are utility companies doing voluntarily to help the community? For example, Connecticut Light & Power Co. supports the Special Olympics. Whatever they are doing, their spokespeople will love to talk about it.

On the job

Interview the people who are the utility's most visible employees in the community — those responsible for making sure your lights stay on or your telephone does more than hang on the wall. Follow a line crew around after or during a storm. Or talk to crews repairing broken water or gas lines. They make a living doing what most of us try to avoid. The story may make an interesting real-person profile.

Some hot topics

Electricity

The industry continues to study whether the electromagnetic radiation from power lines and substations contributes to the incidence of rare cancers. Is this an issue in your community? It usually comes up when a utility is trying to build a new transmission line or microwave tower. In Connecticut, the Connecticut Siting Council is the place to check for pending projects. Make sure you know where to check in your state.

Are local companies or developers trying to develop their own electrical generating stations to use the power themselves or to sell to the local utility? Privately owned small hydroelectric projects can make interesting stories; there are several in Connecticut.

Gas

The effort to clean up the air is making natural gas an increasingly popular fuel choice. Eventually this may force the gas pipeline companies to add facilities — building new pipelines or expanding the capacity of existing pipelines. This generates a lot of local controversy and raises a lot of environmental questions.

If a pipeline passes through your community, why not walk the right of way? Is the company keeping its promise to undo environmental damage? Are the herbicides it uses to keep the area free of trees and brush threatening wildlife and surrounding areas? What do local conservation and environmental groups think of what the company is doing? Has the area benefited from pipeline companies' contributions to conservation and open space programs?

Whenever anyone digs up a road or an area where underground utilities are located, they need permission and a permit. Contractors have been hit with stiff fines for failing to do this. The next time you see a backhoe dig-ging up Main Street, why not check if a permit has been issued?

Telephone

New services or changes in local calling areas are fertile ground for local stories. People always have complaints about telephone services or lack thereof. In Connecticut, for example, complaints are filed with the state Department of Public Utility Control. Or check with local officials about any dissatisfaction they know about.

Municipal governments get revenue from the long-distance companies they choose for municipal pay telephones. Several cities in Connecticut have cashed in by negotiating new deals. This could be a good local story.

Cable

Cable services and community access programming are another source of stories. What do cable companies provide? Are there any "Wayne's World" aspirants out there producing interesting local programming? Is the cable company doing enough, or are local residents or school officials looking for more? Does anyone watch the local programming? Do schools in your area share classes with other schools over cable stations or other linkups? Educational programming and local access have been hot topics for cable companies seeking franchise renewals. The companies are under legislative and regulatory pressure to do more. Cable companies have local advisory groups, and that would be a good place to start.

Water

Municipal and private water companies with reservoirs and other above-ground sources have to invest in new filtration plants and other facilities to meet new federal drinking water standards. This also means a sizable increase in rates. Check for any projects in your area. Also check with local health officials on quality of the water, bacteria counts, lead in the water supplies. Are pipe replacement projects planned? Supply is also always of interest. Have winter storms left the reservoirs brimming, or are we apt to have a ban on watering lawns and washing cars this summer? In the Western states, issues of water supply and water rates are far more complicated than in the East; in fact, they are among the most complicated and political of all issues from Kansas to California. Do a lot of studying before you decide to take on any major water rights stories.

Finding sources

Sources are the key to any story, and utilities are no exception. In addition to company representatives, get to know regulatory officials, legislators, industry trade groups and consultants. Many newspapers have compiled lists of contacts, and some of them, including The Courant, have even stored them on the newsroom computers.

Susan E. Kinsman began her career covering the town of Redding for the Danbury (Conn.) News-Times. She is now the energy and public utilities reporter for The Courant. She is a lawyer and former state capitol bureau chief for The Courant.

CHAPTER 16

Flames, downed planes & hurricanes

By Paul Stern

Disasters are great news.

It may be an insensitive thing to say, but covering a public emergency can be one of the most exciting experiences in journalism.

Properly covering a big fire or a plane crash or a hurricane requires speed, accuracy, ingenuity and resourcefulness. It also takes keen powers of observation, insight into the human spirit and the ability to portray the action and emotion of the event in clear and human terms.

Get there — fast

Nothing is more important than getting there quickly. It can make the difference between getting access to the scene and being herded into the controlled media zone. It can mean talking to witnesses before they leave, or before the authorities tell them not to talk. It can mean watching the daring rescue in person instead of asking a tired and inarticulate spokesman to give a laundered narrative of events.

True, there will be plenty of times when you race out of the newsroom to a fire that did little damage, or a gas leak you can't get near, but the odds are on your side. One day you'll be there first when it counts most.

Use your senses

When you get there, take plenty of notes on what you see, hear, smell and feel: the colors, the smell of things, the direction of the wind and anything else that will help you re-create the scene later.

Count things. Make sketches if they will help you or your graphic artists later.

Write down license plate numbers, identification numbers on planes or boats and other such information that might help you in a background investigation later. Note the time occasionally, too.

Whom to talk to

Do not rely exclusively on official sources. Neighborhood people are much more likely to tell you the kinds of things that will provide the human touches to your stories or disclose the marginal information that later, with proper research and corroboration, will illuminate the cause or deeper significance of the incident.

In spectacular emergencies such as airplane crashes or skyscraper fires, look for angles the broadcast and video media can't easily handle. To compete successfully with the power of the camera, you will need to report not only the obvious and tangible, but the intangible. Find sources who can explain the reasons for things, or reveal the ironies of developments, or expand your understanding of the context of the event. (Example: The firefighter who rescued the youngster from the burning building tells you he was frightened, but gained the courage he needed by picturing the child as his own.)

As a general rule, try to cooperate with public safety officials; you'll probably need their cooperation later. On the other hand, don't let them herd you around without an explanation and don't take what they say at face value.

Stay in touch

Try to stay in touch with your editor and/or colleagues. There are plenty of devices on the market for this — beepers, mobile telephones, two-way radios and even the old "land line." Regular contact will enable you to manage your time in the field, guide photographers to areas of interest, or stay apprised of changing conditions and deadlines.

It is especially important for you to notify your editors when there is a dramatic turn of events. ("Boss, the flooding just washed out the Main Street bridge.") This will enable editors to order more space for news or decide on a photo page.

Records and experts

There are plenty of public records that can help you report on a disaster or public emergency, depending on the size and scope of the event. Some include: town land records, all code violation reports, state automobile registration information, national census data and global weather information.

Talk to the officials who usually bring their expertise to these events: the medical examiner, the fire marshal, building inspector, police, national transportation safety inspectors, etc.

Follow up

Each incident is different, so each needs to be analyzed individually for angles to pursue. Many disaster follows focus on establishing cause and culpability, what it will cost to clean up and what the damages were in human as well as financial terms.

Talk to the victims of disasters as much as possible. This can be awkward, but people who have suffered losses are often more open to talking than you might think.

Paul Stern began learning his trade as a community reporter for the weekly Nutley Sun in Nutley, N.J. He is now deputy state editor for The Courant. The highlight of his career was exposing wrongdoing as a white-collar and consumer-crime investigator for the Fort Lauderdale News and Sun-Sentinel.

CHAPTER 17

Go to the head of the class: Better local school reporting

By Robert Frahm

Covering local schools means writing about budgets, preschool programs, poverty, race relations, testing, teacher strikes, the teaching of values, programs for handicapped children, censorship of library books, the use of classroom technology.

There are feature stories about outstanding teachers or trends in the teaching of reading and math. And investigative stories that examine how schools spend their money or how well they prepare their graduates.

The challenge is to find these stories and bring them to life. Here are some tips.

Getting started

You will be expected to attend and cover local school board meetings. These meetings should be a jumping off point.

If board members debate whether to adopt a particular math textbook, you should visit a math class, talk to teachers, find the head of the math department, interview a mathematics professor from the local college.

If the board worries about school violence, visit schools that are trying to deal with the issue, check with the local police, interview parents and counselors and talk to students.

One of the most important documents you will receive is the school budget. Don't be intimidated. Ask the school system's budget director to help you understand it. The simplest approach is to figure out how to compare this year's budget categories with those from last year or from 10 years ago, for example.

How much does the district spend per pupil on special education, on busing, on textbooks? If there are big changes from one year to the next on any specific category, start asking questions.

One story that always seems to work is the comparison of your town with others. The gap between wealthy and poor school systems is always a story. The best way to start is to ask for spending statistics from the state Department of Education. The department can tell you how much each district spends, per pupil, on textbooks, maintenance, or busing, for example. Another telling statistic you can get from the state is the ratio of students to computers.

Armed with these numbers, you can interview teachers, librarians, parents and others. Look for signs of the differences between towns. Are your town's library shelves half-empty? How old are the history textbooks? Is the paint peeling?

Here are some other stories that come up repeatedly on the beat:

Testing

In Connecticut, the state-mandated Mastery Test is big news. This test of reading, writing and mathematics is given annually to children in grades 4, 6, 8 and 10. You can get the scores school by school.

Such comparisons lead to other questions. If one school's scores seem way out of line — high or low — start asking questions. Is that school's population from a different economic class from others? Does the principal put an unusual emphasis on the test? Has the curriculum been changed to meet the goals of the test?

If the scores are really out of whack, ask the state Department of Education whether anyone is under investigation for cheating. One warning: When you make any comparisons using test scores, be sure to ask someone, such as the principal, about the limitations of such comparisons. Educators generally believe — with some justification — that the public puts too much emphasis on test scores and does not consider some of the other measures of a school's success.

Race and schools

Despite all of the efforts to promote school integration by civil rights groups, politicians and others, schools in many states — including Connecticut — remain remarkably segregated.

School officials track racial balance numbers from one year to the next, and you should, too. Follow the efforts to establish partnerships with nearby school districts to achieve integration. Watch for gradual population shifts in your town. Is one racial group concentrated at a particular school or schools?

An important story is how racial minority groups are treated within schools. Some studies have found that black and Hispanic students are poorly represented in top academic classes and school activities but have a disproportionately high representation in disciplinary incidents and special-education classes.

Special education

Schools and parents sometimes disagree whether handicapped children should have special classes of their own or should be placed in regular classes. This volatile debate is happening nationwide, and there are plenty of experts on both sides. This story is best told by finding parents who are fighting either for special placement or regular classes.

Another important issue is whether schools are identifying too many children with poor English skills, or children who are discipline problems, as special-education students.

Curriculum

The way you and I learned to read, write and do math is not the way schools teach those subjects today. In areas such as math, science and even history, teachers often are putting textbooks aside and asking students to tackle real-life problems.

The movement has begun to show up in new kinds of tests that avoid multiple-choice questions in favor of actual performance tasks. Watch a class or two. Ask teachers why these methods seem better. Ask students and parents what they think.

Get out of the office

The best advice for any reporter who covers schools is to get out of the office and into the schools.

Make a schedule of regular contacts. These should include official contacts such as the school board president, superintendent, the school district lawyer, head of the personnel department, chief curriculum supervisor and the president of the local teacher union. Many large school districts have a research department or at least one person in charge of research and testing.

Researchers can give you statistics on everything from teacher pay to graduation rates. Ask them regularly what studies are under way. These studies are often indicators of the trends educators think about and worry about.

You should also build a network of unofficial sources, including principals, teachers, parents and students. PTA or PTO groups usually will put you in touch with parents. Good student sources often include student government representatives or student newspaper editors. Don't forget to cultivate other school workers, too, such as secretaries and custodians.

Finding a story

The best reporters are the ones with a knack for stumbling on the unusual. How do you do this? Listen, listen, listen. You never know where the next idea will come from.

Here are some actual examples:

▶ During a speech about special education, a superintendent made a passing reference to a new computerized telephone system to catch truants. On further investigation, I learned the system had glitches, such as making recorded phone calls to parents in the middle of the night.

▶ The back cover of a mathematics journal carried an advertisement for a murder mystery written by a local mathematics professor. A telephone call and an interview turned into a good feature.

▶ At a school desegregation conference, I struck up a casual conversation during lunch with a teacher. The teacher, a man, taught preschool children — a field dominated by women. The conversation led to a story.

Looking for the unusual

Sometimes, the best stories run counter to conventional wisdom. For example, a few years ago teachers were bailing out of the profession because of low pay and low morale. Against this backdrop, I wrote a feature about a former salesman, weary of the business world, who gave up a lucrative career to teach high school math.

Sometimes educators try things that have unintended effects. Connecticut, for example, adopted a law in 1986 that raised teacher salaries dramatically. The goal was to attract new teachers, but the salary raises instead prompted older teachers to postpone retirements and hang onto the jobs. In addition, the cost of teachers eventually forced many systems to increase class sizes.

Putting things in context

Now that you have an idea, where does the story fit in the larger scheme of the education world? Or the world in general? Chances are, whatever your local schools are doing, some other school system in your state or in the nation has done the same thing. Is it a trend, and what does it mean? Has it been successful? Include some background in your story.

There are plenty of state and national organizations that can help. Cultivate sources in your state education department and the U.S. Department of Education. One of the best source books available for national education organizations is "Covering the Education Beat," available from the Education Writers Association. The address is 1001 Connecticut Ave. NW, Suite 310, Washington, D.C. 20036.

To stay on top of education trends, you should read other publications regularly. Among the best are "Education Week" and "Phi Delta Kappan."

Getting life into your story

It's easy, but boring, to write about most any sort of education story by interviewing and quoting official sources, such as the superintendent of schools or the school board president.

Get into the schools. Describe the classroom. What posters are on the wall? Is the room cluttered? Noisy? Crowded? Look for detail that adds meaning to the story. What does the teacher do? Is she animated? Stern? Whenever possible, include the voices of teachers, students and parents in your story. These are the things readers will remember.

Robert A. Frahm, a former high school English teacher, began his journalism career covering local schools for the Racine (Wis.) Journal-Times. He is now education writer for The Courant. His honors include the National Grand Prize awarded by the Education Writers Association.

CHAPTER 18

Town & gown: Covering the local college

By Katherine Farrish

If there is a college in the community you cover, it offers you an inexhaustible supply of stories.

Many national issues first manifest themselves, or are most sharply drawn, on college campuses. They include date rape, censorship and free speech, race relations and alcohol and drug abuse.

Furthermore, colleges offer their own special subject matter: important research and new discoveries, the use and abuse of research money, questions of access to higher education, debates over what should be taught, technological advances and quirky student life stories.

When I begin a story about a college issue, I think hard about what it means and why readers should care.

What does the opening of an Asian-American cultural center at the state university show us about the way our state's population is changing? What does an effort by professors to keep Camille Paglia off a reading list tell us about free speech in this country? How is a recession forcing colleges to rethink what they teach and who they serve?

Understanding the institution

To find such stories, it helps to understand how colleges operate.

They are not run from the top down, like corporations. By tradition, a college is managed by a president and administration in collaboration with faculty members and with the frequent advice of students, alumni and employees. If you're familiar with this model, brought to the United States from Germany in the 19th century, you'll understand how to cover a college.

You have to tap into all these constituencies.

Getting started

To begin, arrange a meeting with the college president and top administrators to explain the kinds of stories you're interested in. You can arrange such meetings with the college's public relations office.

Most colleges have at least part-time public relations people who range from useless and annoying to really helpful sources of story ideas. Get to know them.

Then, find out how the faculty members govern themselves. Usually there is a faculty senate or executive committee that the president consults frequently, and these leaders can be some of your best sources. Faculty union leaders can also be helpful.

Talking to students

You also must get out of the office and talk to students. That's the most interesting, and frustrating, part of this beat. You can get some great story ideas from students because they're so unpredictable. One day I got a call from a student who was starting a campaign to bring back "Schoolhouse Rock," those little vignettes about grammar and history that ran on television during her childhood. That made a neat story.

Students typically have mundane concerns about dorm food, long registration lines and parking tickets, but they can also surprise you. I noticed that at several selective colleges, students were protesting the threatened loss of need-blind admissions, a seemingly esoteric policy of admitting students without regard to their ability to pay. By talking to students at Brown and Wesleyan, I found the protesters were genuinely concerned about a return to campus elitism after years of hard-fought gains by the middle class. That made another good story.

Each year, you need to get to know a new set of student leaders and convince them you're interested in their concerns. Don't neglect the cultural groups, like the black or Hispanic student associations.

The worst part of the job is finding students during the summer and winter breaks, but it's important to try. Only by quoting students and their parents will you humanize dry budget, tuition and financial aid stories. When I can't track down student leaders, I call the nearby doughnut shop or convenience store, where you can usually find college students working.

Read the student newspapers and get to know the editors. They're often around in the summer, and they usually have a sense of what many students are thinking. Sometimes it's helpful to offer these budding journalists some advice or a tour of your newspaper, too.

Public vs. private

Private colleges are more difficult to cover than public colleges. There are some things, such as budget information and salaries, that public colleges have to give you but that private schools do not. However, I have found that most private colleges are willing to share financial information and changes in policy if you have developed a reputation for fairness.

Take a chance and ask for access; the worst they can do is say no. I asked Wesleyan, one of the most selective colleges in the nation, to open its admissions deliberations to me. A public relations official thought the school could benefit by having the public understand its admissions procedure, and argued on my behalf.

I was surprised when school officials said yes and allowed me to sit in as a committee decided whom to admit and whom to reject. After agreeing to cloak the students' identities, we ran a story along with a "you be the admissions director" box that was fun for readers. It made for a rare inside look at a selective college and ran in newspapers across the country.

Two-year colleges

Most town reporters will be covering two-year community colleges. There are issues particular to those schools. With the growth of community colleges in the past 30 years, more people have access to higher education than at any other time in the nation's history. But the students are different from those at Yale and even the large state university.

Often they are older, black or Hispanic, new immigrants or from the so-called "forgotten half" — those students who got little guidance in high school because they were not on the traditional college-bound track. Many of them come out of high school with pitiful skills and require extensive remedial courses. Take a look at how many need help and how many have made progress after two years. Look at retention, graduation and transfer rates. These can turn into powerful stories.

Many students at two-year colleges also have unusual life stories, and you can train the public relations people to think of you when they hear about such students.

Scholars and personalities

Colleges attract a parade of people with something to say. One week it is Henry Kissinger, the next it is Spike Lee, then comes Toni Morrison. Make sure the public relations office lets you know who is coming and when. You might want to cover the speech. You might get an interview. You might even want to ask the students what they think of what the speakers have to say. At the very least, you might want to ask how much they pulled down in speaking fees and who paid.

Research and new knowledge

Colleges and universities do more than teach. They are the world's major source of new knowledge. Get the public relations office or heads of various academic departments to let you know who is doing particularly interesting work. Most often, these will be science and engineering stories. But don't neglect other fields: the English scholar who has unearthed never-before-seen letters by Mark Twain; the biblical scholar who has developed a new interpretation of a book of the Bible; the historian with a revisionist theory on the Truman administration.

Two cautions about these stories: You have to translate the researcher's jargon into words that are understandable and explain why the discovery is important to your readers. And if somebody is claiming that his or her work is original and important, do a reality check. Ask prominent scholars in the same field, but from other universities, for their assessment.

Town and gown

Look for ways the university and its home community intersect. Are neighbors angry about loud frat parties? Are townspeople irate that a college is tearing down historic homes for a dormitory or bulldozing a park for an athletic field? Are local restaurants losing business because the university has started a seven-day meal plan in the dorms? How much is the local tax base hurt by having a college — a large, nonprofit, tax-exempt entity — within its borders? Are local leaders asking the school to make annual payments in lieu of taxes? Is the college education department helping the local school system improve the way it teaches physics? Are college experts helping the town track down the source of contamination in its water supply?

The love-hate tug implicit in many town-gown stories can lead to wonderful stories.

Perspective

Finally, don't forget to put your stories in context of what is happening in the state or the nation.

It's especially good to compare tuition increases and budget cuts to those in other parts of the country. Read the Chronicle of Higher Education. Talk to people at the American Council on Education in Washington, the College Board in New York or the state and national education departments.

Above all, really think about what you're writing and why you're writing it.

Katherine Farrish began her career as a sports editor for the Tri-Town Reporter in Vernon, Conn., and as a local news correspondent for The Courant. She was higher education writer for The Courant, and now is the Assistant Bureau Chief in the Eastern Connecticut Bureau.

CHAPTER 19

Covering the
world of difference

By Jeff Rivers

It would be a presumption for anyone to try to tell you how you might go about covering the great community of difference.

What I will do is present a few broad propositions that I think can help you write with greater sensitivity about people in our ever evolving and increasingly multicultural society.

Mainstream

Too often, we fail to recognize that senior citizens, young people, gays and lesbians, Asians, African-American, Latinos, disabled people and other Tops (traditionally oppressed people) can and should be included in general-interest stories. Among other things, they shop, root for local sports teams, mow lawns, fall in love and pay taxes.

Consequently, there are few stories about universal themes that could not include quotes from Tops, whether they are experts or everyday people.

Unfortunately, we often limit Tops to what we view as their stories. Depending on the group, those stories include teen pregnancy, urban violence, AIDS, immigration issues, incidents of discrimination or specfic observances related to those groups.

When and where they enter

At the same time we limit Tops to what we believe are their own stories, we often include them in universal stories in limited ways.

For example, in a series of anniversary pieces about World War II, do we quote people of color as to how they felt about the onset of the war: Were they afraid or stirred by patriotism like everybody else? Or do we talk about black folks as objects of discrimination in the workplace, as if that's the only way they experienced the war?

"Blacks and other minorities"

Too often, newspapers, if they seek a "minority perspective," think solely of African-Americans.

In a nation and state in which the Asian and Latino populations are growing faster than the African-American population, that's a mistake.

Recognize the diversity within various groups of TOPs

Which is to say, Puerto Ricans differ from Cubans, the Japanese differ from the Chinese. Additionally, there are great differences within the various ethnic groups. Thus Puerto Ricans, for example, like other people, cannot be written about as if they are a monolith.

One voice

One way to make sure we don't present Asians or some other group as a monolith is to seek several different people as spokespeople.

In Connecticut, for example, we should not return repeatedly to Paul Bok, an emeritus University of Connecticut professor "and a leader in the Asian community," as if he were the only person who could comment.

Let's Not Forget To be Sensitive to Mainstream White Folks

Let's not assume that white athletes in sports dominated by black or brown people will be slow or awkward. Let's be careful with "white men can't jump," or "white man's disease." Let's not be too quick to paint mainstream white folks as intolerant when they are at loggerheads with other groups. Let's not glibly say their lives lack of imagination. We can appreciate and repect the institutions venerated by Tops without becoming disrespectful of the institutions many mainstream white Americans hold dear.

The name game

We should be sensitive to the various name changes groups have made or will make.

Over time, Orientals have become Asians, those who had been called crippled have opted for the term disabled, and so on.

These name changes are not frivolous. Each name change of each group has signaled that the group sought to see itself and present itself different-ly from before.

Also, where possible, be specific in naming folks: For example, you can get around the Latino/Hispanic debate by calling Puerto Ricans, Puerto Ricans.

Language biases

We should examine how we use language and how that usage betrays our biases and sometimes rankles or even injures Tops.

Who do we say are boys or girls next door? Who do we say are exotic or offbeat? Who has housemates, roommates, live-ins and fiances and who has common-law spouses? Who gets divorced or separated and who is abandoned? Are Asian business people who buy domestic properties pre-sented as invaders while European buyers are not?

Are black male athletes described as animals, monsters, menacing or intimidating more often than their white counterparts who are of similar size and exhibit similar behavior?

Are bad days referred to as "black days?" Are boring things called "whitebread."

The language of limits

Why is Michael Jackson, one of the most popular performers in the world, a black singer, and Elvis Costello, with a much more limited audi-ence, a singer?

Historically, we have used words that portray nonwhite maleness to limit. We have also used words from artistic genres that Tops dominate to limit. Which is to say, a white ballet dancer dies and he's described as one of the world's great dancers. A black jazz trumpet player dies and he's described as one of the world's great jazz musicians. Why wasn't the trum-pet player called one of the world's great musicians?

Formulas

There are formulas that we return to again and again in writing about Tops.

Jamila, the black athlete, who (through sports) overcomes the violence (and "mean streets") of her urban upbringing to make a life for herself. Jin-Jin, the Asian achiever, who came to the United States not speaking a word of English but is now a . . .

Those formulas often allow folks to tell compelling stories. On the other hand, relying upon those formulas often stops us from exploring other ways we can write about Tops.

We have become fond of saying things like "Jamal, the grandson of slaves, has become the first black person to . . ." By saying that the person is the grandson of slaves we seek to represent how far our subject has come or how much things have changed. Still, it must be recognized that if a black person is 60 years old with roots in the American South, she almost certainly is the granddaughter or great-granddaughter of slaves. Saying so, in and of itself, can be no more illuminating and interesting than saying she is the decendant of other black men and women who had knees.

Photographs

Please make sure that photographs of Tops be included in coverage of universal events such as the state fair and so on. Please recognize that different histories could make a photo that would be harmless depicting one group insensitve or even racists to another. Which is to say, the reaction in the respective communities to our running a picture of affluent white children eating watermellons might not be the same as a similar photo of poor black children.

Whad's up wid dat?

Too often, writers get caught up in trying to replicate the speech and speech patterns of various groups. It is hard to do accurately and well. Too often, efforts to authentically portray how people sound gets in the way of our representing what they mean. (Moreover, journalists have had the habit of "cleaning up the quotes" of some classes—influential white men in particular—while seeking to replicate the speech, sound for sound, of others.) This caution is not meant as proscription. If you fancy yourself another Eudora Welty in regard to capturing the rhythms and sounds of everyday speech, go ahead and try; however, please consider to what purpose you are making the attempt.

Contrast ledes

Contrast ledes betray reporters' biases. When we say that an elderly woman "doesn't look like a person who would/could . . ." Or when we allow as how this or that tree-lined suburban street doesn't seem to be the kind of place where this or that could have happened, we are reinforcing stereotypes about people and places.

Besides, tree-lined suburban streets are precisely the places where men go berserk and kill their loved ones and then themselves.

Windows of the other world

Like other Americans, too many of us don't spend much time around people very different from ourselves unless a story dictates that we do.

It is easy to recommend that you take the initiative to attend houses of worship, bars, restaurants and social events that cater to people unlike you. While you prepare to do that, you can:

Read these books:"From Slavery to Freedom", "Jews in America", "Latinos", "A Different Mirror", and these magazines: "Emerge", "Asia Week", "Mother Jones", "The National Review", "Hispanic Business", "Out Magaizine".

Try to Watch TV shows that are popular with folks whose tastes and demographic profiles differ from yours. If you are a "Seinfeild" person, sample "Living Single." If "Martin" is one of your favorites, watch "Friends" for a change.

Each week, choose a different radio station and listen to the morning drive discjockey. That way, you can stay abreast of the vouge phrases, jokes, popular songs, issues and other trends in different communities.

Jeff Rivers began as a general assignment reporter at the Commercial Appeal in Memphis. He is now a columnist as well as associate editor for recruitment and development at The Courant. He has twice won third place in the column writing category from The National Society of Newspaper Columnists.

CHAPTER 20

Understanding power in a community

By David Fink

Power.

Power corrupts.

Power is the ultimate aphrodisiac.

Power is given, not taken.

Many people, from Machiavelli to Henry Kissinger (some would argue the latter is the reincarnation of the former), have weighed in with wisdom about power, and you are free to believe what you want.

But you are advised to accept one truth about it: power is real and is employed each day in very basic ways at all levels of business and government. So staying aware of who has it, and how it's exercised, is vital. If you're covering a town and you don't know at this moment who the largest employer is, who is the richest person in town, who is on the board of the bank, who the largest landowner is — and who comes in second in those and similar categories — you have some homework to do.

Two rules

One: Power, truly, is given, not taken. It is bestowed on leaders, everyone from presidents on down. A popular president, like Ronald Reagan in his first term, will rarely be bucked by members of Congress or anyone else. If he is perceived to be popular, and thus powerful, then he is powerful. Perception, as we already know, is everything.

Two: What is given can be taken away. President Nixon won re-election in 1972 in the largest landslide the nation has seen. Less than two years later, he was driven from office, the only president to resign, finally heeding the entreaties of the most powerful members of his party, some of them his previously staunchest supporters. Go figure.

The point is that we give teachers, politicians, even editors power by listening to them, heeding them, following their lead. Now you might say that if you don't listen to your editor, you'll get fired. That's true. But if too many of you don't listen to your editor, the top brass at this place or anywhere else will start looking for someone the troops will listen to.

Power is given, not taken, as I said above. And if you think the guy with the tanks and guns who wrests power from the king in a palace coup really has power, consider this: If he doesn't keep his soldiers in rum and shekels — and does not continue to give the people some reason to believe he will improve their lot — all of them will find another rebel leader to back, and this guy will be history. They'll simply take away the power they bestowed on him.

In the same way, the council president or the teachers' union president or the school superintendent or anyone in town with power will have it only as long as his or her allies and constituencies choose to keep him or her in power. So don't assume that the school superintendent who had everybody on his team in November still has them there in May.

Where do you come in?

First off, you have to understand that, as a reporter, you have power. People tend to believe what they read in the newspaper, no matter what they say. So no matter whom you have to deal with, don't be afraid. That is not to say you should recklessly throw your weight around. You're responsible for accuracy and fairness.

But understand that you are a player in the drama you cover, no matter how hard you may try to be just an observer. And the people you talk to know you have power. A great journalist once suggested that, "If you weren't a reporter, they wouldn't give you the time of day." And that's true. But the fact is, you are a reporter, and so they will give you the time of day, and much more, if you use your power wisely and fairly.

Who else has it?

Take a look around, use a little logic, and then dive into the power elite of your town or beat. It all makes sense. Who's the biggest employer? The largest landowner? The largest labor union? The highest-ranking politician? Who's on the board of the local bank or hospital or largest corporation? (The truly powerful may be on the boards of all three.) Who is chairman of the local symphony board? The local United Fund?

You get the idea. They are the people who have what others want: money, jobs, money, prestige, money, orchestra seats, money, no-bid contracts, and money.

George Washington Plunkitt, a Tammany Hall ward boss in the late 1800s, said power — power in politics, in his case — comes with delivering votes. If you find three or four people who will vote the way you tell them, he would say, you have power. Being able to deliver three or four dozen, or three or four thousand, increases your power that much more.

So the labor union leader's son may get a job in town hall — or a contract to build the new playground — because the mayor would, all things being equal, just as soon get re-elected, and labor support would go a long way toward that end.

Or the large landowner might get listened to by the zoning board, or assessor, or town council or school board, seeing as how he presumably is a big taxpayer, wealthy enough to contribute to campaigns and could sell his property to any number of developers for uses that might be in keeping with the zoning ordinance but not necessarily the desires of the rest of the town.

The big employers, having what others need (jobs), can wield substantial power to win tax breaks and favorable zoning decisions. They influence policy because, if dissatisfied, they can pull up stakes and move. They influence who is elected because, if dissatisfied, they can throw their support, and campaign contributions, to someone else.

The president of the bank also has power: he can give loans to those who are good risks and will cater to his interests, or just to those who are good risks. Whom do you think the president will choose?

Friends, relatives and bedfellows

Two of the most important questions in local reporting are "who?" and "why?"

When someone gets a town contract, for example, you need to know who the person is and why he or she got it. Don't forget to explore clan/family/neighborhood connections. The guy who got the contract might have been the mayor's next-door neighbor or his brother-in-law or his personal accountant or his lodge brother. Find out.

Understanding the personal connections among people of power in your town is vital. Political organizations themselves stemmed originally from extended families and clans. People from the same clan, or who grew up in the same neighborhood, have common interests and tend to stick together. And people, including government officials, tend to want to hang out with and do business with their friends, or at least with people they know.

If a member of the hospital board of directors needs something from the mayor — a zoning variance for his home, a building permit for his business, a job for his sister — might he be inclined to try to sway the zoning board by hiring the mayor's best friend?

It would be impossible to understate the importance of connections to the power game, or underestimate the number of times connections come into play.

Under the administration of Connecticut Gov. William A. O'Neill, you could safely — very safely — bet a week's salary that the person who got a contract was connected: a member of a town Democratic committee, a guy who once served with one of the governor's aides in the legislature, someone who hired one of the governor's friends for legal advice, accounting services or insurance.

Think of these connections as the wire that carries the power from one person to another. A good example was a story The Courant did a few years ago. On a no-bid basis, the state Department of Public Works was handing out hundreds of thousands of dollars in electrical jobs to an electrician from the same town as the DPW official in charge of the work. A good story if a connection could be shown. But how to find the connection.

The Courant reporter looked at building permits in the electrician's home town. And sure enough, there amid the dusty pile were permit applications that showed the DPW official and the electrician had worked on many jobs together. They were friends and business associates.

The point here is that power is exercised through connections. And while it would be incorrect to assume that things never happen — contracts let, zoning decisions made, etc. — based on merit alone, it's your job to understand why things happen and who is involved. So ask "who?" and "why?" and look for the connections.

The bottom line

Which brings us to the biggest group with power: the voters.

All the talk in recent years about term limits for officeholders and other built-in checks on the political system ignore that people can vote politicians out of office whenever they want.

The perception that they would vote out Connecticut lawmakers who supported an income tax was so strong that it took until 1991 for the state legislature to enact a levy on income. Of course, we later found out, the sentiment was never that strong: Incumbents who voted for the income tax were re-elected.

But isn't that the point? The voters spoke, will continue to, and the politicians and business people who depend on the public to buy their products or re-elect them are very sensitive to the people. So pay attention to the voters even though apathy sometimes saps them of their own power.

Cultivating the powerful

People with power hear things.

The mayor, for instance, tends to know what's going on in town. The president of the largest real estate brokerage tends to know what's going on in the assessor's office and on the zoning board. A member of the hospital board tends to know what's going on not just at the hospital but elsewhere in the city. And the bank president or board member knows who has sought a loan for a new development or isn't current on his loan payments or is depositing cash into his account.

They hear things quietly, and they do things quietly. Powerful people don't need to picket, or hold demonstrations, or write letters to the editor. They get things done with a phone call, or a brief conversation at the golf course or the theater.

They know what's going on, so identify them and get to know them. Have lunch where they have lunch. Never pass up an opportunity to play golf at the country club where they play. Always watch who's with whom. If you see someone powerful that you know, but don't recognize the person accompanying him or her, find out who it is. Powerful people hang out with powerful people. Together, they form a power structure. It's your job to know how it all fits together.

Read all about it

George Bernard Shaw once cautioned that, "You cannot have power for good without having power for evil too." In your town, the powerful may not go so far as to exercise their power to do evil, but they almost certainly, at least some of the time, will exercise it in their own interests. And that's where you'll come in — to tell everyone about it. And when they use their power to do good, you can write about that, too.

David Fink began as a legislative reporter for the Schenectady (N.Y.) Gazette. He is now government editor of The Courant. His honors include The Master Reporter Award, given by the New England Society of Newspaper Editors in recognition of excellence in a body of work over a career.

CHAPTER 21

Budgets: A window on community values

By Larry Williams

I had been a reporter barely three months in 1973 when The Hartford Times assigned me to cover West Hartford. The editor welcomed me to the beat one Friday afternoon, handed me a thick book and said I should read it over the weekend. It was the town manager's proposed budget for 1973-74.

"Maybe you can find some stories in there," the editor said.

I opened the book, skimmed a few pages and quickly grasped the situation: I was a dead man. I could study that tome all weekend and return to work Monday just as ignorant. To me, a "mill" was a factory, a "bond" was friendship, and "revenue" was the middle name of the IRS.

It made my stomach turn as I considered how much I didn't know, and all I would have to learn, virtually overnight, to cover the budget intelligently.

After two decades of writing innumerable stories about government finances, I still fight off a crippling anxiety every time I cover a budget presentation.

Although it helps to know how to do it, it's also helpful — though you'll have a hard time persuading yourself — to be ignorant and nervous.

It's as if you're walking through a foggy cemetery at midnight, your senses so keen you can hear a leaf rustling against a tombstone at a hundred yards.

You'll never be more alert to the story possibilities around you than you are on your first pass through the town budget process. As you get accustomed to budget coverage, you also can get too comfortable. Everything begins to look the same. Every story seems like one you've written before.

Get too familiar with the budget process, and the minutiae and esoterica may distract you from your mission. Some experienced reporters get mired in side issues of more interest to accountants or Wall Street analysts than to the public.

I recall more than one state-budget press conference in which time was wasted dealing with questions such as whether highway overlays should be financed by bonding, and if so, whether they should be five-year bonds or 20-year bonds. I'm not making this up. A novice is less likely to write about things like this — things readers don't care about.

So, while you may feel you're inadequate to the task of covering the town budget, the truth is that your inexperience is to your advantage. Honest.

Your first budget story

As I remember my editor's advice 20 years ago, as he handed me that book, I realize how wrong he was. The worst thing a reporter can do is try to figure out a town budget by reading the book.

So here's my advice: Don't read the book until after you've written your first story about the budget.

Let's say you're the new reporter in town. You go to town hall one March day, stop by the town manager's office (or mayor's office, depending on the local system of government), and the secretary hands you a copy of the proposed budget for next fiscal year.

It seems as thick as a brick, and it's written in budget-speak — a language to confound the uninitiated. Even the initiated don't understand all of it.

Now what?

If you haven't arranged for an interview with the town manager or the finance director — somebody in charge of the budget — then you've got some catching up to do. That appointment should have been made the previous day because, no matter how much you think you know, you won't be able to write about the budget without the help of an expert.

To get started, review the summary pages and, if there is one, the town manager's budget message. These should give you the highlights you need to do intelligent interviews and write the first-day story.

You can leaf through those pages while you're waiting for the interview you just requested. You've been told, by your predecessor, that the manager or budget director hates reporters, never makes time for them. You settle in for a long wait, figuring you may have to convince him you won't leave before he'll consent to see you.

One thing you'll notice is that the book provides details of proposed spending for every town department except the most expensive one: the school system.

In Connecticut, as in most places, the school budget is up to the board of education. The board makes a lump-sum request to the municipal government, which has discretion to change the lump sum but not to tell the board how to spend it.

So, as you scribble your questions, you make sure to include a few about the school budget and how he settled on his lump-sum proposal. In most years, those questions will get you to the core of the conflict about to unfold over the town budget.

What else do you want to know?

It's easy to think of the right questions to ask about a proposed town budget. They're the simple questions any taxpayer would ask. They are the questions you would have if you owned a home and car in town.

But sometimes reporters don't ask those questions. They think up more exotic lines of inquiry that end up wrecking their stories. Why? My pet theory, based on no research, is that most reporters find budget stories boring, so they figure readers also find them boring. Rather than write a story they're sure is boring, they try to find some way to jazz it up.

My advice is: Don't worry about your story's being "boring." It has a ready audience of taxpayers who, I assure you, will not be bored if you answer their basic questions and do so in clear, simple language.

The first questions

Here's a checklist for Day One:

▶ Would there be a tax increase? If so, get it both in mills and in a percentage. (Note I said "would," not "will." This is a proposal, so it should be described in those terms. "Would" doesn't become "will" until the budget is approved by the appropriate body — the town council or perhaps the town meeting, depending on the local system of government.)

▶ How much would the tax increase cost an average homeowner? (The assessor's office can help with this.)

▶ What is the estimated spending this fiscal year, and how much is requested for next year? Get the increase in both dollars and percentage points.

▶ Where would spending be increased, and why?

▶ Are any programs recommended for reductions or increases in the level of services provided to the public? This is not the same as asking where more or less money would be sent. The manager may argue, for example, that it will cost more money next year to provide the same level of services.

▶ Are any new programs proposed, or would any programs be eliminated?

▶ How does the money for schools in the budget compare with the amount the board of education requested? How was that decision made? Would school programs be affected?

▶ Are there any capital projects proposed, such as road repairs or construction or renovation or buildings? How would they be financed — by allocating current revenue, or by selling bonds?

You're barely finished writing down your questions when the door to the manager's office swings open and out he strides, smiling generously at you.

"Come on in. I've called the finance director to come join us," he says as he waves you into his office.

What is it about Budget Day that improves the social skills of so many town managers?

Obviously, they'd like to see their spin on things reflected in your story. But most would settle for your getting the facts straight. Don't be shy about exploiting their concern. Stay as long as necessary to get what you need.

A few cautionary notes:

▶ The manager may say that spending would be "cut," even though the budget would increase. What gives?

The manager started out with a hypothetical figure for what it would cost to maintain all existing programs for another year. Then he reduced that figure and called it a "cut." All governments use this concept. The question you should try to answer is whether that hypothetical figure was realistic, or was it puffed up so that the final proposal would look lean by comparison.

▶ Perhaps the budget would freeze, or even cut, "positions." Does that mean people will be fired or nobody will be hired? Perhaps not. This is a tricky area. Government managers don't like to count employees. Instead, they count positions. You should make a point of trying to blow away that bureaucratic smoke screen and find out what would happen to real people. Cuts or freezes that affect only vacant jobs are false economies.

Once liberated from the manager's office, you should collect your thoughts, then gather comments from as wide an array of people as you have time for.

These would include council members; leaders of advocacy groups such as the PTA or local taxpayers' association; perhaps the heads of some town agencies or leaders of town employee unions.

Cast your net wide, so you capture a range of views. Don't worry too much about the quality of their comments. Nobody's going to scale new heights of eloquence in an instant analysis. Just grab the "usual suspects" to shovel some quotes into the story.

At the same time, keep in mind the political angles being played by the people you're interviewing.

The council minority leader wants "deep cuts." Sounds good, but press for details. In Connecticut, as in most places, the politics of budgets are partisan. Majority parties pass budgets. Minorities oppose them, hoping to tap public anger and pick up votes in the next election.

Similarly, school board members often enjoy a degree of political immunity that allows them to plead for big budget increases. In Connecticut, as in most places, there is little risk to them because they don't raise tax money. The council does not have this luxury. If it gives the school board what it wants, and raises taxes to pay for it, it will be the council members who could lose their seats in November.

Incidentally, you should be thinking about graphics from the moment you open the budget book. A chart of budget highlights will ensure more readers see the key numbers and, since numbers impede readability, you're better off with fewer of them in the story.

Drudgery pays off

The day ends with you frantically banging your story into the tube, barely making deadline. Now what?

It's time to read the budget book.

Don't skim it. Study every page. You'll find it's tough going. You'll feel yourself nodding off. Jump-start yourself with this thought: You are a great reporter. You are putting forth the extra effort that budget coverage really requires, and it's an effort television reporters and competing newspapers probably won't make, giving you an edge as the story develops in the next few weeks.

And it's even more important than that.

The budget is a window on the community's values and priorities. Every year, the townspeople, through their representatives, decide what's so important to them that they're willing to spend money on it.

Drudgery usually pays off. Those who put in the time are rewarded. First, you can hardly learn too much about a topic as important as the town budget; your expertise is bound to improve you coverage. Second, you will find leads to stories along the way. Guaranteed. And third, your effort will build respect for you at town hall, which will help you in the long run.

Scouring that book isn't the only unpleasant task that falls to a diligent reporter. You also should attend all public meetings, especially the ones in which town department heads plead with the politicians not to cut any more money from their budget requests.

These sessions are not to be missed, but they're also not necessarily to be written about unless an obvious story emerges. The purpose of being there is to scout for leads and develop sources for future stories. The same advice applies to sessions between the school board and school administrators.

Perspective

As you get into covering your first town budget, it's helpful to consider how much in common it has with the budgets of comparable towns in your state.

The biggest use of public money in every town is for education, although the schools tend to dominate small-town budgets to a greater extent than they do the budgets of large cities.

In some states, big cities levy their own income taxes. But in most states, the biggest source of local revenue is the local property tax.

In Connecticut, for example, it accounts for 64 percent of all local revenue.

The second-biggest source of revenue to towns is state aid. In Connecticut, for example, it averaged 26 percent of local budgets in 1990-91. Other revenue sources include service charges, licenses, fines and interest on investments.

The property tax is levied in "mills." A mill is $1 of tax on each $1,000 increment of assessed value, which typically is 70 percent of market value.

In most places, including Connecticut, motor vehicles and personal property — office furnishings, business equipment and the like — are assessed annually, so their value for tax purposes is kept current.

Because real estate prices rise and fall, land and buildings have to be periodically reassessed in what is known as revaluation. In Connecticut, revaluation is supposed to occur every 10 years, but towns may postpone revaluation or phase in its effects over several years. As a consequence, real estate assessments are rarely up to date.

Ask your local politicians why they want to postpone a revaluation, or why they want to phase in the new assessments. Whatever they tell you, bear in mind that homeowners — the people who benefit from delay if property values have risen — usually dominate the turnout in local elections.

Local officials always complain that they don't get enough money from the state. In Connecticut, for example, you may hear that the state sends less aid to municipalities than most other states. Statistically this is true, but be wary of such comparisons. The structure of government varies so much state to state that statistics may not give an accurate picture of how state and local taxpayers share the burden.

Keep in mind, as you listen to these complaints, that local officials have a political interest in blaming the state for their financial problems.

On the spending side of the local ledger, education is usually the big-ticket item. In Connecticut, for example, it absorbs 52 percent of the average budget. Public works and public safety tie for second at 10 percent each, and employee fringe benefits and debt service follow at 7 percent each.

I said earlier that a budget can be read as an annual statement of the community's priorities and values. This interpretation should be tempered by an awareness of other factors that can affect the budget.

For example, big cities spend a smaller proportion of their budgets on education than do small towns. Does that mean they value education less? Not likely. It means they have to spend more on streets and cops, so that shrinks the percentage going for schools. It's not a fair comparison.

Neither would it be fair to say that small towns care less about public safety than big cities. They need less police protection, so they spend less.

Town-to-town comparisons can be useful, but make sure you compare your town to others with a similar population and character — urban, suburban or rural. Comparisons never tell the whole story, and there may be explanations for disparities that are not immediately apparent. But if your town spends a lot more or less on education than similar towns, that may be the key to a story about your town that goes well beyond its budget.

Attempting to compare tax burdens, even among towns that seem almost identical, is a risky business. If the tax rate is 50 mills in one town and 25 in another, it may not mean one town's residents are taxed twice as heavily. It depends on how recently each town revalued its property.

Comparative statistics by the carload are available. You just have to track down the right sources in your state. In Connecticut, for example, there are:

▶ The Connecticut Policy and Economic Council, which publishes a book on municipal budgets every year or two.

▶ The Connecticut Conference of Municipalities.

▶ The state Office of Policy and Management, which has a staff of experts on municipal finances.

▶ The state Department of Education, which publishes data on school spending.

Use the numbers you get from them as clues, not answers. It takes detective work to puzzle out what they mean.

The state aid conundrum

To return to the annual budget-adoption process, the town council (or board of finance, or town meeting, depending on the town charter) has to pass a budget by the time the new fiscal year begins. In Connecticut, as in most places, that means by July 1.

Usually, most towns easily beat their deadlines. Hartford, for example, usually adopts its budget in late May, and most smaller communities in Connecticut finish well before then.

Often, they are acting without knowing exactly how much state aid they will receive in the next fiscal year. They have to make an educated guess. That's because (in most states) the state legislature is working on the state budget at the same time that local officials are working on theirs, and local officials usually finish first. In Connecticut, the legislature never adopts a budget before May and often takes until June.

State aid is a fairly significant figure not to have nailed down when the local council adopts the new budget. In Connecticut, for example, it represents more than a quarter of the average town's revenue.

And when the manager proposes his budget, six weeks or so earlier, he knows even less about how much state money he'll have to spend.

One thing you can do with a manager's budget is to question the validity of assumptions being used to estimate state aid.

In 1991, Simsbury, Conn., a wealthy bedroom community, based its budget on an assumption that it would get a certain level of state aid for education, even though the legislature was working on changes to the grant formula to take money away from rich towns.

The legislature didn't approve the new grant formula until September that year. Suddenly, Simsbury had a big hole in its budget.

The explanation for that snafu was that the town got some bad advice from Simsbury's state representative, a Republican who didn't have a clue, apparently, as to what the Democratic legislative majority was doing to the grant formula. The town selectmen should have read The Courant, where the legislative issue was well-covered.

Years ago, when I covered Hartford, the city manager proposed budgets that assumed the state would give the city no increase in aid. It was, at the time, an unlikely, if not absurd, scenario.

The manager said he was simply playing it safe. But what he was really doing was squirreling away money so he could pull it out of a hat at the propitious moment — the eve of the council's vote, when members would be desperate to avoid a tax increase.

To run a reality check on the estimates in your town manager's budget, check them out with your local state legislators, but be careful to weigh their opinions according to whether they're in the majority at the Capitol and whether they hold leadership posts.

You could also check with groups that lobby the legislature on state-grant issues. In Connecticut, for example, you could call the Connecticut Conference of Municipalities and the Council of Small Towns.

While state aid may be uncertain even after a town budget is adopted, there's much less guesswork involved in projecting revenue from the property tax.

The town "grand list" — the assessed values of all properties — is a known figure. In Connecticut, for example, it is required to be completed by Jan. 31. To calculate revenue, just multiply by the tax rate. Right? Almost. The town manager does have to estimate the collection rate — the proportion of taxes billed that will be paid.

You should check that estimated rate and compare it to the actual rates in previous years. A big change would warrant an explanation and probably a story. An increase in collections might mean the town has gotten better at enforcement; a decrease might be the effect of job losses. Even a modest change could be a story if it's part of a trend. Let's say collections are dropping. You check delinquency records in the tax collector's office and find them decorated with the names of prominent developers. Bingo.

The spending side

As for the spending side of the budget, you should be looking for stories on the consequences of the proposals made by the manager. This should be done with extreme care, lest you appear to be an advocate for spending.

Let's say the manager proposes a cut in the senior center budget. You go there and the seniors tell you how much they need that money. You write that and you're in their corner, lobbying for their cause. If you do these types of stories, be sure to give prominence to the other side. Too often, in stories I read in the paper, the argument favoring a spending cut gets short shrift.

The same danger awaits the reporter who goes out to interview homeowners about the manager's proposed tax increase. It should come as no surprise that almost everyone is opposed, and that most say they can't afford it.

Maybe the truth is they can afford it. If taxes have not gone up in years, and the folks who complain are living in mansions, you can point these things out.

And ask people who oppose higher taxes where they think the budget should be cut. If they aren't sure, put that in the paper.

Prying closed doors open

While you document the human drama outside town hall, the action inside shifts from the public to the private domain, as politicians start making decisions in closed caucuses instead of open meetings. The two parties stop pretending that the budget is a bipartisan issue. In fact, the majority party will make decisions. The minority party's role is to complain about the decisions and vote against them.

Is this always the way the budget process unfolds, and does it happen in every town?

Yes. If you find otherwise, write about it. It's a remarkable exception.

The secrecy of party caucuses (they nearly always are exempted from any open meeting laws) forces reporters to play cat-and-mouse with council members and key administrators to find out what's going on. Sometimes the minority will know what the majority is doing. Sometimes town political leaders also know. If your town hall sources go cold, try prospecting on the fringes and use what you learn there to pry more out of the insiders.

Obviously, in using leaks from the inner sanctum, you should be careful not to misinterpret what you're told. As you'll learn, if you haven't already, politicians who are violating a code of silence often try to convey information to reporters without baldly stating it. Sometimes, their winks and nods are given to varying interpretations.

I'm stressing this partly because the biggest error I ever made in print resulted from my inability to read the signals of a West Hartford council leader on the morning before the final budget vote. (At the time, I worked for The Hartford Times, an afternoon newspaper, so I had to get the results of that night's meeting before they happened if I was to beat The Courant.)

The councilman was trying to tell me there would be no tax increase. I misunderstood and reported that the tax rate would increase by 1 mill.

A great scoop. Too bad it was wrong.

I can't remember what he said, or how I misunderstood it, but I sure remember the sick feeling in my stomach when I realized I'd goofed.

Once the final budget vote is taken, you should be prepared, again, to give the public answers to basic questions, such as how the final product differs from the manager's proposal and why. If a tax increase is approved, you should state it in mills and as a percentage, and you should provide an example or two of the effect on property owners.

A good technique, if there's time, is to set out the major changes in a chart. That makes them easier for the reader to understand, and frees you of the obligation to use all those figures in your story.

If it's a typical budget in a typical town, it will be approved by a party-line vote. This is especially true if a tax increase is involved. That's the price of political power in Connecticut. The majority party gets the spoils, but it also gets the job of making unpopular decisions.

I hesitate to lecture too long on this because it makes me seem more cynical than (I believe) I really am. The thing to remember, though, is that what the Republicans say they're for when they're in the minority may not be what they would do if they were in the majority.

Between budgets

With the budget in place, and nine months to go before the manager will propose another, a period of benign neglect is appropriate. Give the budget four or five months to ripen, then check on how things are going. If revenue or spending are way off the estimate, you've got a story.

Aside from bringing the big picture into focus periodically, there are numerous little pictures you can develop on the local fiscal beat.

You should cultivate sources among town employees who buy supplies and services, assess property, collect taxes, perform audits and monitor the town's income and outgo throughout the fiscal year.

Some things to look for:

▶ Who are the big tax delinquents in town? What is being done to make them pay?

▶ Are some of the town's political leaders, especially council or board members, among those behind in their taxes?

▶ Who has contracts to provide goods and services to the town hall, police department, school system and so on? If there are political luminaries among them, are there any questions about how contracts were awarded? If the town has set-aside rules to favor minorities, or local-preference rules to favor local companies, who has benefited and at what cost? Also, fraud is rampant among the people who exploit these rigged systems. White-owned companies masquerade as black-owned. Out-of-town firms create a town "office" that's no more than a mail drop. Local officials often know what's going on but do nothing about it.

▶ Are some businesses that have contracts with the town behind in their taxes. Some towns have rules against doing business with tax delinquents, but you can bet it happens anyway. Others require the amount of tax delinquency to be deducted from payments to a contractor, but somehow those deductions don't always get made. Look for political connections among the contractors who benefit from the town's laxity in enforcing those rules.

▶ What expenses have been submitted for reimbursement by elected and appointed officials? Do they dine out at taxpayers' expense? Do they spend lavishly for out-of-town trips while the school system is short of supplies?

▶ Which town agencies and programs have been audited and what were the results? The audits you're looking for are not the ones done by an outside accounting firm and attached to the town's annual report. Those audits rarely go deep enough to catch waste, fraud and abuse. You need to speak to the auditors who work for the government. Some towns don't have them, but if your town does, cultivate a relationship with them right away.

▶ How have the local employees' unions fared at the bargaining table compared with employees in other towns? If your town's unions are getting bigger raises than workers in other towns, try to find out why. (Information on comparative raises should be available from the people who negotiated the contracts. It's generally on the table during the talks.) Check out the political activities of unions that are being treated well. You'll have to look beyond the campaign finance reports filed in the town clerk's office. Unions often contribute more people to the campaign than they do money. In Hartford's Democratic primary in 1985, city firefighters ferried voters friendly to the party-endorsed slate to the polls. They were unpaid volunteers, so that contribution did not appear on any finance report.

Larry Williams got his start covering municipal government for The Hartford Times. He now covers state politics and government for The Courant. His reporting on the Connecticut state budget is widely regarded as some of the finest budget coverage ever produced.

CHAPTER 22

A budget story checklist

By Leslie Gura

Things to include in all budget stories:
▶ Total proposed budget and percentage increase from current year.
▶ Total current budget.
▶ Proposed tax rate .
▶ Expressed in mills, and percentage increase from current year.
▶ Current tax rate.
▶ Effect of proposed tax rate.
What would it cost people? Example: If the average home in your community has an assessed value of $40,000, a 3-mill increase in the tax rate would add $120 a year to the average tax bill.

Define key terms
A mill is $1 for every $1,000 of assessed property value.

What is the next step in the budget process?

What are all the rest of the steps in the budget process?
A simple sentence, such as: "The budget must still be approved by the board of finance, the town council and voters at a town meeting," would suffice.

Something that would be nice to include in most budget stories:

Winners and losers.
A sentence saying something like, "The proposed $XX million budget includes no money for new police but gives $3 million more to the board of education."

Things to avoid in budget stories:

Jargon, official-speak:

Such as: "The board's subcommittee on budgetspeak recommended that the document's fund balance handle all bond issue deferments and other possible future expenditures."

Number-speak:

Such as: "The town council Tuesday approved a $49.83 million town budget for 1991-92 that includes a 14-mill increase in the tax rate, a 13 percent hike over the current, 1990-91 spending plan."

Cliche-speak:

Tight budget, lean budget, no-frills budget, austerity budget. Every administrator claims his or her proposal is a no-frills one, and that 'austerity' is the key word this year. They always say that.

Leslie Gura began his career as a reporter covering Kaiser Steel Corp. in Fontana, Calif., for the Fontana Herald-News. He is now the Assistant City Editor at The Courant.

CHAPTER 23

Taking the Zzzz's out of zzzzoning

By Mark Pazniokas

Face it. Zoning stories bore you.

Don't feel too bad. You're no different from most reporters. We tend to glaze over when confronted with land-use issues, and we cover them superficially and oh-so-dryly. It need not be so.

Zoning is about money and power. Zoning is about politics. Zoning can be about vision and foresight, but too often, it is about shortsightedness and indifference.

You know all those variances the local zoning board of appeals grants each month? If your town is typical, as much as 90 percent of them may be illegal.

How can that be? Easy. Zoning officials are used to making their decisions with relatively little public oversight. I'm told by a prominent land-use lawyer that a suburban Hartford commission routinely retires to an anteroom for private deliberations, an illegal act that apparently never has been challenged by a reporter.

Reporters tend to cover land-use stories case by case. We go to the hearing on a controversial zone change or site plan, but too often we do not explain the big picture.

Land-use trends dramatically change the character of the community and region you cover. For example, the death of the New England landscape is a major, continuing story that goes underreported. Rural and suburban sprawl is quickly changing eastern Connecticut, where some towns have doubled in population in the past decade.

A little background would enable reporters to compare what is happening in their region with what is happening elsewhere. For example, compare suburban sprawl in Connecticut with land use in states where creative zoning encourages the preservation of open land by forcing development to be clustered together.

Zoning is alchemy. Rezoning a piece of land can increase its value ten-fold over night. That alone is reason to closely cover zoning commissions. Do you know who is making those decisions? How well does your local commission justify those decisions? Do they follow their town's plan of development? How good a job do they do? There are ways to judge them, even if you are not a planning professional. First, a brief overview.

What the heck is zoning?

Zoning is the regulation of land use, and it's a relatively recent develop-ment in American life. It was first developed early this century to protect residential neighborhoods from industrial development. The essence of zoning is separating incompatible land uses.

It is a simple concept, but some folks felt the proposition was downright un-American — and there are still towns without zoning. They apparently share the attitude of my first editor, a cantankerous sort who used to rou-tinely denounce zoning as "fascistic." What right, he thundered, does a local board have to tell anyone what they can do with their land?

Without question, zoning is an incredible power for local officials. How big can a house be? How small can a house be? How much of a lot can be covered? How little? Residential? Commercial? Industrial? How much parking? Are apartments or other types of multifamily housing allowed? All these factors determine how expensive — and how exclusive — a com-munity might be.

Zoning determines if mobile homes are allowed. It also says whether you can park a boat or recreational vehicle in your driveway or yard. Zoning says you can't live with three other people who are not family members, no matter how big the house. You'd be amazed what is in your town's zoning regulations. Maybe you ought to read them.

My old editor's qualms notwithstanding, communities can pretty much tell landowners what to do with their land. Courts have held zoning to be a valid exercise of municipalities' police powers since a landmark 1926 Supreme Court decision upholding the constitutionality of zoning.

There are limits, of course. The U.S. Constitution guarantees everyone due process of law. Even real estate developers. This means that zoning commissions must follow fair procedures (you'll hear lawyers call this pro-cedural due process), and their actions must promote a valid public purpose (substantive due process). Sound vague? It is. Basically it means zoning authorities have wide latitude.

You may occasionally hear a property owner complain that a zoning decision amounts to "a taking of their land." They threaten to sue. Forget it. These things rarely happen. To win such a case, the property owner must show that the zoning decision left the land without ANY value.

Where to start

Go to town hall and ask where you can buy a copy of the zoning regulations. Don't sweat the technical stuff; just familarize yourself with the different types of zones. In most places, the regs will come with a zoning map.

Make an appointment to see the town planner. (If you are covering a town without a town planner, call the regional planning association and seek a briefing. Other possibilities are the land-use consultants who may be active in your area, or planners from neighboring towns. These folks tend to take a regional view.)

There are exceptions to the rule, but generally planners are among the most reporter-friendly people on the planet. Most planners are used to being ignored by their local zoning commissions, and they are all too happy whenever someone, even a reporter, is willing to use the planner's expertise.

Ask the planner to give you an overview of the land-use issues in town. What are the trends, locally and regionally? Is farm land being gobbled up by subdivisions? Is the town trying to attract industry? Retail? Are any developers sniffing around for shopping mall sites?

Have the planner go over the zoning regulations. When were they last changed? How relevant are they to what is happening in town today? Have the planner go over the community's plan of development. In many parts of the country, as in Connecticut, state law requires every town to have one and update it once every 10 years. This is the town's vision of what it wants to be. By law, zoning officials must take the plans into account, but they do not have to strictly follow them. The plans typically are thoughtful documents. Use them as a yardstick by which you can measure the decisions of the town's zoning officials.

On a background basis, ask for a rundown on the powers and members of the boards that control zoning and planning in your town. In Connecticut, those boards are called the zoning board of appeals and the zoning commission. (Some states use different terminology.) The zoning board has the power to change zoning on a broad basis; the zoning board of appeals is just that, the place where decisions of the zoning board can be appealed. ZBAs also are the entities that grant variances.

How long have the members been serving? What are their backgrounds? Their strengths? Weaknesses? Someone who has been running a zoning commission or a zoning board of appeals for a long time can be an overlooked political power in town. Talk to them. What is their vision for the town? Do they have one?

What is the ZBA practice regarding variances? Is there any strain between the zoning authority and the ZBA? ZBAs, by issuing variances, often undo the work of the local zoning commission. In West Hartford, Conn., for example, town officials have actually sued the ZBA, which was routinely giving developers waivers from the town's regulations on parking.

Pay attention to ZBAs

A variance, which is granted by the zoning board of appeals, allows land to be used in a way that is otherwise forbidden by a zoning ordinance. They are a way to circumvent zoning, and they often result in major changes to the character of a neighborhood or municipality — for good or bad. By their very nature, a request for a variance is a request for a special favor.

The mish-mash of development along Franklin Avenue in Hartford is a good example (or bad, depending on your point of view) of zoning by variance. How did those restaurants get stuck in the bottom of three-family homes? Variances allowed them to be opened, then expanded as requirements for front yards and side yards were waived. Bit by bit, a commercial corridor was established and a residential neighborhood eroded.

On a smaller scale, the same thing can be found on any thoroughfare in any suburb. Ever notice all the homes around hospitals that have been converted to doctor's offices?

Most variances are improperly granted — in a strict legal sense. An applicant should be able to show that strict compliance with the zoning ordinance would impose an "undue hardship" on the property owner — meaning there is little he or she could do with the property without the variance. The claimed hardship should be unique to the property, not general to the area. The landowner should not have known of the hardship when the property was purchased.

You will find that few applications for a variance meet those standards. In most instances, your proper reaction probably is, "So what?" But look for patterns. They will help determine if the ZBA's actions are newsworthy.

Are a lot of variances being granted in one neighborhood? Are they changing an area? Are they subverting the policy of the town council or zoning commission?

Is the same developer or lawyer involved? If so, the reason may be innocent: In a small town, sometimes there are very few players. Of course, maybe the reason is not so innocent. Look for obvious conflicts: personal relationships between ZBA members and the applicant, or between ZBA members and the lawyer. As a matter of practice, it is a good idea to know where the members of the ZBA and zoning commission own land in town.

This does not mean you need to undertake a major background investigation on everyone who appears before a local zoning authority. That is the good news. Now for the bad news. There is no substitute, especially when you are new to a town beat, for going to all the meetings and observing first hand how things work.

Even if the agendas have very little that seems interesting, go to the meetings to educate yourself and develop sources. You will learn how perfunctory, or how diligent, the local boards are in their consideration of business before them. Do the board members seem to come into meetings with the decisions already made? If so, ask the obvious: When and where did they discuss the material so they could come in and vote so quickly? You will learn if there are local gadflies or other watchdogs who attend all the meetings.

When to write

Before anything can happen on a proposed zone change or variance, there must be a hearing. Write an advance on any proposal you deem to be important to your readers or potentially controversial. The town planner can help you with this. No one just waltzes in with a zone-change request. The planner is going to know what the applicant has in mind.

The application and associated materials are public record and will contain the basics: The location of the land involved; the nature of the zone change or variance; the names of abutting property owners.

Covering the hearing

Never just show up at a zoning hearing and wait to see what happens. See the town planner the day before. Ask the planner to identify the specific issues before the board. A mob might show up at the hearing to oppose a shopping center, but it may turn out that the issue is the design or the size of the center — not a question of whether something can be built. Your advance story should clearly explain the issue that is before the board or commission.

Whenever possible, walk the site. You may find wetlands that are not on a map. You may find that site work already is started, even before the approvals are granted. Either may give you an immediate story. At a minimum, walking the site will make what you hear and see at a public hearing clearer to you.

Read the traffic studies that are usually required for commercial site plan approvals. They are daunting at first glance, but they will tell you if construction of the project will result in gridlock on certain roads at certain times.

Zoning enforcement

Zoning is meaningless if there is no zoning enforcement. Illegal dumps, junkyards, repair shops and other uses spring up all the time. Is your town doing anything about it? In a large community such as Hartford, these things sound trivial, but they are not. They affect quality of life and can speed the deterioration of a neighborhood. Periodically check on the performance of your town's zoning enforcement officer. Ask him what enforcement action he has taken lately. Ask the town planner for his pet peeves about zoning violations that are being ignored. Let him go off the record, if necessary. If he tips you off on where they are, it is easy enough to go look at them yourself.

Other sources

Find the land-use experts in your area who will be willing to share their expertise. In Connecticut, for example, Dwight H. Merriam, a lawyer with Robinson & Cole in Hartford, has a national reputation in land-use law and is willing to talk to reporters. Terry J. Tondro, a professor at the University of Connecticut, specializes in land-use law. Tom Byrne, a lawyer in private practice in Farmington, often is consulted by other lawyers on land-use questions. You can find experts like them in your state.

Books

There are a number of books that explain the basics in plain English. Every newsroom and news bureau should have one.

"The Citizen's Guide to Zoning." Chicago: American Planning Association, 1983, is a primer.

Merriam recommends the "International City Manager's Association Green Book, the principles and practices of urban planning."

If you are covering a rural town that is going suburban, you can get ideas for what your town should be doing by checking out "Dealing with Change in the Connecticut River Valley: A Design Manual for Conservation and Development," by Robert D. Yaro, who works for a Fairfield, Conn., planning agency.

For urban issues, try the Urban Land Institute in Washington, D.C. It publishes a wide range of books and pamphlets on zoning issues. The number is 202-624-7000.

Mark Pazniokas started his newspaper career covering local news at the Journal Inquirer of Manchester, Conn. He is now the federal court reporter for The Courant. His work was published in The Poynter Institute's "Best Newspaper Writing of 1990."

CHAPTER 24

Filtering the rhetoric:
Covering a political campaign

By Michele Jacklin

When we judge greatness in a political writer, I think our standard should be different from the one we use to judge greatness in a TV quiz show contestant: The idea is not just to leave the stage with the most right answers, but to have shown the audience how to interrogate the world in a new way.

The author of the above quote has never been identified, though I first read it in the New Yorker. But, for years now, I've had a dog-eared photocopy hanging above my desk at the Capitol, a constant reminder of what my job is about.

There's no mystery to covering politics; it doesn't take great talent or insight or intelligence. What it does take is an abiding love of democracy. If the greatest form of government on earth is to succeed, it's essential that voters make educated and informed choices.

Voters can't make informed decisions if they simply listen to candidates' stump speeches or watch slick TV ads produced by armies of highly paid consultants. They need someone to filter out the rhetoric, to act as a reality check. If we don't fill that role, who will?

Some basic precepts

Having covered campaigns and elections for the better part of 16 years, I've found its useful to keep some precepts in mind. At the risk of appearing naive, battle-hardened or cynical beyond redemption (accusations that have all been leveled at me), I'll share them:

All politics is local

If there's nothing else you glean from this essay, it should be this. From

Congress to town hall, everything emanates from the ground up. Grass roots may be a cliche, but if politicians don't nurture those grass roots, all the polling, high-paid consultants and media buys won't help. Local. Local. Local.

Don't be discouraged if it seems that not many people read your campaign stories.

Tell yourself as I do: What you're doing really is important; and you'll get your paycheck anyway. It's true that political stories are among the most poorly read in the paper. Many readers don't care about issues. It is, however, our obligation to write about them. Even if not many people read political stories, those who do tend to be the Very Important People: the candidates, the movers and shakers, the campaign strategists and the money-givers.

All politicians are not crooks.

They also are not power-crazed lunatics or egomaniacs. Most are driven by a desire to shape a small piece of the world in a positive way. As one former state rep said to me recently: "We're not serving because we get a special license plate. We're serving because presumably we're trying to do something that will better our state." The former state rep now makes a ton of money working for a brokerage house, but he's thinking of running for state treasurer, a job that pays $60,000. You say to yourself: "What is this guy smoking?" The truth is, most politicians are not in it for the money. In Connecticut, for example, our highest-paid elected official, the governor, earns the unprincely sum of $78,000 a year. State legislators here earn roughly $20,000. Town council members earn pin money, if they're lucky.

But let's not be Pollyannas, either. Some politicians get intoxicated by the power. "So what if I break this teeny-weeny inconsequential law," they say to themselves. "It won't really hurt anyone and no one will be any wiser for it."

Well, every time they break a teeny-weeny inconsequential law, it degrades all politicians and erodes public confidence in our governmental system.

Politicians are made, not elected

To cover the political process intelligently, you need to understand how candidates for office get to be candidates in the first place. The process varies from state to state.

In Connecticut, for example, most important political entities in a municipality are the political parties' town committees. They can range in size from a couple of dozen people to about 70. Generally, anyone over the age of 18 who is registered with a political party can join. Officers are elected by the members.

It is these groups that nominate candidates for local office. Depending on the size of the municipality, nominations are done by town committee elections or by caucus (in which any registered party member can show up at an appointed time and place and vote.)

In Connecticut, town committees also elect delegates to state and congressional nominating conventions. Different delegates are generally designated to select candidates for governor, attorney general, secretary of the state, treasurer, comptroller, U.S. Senate and Congress.

It may work differently in your state, so be sure you learn the rules of the game. In some states, for example, many municipal elections are nonpartisan, meaning that political parties play no formal role in the nominating and election process. If you do not understand the election laws in your state, you (and your readers) will be utterly confused.

In Connecticut, for example, we have a nominating system that was designed by Rube Goldberg's cousin.

In a single-town House or Senate district (that is, a district that does not cross town boundaries), a person who is denied the party endorsement may get on the ballot through a petition. If the designated number of signatures is reached and verified by the town clerk, a primary is held pitting the endorsed candidate against the challenger. (This is very important: If there is a primary, a person does not become the party NOMINEE until he or she wins the primary. Before that, he is merely the ENDORSED candidate.)

In multi-town districts for the state House and Senate (that is, districts that include parts of two or more towns) and for higher office, a candidate needs 15 percent of the convention delegates to force a primary.

In Connecticut, delegates are chosen in February, March or April, depending on the office. Nominating conventions are held in June or July;

primaries are held uniformly on the first Tuesday in September (unless it falls on the day after Labor Day, in which case it is the second Tuesday in September). Become familiar with the election year calendar for your state.

Delegates are the people who get courted and threatened and whose arms often get twisted by party pooh-bahs and incumbent governors. As such, sometimes they're likely to talk about such tactics; often they're not. But if you spot any delegates with their arms in a sling, it wouldn't hurt to ask why.

All together now: make sure you understand the nominating process for the races you cover.

They're all connected

Get to know the town committee chairman or chairwoman. They are apt to know a lot about who's doing what to whom and who's about to get what from whom. Most political patronage jobs go through the local town chairmen. They are also in constant touch with the state party chairman.

They will know if their local races are targeted by the state party and how much money is being channeled into town.

It is also good to get to know the local members of parties' statewide governing bodies, which in Connecticut are called State Central Committees and have 72 members each. In Connecticut, not every town has a State Central member; they are apportioned by state Senate district, with each of the 36 districts getting two. Although State Central members tend to be old and out of touch, sometimes you will strike gold.

Documents, documents, documents

The best place to start checking out a candidate is the paper trail. Here are the documents worth reviewing:

▶ Resumes.

As incredible as this may seem, candidates sometimes exaggerate or even lie about their accomplishments. Check whether the candidate really graduated from Harvard Law School or served in Vietnam. A candidate who lies on a resume may lie about other things.

▶ Campaign finance reports.

In many states, candidates are required to file campaign finance reports periodically. In Connecticut, local candidates file them with the town clerk.

Town commitees and candidates for higher office file with the secretary of the state's office in Hartford. (The dates can change from year to year, so it is best to call the secretary of the state for the filing deadlines.)

A wealth of information can be wrung from these reports, beginning with the obvious: who's ahead in fund-raising and who's behind.

Write about it; it's a story. For one thing, fund-raising attests to a candidate's viability. If Candidate X has raised only $100, $50 of it from his wife, chances are he's not being taken seriously, or is not taking the election too seriously himself. Conversely, if Candidate Y has raised thousands, hired a consultant and bought air time to run ads, she's probably the Real McCoy.

Follow that money. Who is giving? In my Connecticut hometown, for example, Democrats are closely allied with the bigshot real estate developers. The names of the developers routinely show up on the Democrats' campaign finance reports. Is it any surprise that Democrats generally vote for proposed subdivisions? No sirree. To whom are the builders and merchants giving, and what do they want? Zoning variances? How about the bankers and lawyers and the state Capitol lobbyists? You get the drift.

▶ Ethics reports.

Some states require candidates to file financial reports showing assets and debts. In Connecticut, there's not much to help you here in municipal elections, but state House and Senate candidates must file reports with the State Ethics Commission in Hartford. It doesn't hurt to take a peek.

▶ Court records.

Has the candidate been sued or has he sued somebody? Has he been divorced? Court files from such cases may contain interesting fodder about personal finances and other stuff, such as domestic violence. Probably, much of this won't ever find its way into the newspaper. But it never hurts to know as much as you can about a candidate. At The Courant, as with several other major newspapers, you don't even have to leave the newsroom to find out if your candidate is involved in a civil case. The newsroom has access to computerized federal and state civil court records that will show that. However, to see the case files themselves, you have to go to the courthouse.

What to write and when to write it

A campaign officially opens when a candidate announces he or she is interested in seeking a specific office. Announcement stories are fairly pro forma. If the candidate is a newcomer to politics, this is the first time he is being introduced to the community at large. Stick to the basics: who is this person, what is his background, how old is he, why is he running?

Sometimes, there may be a need to write a story before someone formally enters the race. This is especially true if the potential candidate is well-known, is challenging an incumbent, is a carpetbagger or has some other trait that makes him unusual or interesting.

There may be more than one person competing for the same party's endorsement. If so, a "horse race" story, plumbing the dynamics of the contest, is what's called for. Ask yourself: What's at stake? Whom are the political leaders backing? Is there a potential for a primary? Will a bitter fight divide the party, making it easier for the opposition party to win in November?

Focusing on the horse race doesn't mean, of course, that the candidates' positions on the issues should be ignored. But readers love a good fight, and this is an opportunity to get inside the ring.

The next defining moment comes when the candidate wins, or is denied, his party's endorsement. For local candidates in Connecticut, that comes when the local town commitee selects a candidate, usually in late spring or early summer. Obviously, the party's decision calls for a hard news story.

If there is a primary, there will be a campaign to cover during (by the Connecticut election calendar) the dog days of summer. If there isn't a primary, the summer months are typically quiet. It is a time for the candidates to raise money, paint lawn signs, bone up on the issues and otherwise wait for voters to return from the shore.

This lull before the general election will give you a chance to examine resumes, ethics reports and court records, and to begin following the fundraising trail. It's also a good time to gather material for personality profiles.

A few days before the primary (held in September in Connecticut) is an appropriate time to write a setup piece, putting the race in perspective, summing up the candidates' positions and reminding voters why the election is important to their towns, their children and their future.

On Primary Day the story is simple: who won, who lost and why.

With the primary over and the candidates chosen, the fall campaign will be in full bloom. Between mid-September and the November Election Day (by the Connecticut election calendar), there should be ample time to run profiles, issues comparisons and more horse race stories.

If the candidates are both serious and savvy, they will periodically release statements and hold press conferences. Some will be worthwhile; some a waste of time.

Remember, a newspaper is not a bulletin board and is under no obligation to print every utterance from every candidate. This is where judgment is crucial. You must determine what is new, what is newsworthy and what is important.

Fairness and balance are also incredibly important. You'd be amazed how many candidates actually measure the length of stories and count the number of times they're quoted in stories in an effort to prove that a newspaper is somehow biased against them.

Don't be intimidated. When a reporter begins focusing on the number of quotes in a story, he is in danger of missing the forest for the trees. What counts is whether the coverage of a race was balanced over the course of a campaign: that both candidates had roughly the same number of stories and that they were played in a comparable way, and that for every accusation there is a response.

Be sure to smoke out rumors and whispering campaigns. Don't allow a candidate to disavow a rumor if you know that he, in fact, is responsible for promoting it. Particularly in local races, rumors — true or untrue — have a way of becoming part of the fabric of a campaign and can do as much to derail a candidacy as statements made in the light of day.

Keep your eyes open and your ears tuned to events and developments that may be quirky, mean-spirited or downright funny. While the main job is keeping readers informed, there is nothing wrong with entertaining them, as long as we always remember to be fair.

As Election Day nears, even if it seems repetitive, don't hesitate to sum up the campaign, sizing up the candidates, the issues and the personalities.

Polls have shown that the vast majority of voters don't pay attention to campaigns until the waning days of October and often don't make up their minds until the 11th hour. So the more information you can give voters in the week or two before Election Day, the more of a public service you have performed.

A few final words

Given the inherent differences from town to town and from election to election, it is impossible to offer a laundry list of story ideas. To the truly observant, the ideas will come. However, there are two points to keep in mind.

▶ Hold the candidates accountable. Don't let them get away with making outrageous claims — don't let them say they are going to repeal the state income tax without making sure you ask them where they plan to get the money to run the state. Don't let them say they want to cut school spending without explaining how they're going to deal with crowded classrooms and deteriorating textbooks. Don't let them say they're going to pave the streets with gold, make everybody rich and eliminate crime without explaining HOW they're going to do these things.

▶ Finally, explain to readers how politics and the issues affect their lives. Illustrate your points; personalize them. Homeowners want to know if a proposal to change zoning standards will result in a shopping center's being built across the street. Parents want to know if their kids are going to be in crowded classrooms. Everyone wants to know if the police and fire departments are going to be trimmed or if taxes are going up.

Michele Jacklin began her career as a local news reporter for The Bristol (Conn.) Press. As a Courant political writer, she provided distinguished coverage of presidential, congressional, gubernatorial and state legislative elections. She is now a member of The Courant's editorial board.

CHAPTER 25

Surviving election night

By Anita M. Seline and Naedine Joy Hazell

The campaign is over. Election Day has arrived. Now what? Here's a check list.

Before the polls close

▶ Know the history. What margin of victory did the incumbent have in past elections? Has the incumbent lost before? How many times have each of the candidates run? Did they win or lose in the past? What have voter turnouts been in the past? High or low?

You may need all this information during the course of the evening as you're putting together your stories. These facts also add perspective, so your stories say more than who won and lost.

▶ Get a map of the town's voting districts. This should be available from the registrar of voters office. The map will show you which neighborhoods vote where in your town.

The map is invaluable for analysing election results. Will the neighborhood that fought construction of a low-income housing project turn out to vote against a politician who was for it? Will the vote go along racial lines?

▶ Look at results from past elections. Figure out which voting districts have the highest vote turnouts and to what degrees they have voted for political parties in the past. Will the vote follow the historic pattern tonight or has something happened that might change it?

▶ Find someone knowledgeable, and as neutral or honest as possible. Ask him about voter turnouts in the city and for clues for signs for early success or failure of the candidates you are tracking. For example, Candidate A needs to carry districts in the east end of the town by 300-vote margins to offset the opponent's strength in the west part of town. That can help you understand the returns as they come in and also give you something to write for early editions if the results come in late.

▶ Find out where the victory/losing parties are held by the candidates and make sure that the candidates will appear there, win or lose. If not, find out where they will be or arrange a place or telephone where you can reach the candidate. Photographers and editors will be asking you for this information throughout the night.

▶ Think of questions to ask the candidates for both scenarios — win or lose.

▶ Editors usually urge that background material be written ahead of time. This is fine to do, but allow yourself some flexibility, especially in a close race. In this case, be prepared to write two versions of background copy, but keep them short. You'll have plenty of material — and more lively stuff — when the polls close.

When the polls close

▶ Be inside one of the polls when it closes, preferably a high-turnout district. Listen and tally the results when they are read off of the voting machines. On the basis of what your neutral, honest person told you, you should be able to get a good idea of who won.

▶ Head to one of the headquarters/parties of the candidates. It's your call about whether you should find the loser or winner first. Head to where the best story is. If a longtime incumbent is headed for defeat, go there.

If an outsider has pulled off a surprise victory, go to that headquarters. If it's a predictable race, then stick with the winner and find the loser before you head back to write.

▶ You also may want to find the best-organized campaign. If they have their act together, they should have runners at all of the polls reporting back with the results from those districts. Often these campaigns will know the results before town hall or, sometimes, even before the newspaper.

Back in the office

▶ If it's an important race that has the interest of your editors, listen to what they want in the story. Do this before you start writing; otherwise, you're going to be re-writing on deadline.

▶ Keep it short and simple. Who won and what does it mean, if anything.

▶ Provide color from both Election Day and the victory/loss parties. Write with authority to give readers some perspective, something more than they can get from the TV. Keep in mind the day-to-day battles of the campaign and how they may have affected the race.

▶ Include voter turnout in the race but don't use it in terms of district numbers. Characterize neighborhoods, such as Candidate X won in the Behind-the-Rocks neighborhood, not Candidate X won in voting district 12. Few know what voting district they reside in but almost everyone has a neighborhood affiliation.

▶ Don't blow your deadline. Unless there has been some tremendous foul-up in the election results, there should be no reason for missing your deadline. On election night, making deadline is critical because of the amount of late copy that is handled in a short amount of time.

▶ Keep calm. There will be enough craziness around you. Don't contribute to it.

Election night from an editor's point of view

First you panic. Best to get this out of the way early, as there will be no time later.

Second, and more important to the coverage — start planning early. (Ideally, you start a month in advance, but a week will do in a pinch.)

Election night in the newsroom is like opening night of a play — either everyone knows their parts, and knows them well enough to ad lib, or they don't. After the curtain goes up, the evening takes on a life of its own.

Take a moment to dream

Before you start planning, dream a little. If you could have it all, what would it look and read like? Would there be a main bar with comments from participants and voters, plus an analysis of why so-and-so won? Or would it be better to split this information into three stories and add a sidebar of color from various polling places and headquarters? Color photos of the winners and losers? Charts with everyone's name spelled right and the winners highlighted? A map showing which candidate won which districts?

Then, make a list of your available staff, and anyone else you can borrow.

Now for reality

Place the dream next to reality.

Decide what you can do with the people you have. Sketch a tentative story budget with reporters assigned to each story or part of a story.

Estimate story lengths. It is best to formulate a budget after talking to your lead reporters, who have the best idea what the stories will be that night.

If you want charts, decide what you want them to say and start talking to graphics NOW, NOW, NOW. Give them a mock-up of what you think might work, or what has worked in the past, but remain flexible.

If you want maps, talk to graphics NOW, NOW, NOW.

Ask to see the finished maps and charts (without the numbers, of course) at least a day or two in advance so you can proofread the names, districts, party affiliations, etc.

Photos? Of course. Better alert the photo editors NOW about how many people it looks like they'll have to devote to covering the news that night.

Getting a head start

One meeting among department editors or coordinators about a week before Election Day should help to clarify the game plan. But keep it brief. If possible, have the meeting with everyone standing. This usually speeds up the process.

Meet with the staff at least three days before the election. Make assignments, but be ready to change them if a better idea comes up during the meeting.

Although some people will find this insulting, hand out a sheet reminding everyone that their stories absolutely must include the candidates' names (spelled properly), their party affiliation, their age, their occupation and previous offices held or significant community contributions. Other significant details should include the length of the term, how much the job pays and whether the winner will be in the minority or majority.

Every reporter covering a race MUST (no matter how it dulls their creative edge) pre-write at least the basics of their story. I've known some reporters, myself included, who have gone so far as to write a story based on who they thought would win and just left room for quotes and color. If there's time, the canned story can always be killed and written fresh. HOWEVER, if there is no time (a commodity in short supply on most election nights), and they have to call quotes in from the field, the story is essentially done.

Just in case someone has NOT done the above, editors should have easy access to a paper file or computer file that contains all pertinent information on candidates, including age, party, background etc.

Stay loose

Be ready to redeploy reporters/photographers in response to where the news is happening.

Don't drink any coffee. You'll be high enough.

NEVER, NEVER lose your sense of humor.

Naedine Joy Hazell started her career covering local news for The (Bergen) Record in Hackensack, N.J. She was the city editor at The Courant and now is the paper's travel writer. Her honors include New York Associated Press awards for news and feature writing.

Anita M. Seline began her career as a local reporter for the Waterbury (Conn.) Republican. She covered Hartford City Hall for The Courant before moving to Washington, D.C., to work as a freelance writer.

CHAPTER 26

Meetings, meetings and more meetings

By Peter Sleight

Why do we go to so many meetings?

Well, because we have to. In most community news beats, reporters cover all council meetings, school board meetings and most planning and zoning commission meetings.

But we also cover these meetings because they are an important part of local government.

We know that meetings usually don't make riveting journalism. If we're going to cover so many, how can we make stories about them better?

Here are some suggestions:

1. Prepare.

Preparation starts early in the day — not seconds before the meeting comes to order.

▶ Identify the major issue that will probably lead your story.

▶ Collect any background clips from your own files or from the library.

▶ Write the background in advance. Then you need only write a few topping paragraphs after the meeting. This will allow you the time to make those beginning paragraphs, which carry most of the news, the best they can be. It also makes meeting deadline easier.

▶ Call the people you think will be major participants in discussions and get background and quotes about their positions. That way, if you have trouble buttonholing someone during a meeting, you have their positions covered. This is also a good way to learn about brewing disputes before they happen.

2. Analyze your meeting coverage decisions.

▶ How interested will your readers be in a given meeting?

▶ Are there issues that can be discussed more fully in a well-reported advance?

▶ Will your readers be better served by a different story?

Any decision to skip a meeting must be made with your editor and in light of competitive concerns. But if you've been developing enterprise out of your community, anticipating issues, analyzing trends, looking for human-interest stories, you'll be able to skip meetings offering scant news.

3. Think of your readers' needs.

Most of your readers will be residents of the community you cover. And most of them will be taxpayers.

For the most part, they will be interested in a few key items that could affect their lives and wallets: Are my taxes going to increase? Is my child's education going to get better or worse? Are they going to build a paper mill next to my house? Will my garbage be picked up, will the leaves be removed, will the roads be plowed in the winter? Did my neighbor say something interesting (or make a fool of himself)?

4. Anticipate the results.

You should almost never be surprised by a development at a meeting. It's your job as a reporter to have a good idea of what will happen at a meeting before it happens.

▶ Visit any neighborhoods that might be affected by changes being considered. This might be obvious in the case of major proposals, such as a highway widening project. But the technique can be just as useful for minor things, such as a zoning variance for a horse barn. Getting a first-hand sense of the physical layout and direct quotes from the parties involved can help you interpret technical discussions during the meeting and be more valuable than hours of meeting time.

5. Be alert to the real story.

Just because the council spends 45 minutes talking about campaign signs in the town right of way doesn't mean that's the lede of your story. Maybe you should focus on the $4 million housing rehabilitation grant the council spent five minutes voting to accept with no debate. Which issue will have greater effect on your readers?

▶ Watch for the news happening outside the meeting. There's news happening in the hallways and parking lots of every meeting hall: Countermeasures are plotted, alliances formed, opinions ventured.

▶ Be alert for meaningful political interplay — but don't waste time with petty politics.

Understand that elected officials don't always run the community. The real powers behind local government are often the party chairmen, the directors of large banks and businesses, lawyers, or political contributors with deep pockets. Keep these questions in mind: Who is exercising power? Who makes the final decision? Who's behind the votes?

▶ Seize the drama, whatever it is.

If there's a sharp disagreement, use some sharp quotes. If there's a marked reversal of position, point it out. If there's a big effect for taxpayers, like a waste of money or a tax increase, note it prominently. If someone makes an accusation, use it to frame your story.

Peter Sleight started out as a city hall reporter at a Gannett daily in Poughkeepsie, N.Y. Today he is The Courant's assistant metro editor/nights. He writes freelance articles about gardening, and he has served as assistant director of the National Writers' Workshop/Hartford.

CHAPTER 27

How to get more than grief from the cops

By Andrew Julien and Tracy Gordon Fox

The young reporter walks into police headquarters and stares down the gruff sergeant sitting at the front desk.

"What's going on?" the reporter demands.

"Who are you?" the sergeant asks.

"I'm The Press."

"Call the public relations officer," the sergeant says.

"I tried. He's playing golf."

"Call him tomorrow."

"But I've got deadlines! I'm going to call the chief."

"He's playing golf with the public relations officer."

Readers want to know who's getting burgled, beaten or busted. They are fascinated by the extremes to which people will go to satisfy anger, jealousy or greed.

They want the details. It's your job to get them.

Unfortunately, cops are not the most open of public servants. They are by nature — and profession — suspicious. They often feel embattled — criticized by the public for their inability to stop crime and scorned by the people they are supposed to protect.

You won't get respect at the police department. Not at first anyway. Not until you earn it.

So, when the desk sergeant growls at you, don't take it personally. He's not angry at you . . . yet.

There will be a time to do battle, but if you don't get past the front desk, you won't get anywhere. So be polite, smile. Let him blow off a little steam.

Developing trust

Cops love to schmooze. Instead of blasting in and demanding information, stroll in and ask the sergeant, or any cop for that matter, how his day or night is going. "Busy night? Had time to breathe?"

If he says he's busy, he probably is. Ask when it might be a good time to stop back. If you show him respect, you've taken a step toward breaking down the barrier between cops and reporters.

Developing trust is the key.

Cops love to talk about what they do and how they do it. But they are afraid of being burned, of releasing information they shouldn't, or of making a superior look bad. Show them you're as interested in their concerns as you are in their information and they'll warm up.

Whatever you do, don't burn them.

Don't banter about your sources. Collect home phone numbers at every opportunity, but don't abuse them. Make sure everyone's working off the same definitions of what's background information and what's off the record.

As you develop sources, ask them point-blank if you should leave your name when you call. This shows you take confidentiality seriously.

Earning respect

Some cops, especially those who have been at it awhile, may try to manipulate reporters. They'll tell you not to publish something now and promise to give it to you first later. They'll say you're jeopardizing their chances of cracking a case.

Sometimes it is worth holding off for a couple of days on a story. Sometimes you've got to go with what you have and take the heat that comes with it.

Mutual respect is the best you can strive for. And to get it, you must be fair. If a cop made a good bust, write about it. That way, when it's time to write a story that is hard on the police, you will have a track record.

And when it's time to be tough, don't apologize.

Getting started

Most departments have a procedure for reporters to review the daily arrests and incident reports. Some allow reporters to look at everything; others are more restrictive. Learn the procedure in the community you cover, and if there is no set process, talk to the chief about setting one up.

In addition to getting basic information about what happened, who was arrested, date of birth, age, date, time, etc., try to get as may other details as you can: names of victims and witnesses, the name of the arresting officer, the type of car stolen, etc. If the officer tells you a ring was stolen from a home at 123 Cherry St., ask what kind of ring. Maybe it was someone's mother's engagement ring. With one question, you've punched up a cop brief.

Use the basic information as a starting point. Whenever there is time, and the story holds more promise than a routine police brief, go to the scene and try to find witnesses.

Talk to the victims. Maybe the victim at 123 Cherry St. inherited her mother's engagement ring just a few weeks ago and is devastated by the loss. Maybe the guy who's car was stolen is now stuck without a way to get to the prom. A few extra moves could turn a routine burglary story into an interesting yarn.

Beyond the police report

Many reporters make the mistake of relying almost exclusively on the police to find out what happened. What the police do is part of the story, but only part. Victims have stories, witnesses have stories and very often criminals have stories too.

When you are at a crime scene, and the cops are too busy to talk, capitalize on your opportunity to talk to possible witnesses. Make your questions pointed and specific; group dynamics can turn two witnesses into 40 "wanna-bes" happy to speculate on what happened without bothering to note that they didn't see anything.

To interview a victim, introduce yourself and say you're sorry about what happened. Sound sincere. Better yet, mean it. Throwing questions at someone who is very upset will get a door slammed in your face.

Developing sources

First, find out how your department is organized. Most departments are divided into divisions with a sergeant or lieutenant in charge of several officers or detectives. Get to know the heads of the key divisions: narcotics, major crimes (homicide, etc.), internal affairs, patrol. Then find out who the key detectives are, the ones who get the big cases.

Some departments have community affairs officers who are involved in neighborhood crime prevention projects, programs for troubled youth, etc. The dispatchers often know everything going on.

Get to know as many people as you can. Talk about last night's UConn game, chat with them about something in the newspaper, admire the picture of the kids on their desks. Show them you are a person. Go riding with patrol officers to get to know the officers on the beat. Go on a tour of headquarters.

When you're new on the beat, you have a special status that you can exploit. You don't have to play dumb; you are dumb. You are expected to ask questions. If you find someone talkative, ask who wields the power; who the best cops are; how much political interference there is in the department; the state of morale?

Your honeymoon period won't last long. Once yours becomes a familiar face, questions like those will be regarded with more suspicion from people trying to figure out what you're really after.

Many departments have rules about who is allowed to talk to the media. Don't break those rules in front of a supervisor.

Tell the supervisor that to get the full story, you'll need to talk to the cop who made the bust. Explain why it is important; don't assume that cops understand how reporting works. Ask if you can talk to the arresting officer or the detective with the supervisor present, at first. If they see they can trust you, the rules may slip away.

You can also get to know cops outside headquarters, on the street, in bars, etc. Be careful not to grouse about one cop in front of another; don't join in their grousing about a supervisor. Let the cops do the grousing.

Give the impression that you respect the job they do. When you get to know what it entails, you probably will.

While police "sources" are great, attribution to "unidentified police sources" in the newspaper often suggests a cop-out by the reporter. Cops are public servants, paid by the taxpayers. They are obligated to give out routine information and should have no need to hide behind anonymity to do so. Save the unnamed source for the big expose or the big story where careers of sources may be at stake.

Freedom of Information

If there is one law the police aren't enthusiastic about enforcing, it's the

Freedom of Information Act. Connecticut has one, and there is probably one in your state. Be sure you know what the law entitles you to see at the police station.

Threatening to file an FOI complaint sounds more impressive than it is. In Connecticut, for example, the target of your complaint has four days, by law, to decide whether to give you the information you're after. If the answer is still no, the case is scheduled for a hearing, usually a few weeks or months later. That won't help your daily story any. You will get more, faster, if you work out your own ground rules and relationships with the cops.

If a department is routinely and irrationally obstructionist, talk to the chief and/or arrange a conference with you, the chief and your editor.

Accumulate details

Arrest warrant affidavits compiled by the cops often are highly informative, and all-too-often are sealed by the court immediately after a high-profile arrest. But in interesting cases, always check the court files for them; sometimes they are available.

Keep files on all crimes you think may turn into good stories down the road and squirrel away information as you go. It might seem like nothing at first, but if you accumulate details, you may have in your files the raw juicy bits that can get a story onto Page 1.

Beyond hard news

It is rare that the full story behind any particular crime is told in the piece that reports the event itself. The first rush of reporting is given over to finding out what happened, squeezing information out of the police, tracking down witnesses or trying to coax the victim or family members to talk. Once that is done, however, the best stories are worth more of your time.

The possibilities are vast. Crime stories can focus on victims, criminals, detectives or any of the vast array of social issues that come to light in the arena of crime.

The story might show us how poverty, love, greed, jealousy or even something as mundane as unemployment, drives someone to do the unthinkable. Or, as many novelists and journalists have proved, the story of solving the crime itself is often compelling. Detectives are fascinating people who wade into the muck of society and sift for clues. They are rich characters that, if well drawn, can make a story sparkle.

Whichever angle you take, the key is building a complete chronology of the events. You are going to tell a story so you need to know precisely what happened, when and to whom.

Different players probably were involved at different points, so talk to all of them, or as many as possible — victims, family members, friends, cops, neighbors, co-workers, witnesses, lawyers. If possible, talk to the criminal or his/her lawyer.

Documents can be useful too. If an arrest warrant is on file at court, it will contain names, details, dates and times, as well as the key pieces of evidence. Other court records and police records will help build the picture. A detective may be reluctant to unravel his case for you, but may be more comfortable sharing details that will pad out a warrant you've gotten from the court.

Elicit as much detail as possible. If you want to understand how the victim felt, don't ask, TV-style: "How did you feel?" You will get an answer like, "angry" or "numb." Which will leave you with the bland and boring: "The rape left her feeling angry."

Ask, instead, "What did you do?" Find out what people did and you can write the story as it happened so the reader can watch it unfold. Melodramatic embellishment is not needed. The events themselves are compelling. Just re-create events accurately and completely.

Visit the crime scene, or better yet go there with the investigating officer or the victim. Being there may elicit a flood of memories, and you will see details you may want to use.

If you're talking to someone who has lost a loved one to violence, ask to see their photo album. Let them talk you through it. This will spark vivid emotions and memories.

Detectives are precious sources; chances are they have already done much of the work you are planning to do. They will rarely say anything that might jeopardize an investigation, but after an arrest or a conviction, they might share war stories over food or a drink, assuming you've built a good relationship.

Once you have put together the chronology, experts can help give the story depth. The FBI's psychologists and forensic experts can help you interpret your information. Based on the circumstances of a crime, they may be able to tell you something about the criminal. Universities usually have sociologists who study crime and violence.

Have patience. Family members, victims and cops all talk, but they talk when they're ready. They are not elected officials and have no special obligation to the media.

Social problems

With awareness growing about the relationships between certain social problems and crime, police departments are increasingly turning to specialized divisions to handle certain cases.

Child abuse and youth violence are often handled through a special youth services division. Some departments have specialists in domestic violence or hate crimes. Smaller departments may have a detective who spends part of his time on one of these specialties. The officers who work in these areas often see trends and patterns developing.

Because of the touchy nature of these crimes, it can be difficult to get the cops to open up. And some details, such as names of juvenile offenders or victims of sexual assault, may be sealed by law.

A good way to gain a foothold is to do a generic story about what a given division does, sidestepping the touchy question of confidentiality. That approach might yield dividends down the road, as the cops learn that you're interested and can be trusted.

Police officers in these specialized divisions often work closely with community agencies. The agencies are often more accessible and might put you in touch with victims willing to participate in a story.

Beyond crime stories

Police departments provide not only crime stories but pieces about what happens when politics and money mix with issues of public safety.

Here are some areas to explore:

▶ Technology. From computerized cruisers to semiautomatic handguns to DNA testing, police departments are the place to look for the latest methods to help fight crime. Look for stories that tie technology to a specific case to show the reader exactly what is going on and how the new technology might help police better do their job. Be careful to look at the costs, too. Sometimes, especially in smaller departments, the police want new things just because they're new.

▶ Budget. The annual public safety budget is not only a spending plan but a story tip sheet. A request for a crisis intervention officer could signal an increase in family problems. A request for an extra detective might be a sign that the department is not keeping up with its investigative caseload.

▶ Office politics. Who's in, who's out, whose star is rising and whose is plummeting? Office politics are as much a part of most police departments as guns and badges. Appointments to key spots are often linked to internal networks. Sometimes there are good stories here, especially if questionable appointments are made. Few cops will go on the record with this type of information, but a reporter who knows what's going on will be in a position to write such stories because he or she will be able to see the motives behind the moves.

▶ Unions. Police unions, especially in cities, tend to be powerful, with clout inside and outside the department. That can put them at odds with the administration. Union leaders will often share information about things going on inside the department, but they do so for their own reasons. So, anything they tell you should be checked and used carefully.

▶ Internal affairs. Larger departments usually have a separate internal affairs division, but even small departments will have someone who handles issues relating to the conduct of police officers. The jurisdiction of the FOI laws here is sketchy, but the final outcome of a case should be available. Some departments have independent review boards, which makes getting at these stories much easier. The victims are also often willing to talk.

Andrew Julien got his start at an English-language political monthly in Tel Aviv. He now reports on workplace issues for The Courant, where he formerly had the city police beat. His honors include a Connecticut Society of Professional Journalists award for his column, "Working."

Tracy Gordon Fox began by covering local news for a weekly in West Hartford, Conn. She now covers the town of Colchester and regional state police news for The Courant. Her honors include winning two Steven Gield Awards, The Courant's in-house prize for excellence in local reporting.

CHAPTER 28

The State Police, the FBI and the Mob

by Edmund Mahony

First, the bad news: You will be talking to people who are instructed from the earliest moments of their professional training not to tell anyone what they are up to.

Mobsters subscribe to this practice for a simple reason. If others find out what they are doing, the mobsters go to jail. That is why mobsters kill other mobsters who have big mouths.

State police officers and FBI agents have more reasons not to talk, but they are just as simple. Generally, they believe that loose talk about an investigation can jeopardize the case. They don't want to be killed professionally.

It has become common for defense lawyers, particularly in federal criminal trials, to file motions demanding to know what law enforcement agent provided confidential information to a reporter prior to trial. (It makes no difference to some lawyers that not everything published in the newspaper was leaked by police officers. They act as if everything was because that is consistent with the trial strategy of portraying the defendant as victim of law enforcement run amok.)

The defense motions typically claim that the resulting newspaper articles so hopelessly prejudice jury pools against their clients that the charges should be dimsissed.

In any event, the wedges defense lawyers drive into cases over leaks amount to expensive and time-consuming digressions from the principal issues in the cases. Judges usually do the right thing about such motions: ignore them.

But there is always concern among prosecutors and police that, someday, a judge might accept a defense argument alleging a pattern of leaks and dismiss a case as a sort of symbolic punishment. Investigators, who often work years on cases that cost millions, would not like that.

There are other reasons why state police and FBI agents are leery about talking to reporters. One is that it is against the rules of their agencies. In the FBI, only supervisors are permitted to take calls from reporters. If an agent receives a call, he is supposed to disclose no information and immediately report the call to a superior.

When the contents of confidential, investigative documents appear in the paper, the FBI and most state police departments, including Connecticut's, have internal disciplinary units to determine whether the leakers came from their ranks. The federal leak police actually carry around polygraph machines. In Connecticut, violation of the state law prohibiting disclosure of wiretapped information is a felony.

Finally, police know that many of the crooks they investigate are avid newspaper readers. Gangsters have been intercepted on telephone taps early on Sunday mornings critiquing stories about them. Others keep scrapbooks and clip anything that has to do with the mob. Police and FBI agents are acutely aware that information they give reporters could wind up in the paper and alert the mob about how much the authorities know and where their investigations are headed.

Being aware of law enforcement's institutional bias against reporters is important, not only to understand why cops can be such pains in the neck, but to figure out how best to circumvent the bias.

The mob's bias? It's just interesting to know it has one. When a mobster talks to you, bet he is trying to use you.

All that having been said, there are things you can do to loosen up potential sources in law enforcement and the underworld.

Be prepared

Be as prepared and backgrounded as possible when interviewing someone. The more you know going into a conversation with a cop — and to a lesser degree, a crook — the more you are likely to take out. This is true for a variety of reasons.

First of all, the source is not likely to think he is telling you anything if he thinks you already know it. For example, if you are working on a story about why a connected bookmaker was killed, you can call an organized crime investigator and simply ask, "Why?" But you will probably be disappointed.

But if you called and said, "I'm hearing two reasons why Bustout got killed. One is that his bosses decided he was a police informant. The other is that he committed a breach of etiquette by indiscreetly accusing a high-er-ranking thug of ripping off his office. Are you guys hearing the same things?"

Under the second scenario, the agent is going to want to keep you on the phone to try to figure out how you know what you know. In addition, since you already have that information, he will be able to tell his superiors he didn't tell you anything.

Dope it out

Look at an investigation and make logical guesses about its direction, its target and what offenses are involved. Call around and phrase your questions as if you are looking for confirmation rather than new informa-tion. Make the same kinds of judgments when researching something that may not be under investigation by the authorities.

It is likely that everyone you speak with will provide you with a small bit of information. Incorporate the nuggets into questions for your subsequent sources. Be sure, however, that you do not create a story with your ques-tions. Law enforcement is a small, gossipy community. Your questions to one source can come back as information from another.

Pound the pavement

Cops and agents spend a lot of time and effort finding out what they know. They twist the arms of informants. They spend hours in dirty cars watching comings and goings from dirtier buildings. They spend even more hours in cheap rooms monitoring wiretaps. It should not come as a sur-prise that some think, "Why should I break my back digging up informa-tion just to spoon-feed some lazy reporter."

But, if they think the reporter is out pounding the pavements, too, there is more respect and more willingness to be friendly. Translation: They will try to get information from you.

Hang out

There are lots of ways to get information. If you are working on a mob case, go to a mob bar. Take a friend or two. Sit around. Drink beer. Watch and listen. You'll invariably pick up something you can use sometime or another.

Identify your neighborhood bookie. Watch who drops by to talk to him and swap envelopes. Find the gambling halls in your city or town. Park down the street and watch who comes and goes. Maybe it's an influential politician with a popular radio announcer. (It happened.) Find out who else is parked and watching like you. Ten to one it's the police.

Check the files

Go to court when gangsters are on trial or having hearings. Filings in court, particularly federal court, are voluminous. If there is electronic surveillance in the case, the file may hold the applications. The applications contain, as probable cause, the evidence uncovered in previous court-ordered electronic surveillance.

More than once, clerks have inadvertently included in public files material that courts had previously ordered sealed.

Chat them up

While in court, chat up the criminals. Lots of times they are bored and willing to pass the time with small talk — or at least brag about how bad they are. They probably won't confess, but chances are you'll get something you can use.

When you write about a gangster, try whenever feasible to interview him — in person. It helps him to remember you. Ten to one, the next time he sees you, he'll call your name and make some crack, if only as part of some bizarre effort to impress his flunkies by proving he actually can speak to reporters.

Sometimes the face-to-face pays off with more than color. Billy "The Hotdog" Grant, the late, great tube-steak impresario and bookmaker to the bookies, was once so startled by being questioned at one of his fast-food joints that he blurted the fact that he had spent most of seven years of Friday afternoons playing cards and drinking in a West Hartford restaurant with the fugitive underboss of the Colombo crime family.

In a few cases, it's possible to develop lasting associations with crooks just on the basis of some early courtroom encounters. Gangsters correspond with reporters all over the country. Some write from prison. Some call on 800 lines from the witness protection program. Some just call because it gives them some sort of satisfaction not immediately clear to normal people.

Schmooze the cops

Chat up the cops, too. They're easier to befriend than the crooks. But be persistent, regardless of whom you're trying to reach.

Some years ago I needed to wheedle some information from a state police sergeant, a veteran of the specialty squads investigating legalized gambling and organized crime.

The sergeant did not deign to return my calls. I kept trying. Some days later, a mutual acquaintance called me at the sergeant's behest to find out what I wanted and then to tell me to forget it. I pleaded and the mutual acquaintance promised to lobby on my behalf. As time passed, sources I had spoken with on other matters began calling, alerting me that the sergeant was asking questions about the strength of my word.

Finally the sergeant himself called. He would permit me to eat breakfast with him so he could look me over personally. Breakfast was to be at 5:30 a.m. In Danbury.

We met and he ate and I guzzled coffee and paid. He apparently approved. A few days later we met again, this time in the lot behind a Hartford restaurant. He gave me a package of information more helpful than I had hoped.

The sergeant and I began speaking regularly and became good friends. Although he is now retired, he continues to be a valuable source. Some years back, over a couple of beers, I asked him why, for our first meeting, did I have to make that pre-dawn drive to Danbury. (I had since learned that he drove nearly as far.) He said he figured anyone willing to get up that early with no guarantees probably would work hard enough to get the story straight. In other words, if I had blown off the breakfast, I'd probably still be trying to get the story.

Defense lawyers as sources

Defense lawyers are considerably less discerning about whom they'll speak with, so don't forget them. Sometimes in multi-defendant criminal cases, a defense lawyer will purposely try to taint the jury pool by leaking confidential information. For example, he may be trying to plant an article — to be read by prospective jurors — that he thinks characterizes his client as less culpable than the others on trial. Learn what you can from them, but don't allow them to use you.

Don't be a wuss

Remember that people involved in crime, on either side, tend to regard themelves as coming from the tougher classes. So play it accordingly. Give as good as you get, and don't let anyone push you around. If you want someone to talk to you, he has to trust you. No one will trust you if he thinks you're a doormat.

If you publish something that is judged to be prejudicial or otherwise sealed from the public, everyone in the case, from the cops to the defendants to the judge, is going to turn on you like barracuda to make it look like they didn't leak. If it happens that you got the information from any one source, that person is likely to be the most ferocious in an effort to deflect suspicion.

Don't pull your punches when you write, about the cops or the criminals. They fancy themselves professionals, each in his own way, and, for the most part, don't take things personally. Chances are, if you stumble across something that becomes what is perceived to be "a negative story," they will agree with you about your obligation to report it.

Patience

Finally, be patient. You will have to whether you want to or not. It can take years simply to get well-placed FBI agents to answer the phone when you call. Many times your best police sources will be people you met on your first beat. You might be covering the little town of Putnam and meet some young troopers working the overnight shift at Troop D.

Years later, you will all be assigned elsewhere. You might be covering a big organized crime case, and the troopers might have been promoted to OC squad to work a wiretap. With a little luck they might be listening in on the conversations of a graduate of small-time Putnam crime, and the case will be a reunion.

Edmund Mahony got his start covering local news for The Norwich (Conn.) Bulletin. He now is a general assignment reporter for The Courant. Mahony's accomplishments include helping revive the old newspaper tradition of the serial — a riveting multi-part tale in which each installment ends in a cliffhanger.

CHAPTER 29

Finding your way around the courthouse

By Lynne Tuohy

The people who work in court, especially in the urban courthouses, are overworked and frustrated. You'll be able to spot the defendants pretty easily; they're often the only ones smiling.

This does not excuse the rudeness you may encounter, or the 10 minutes you may wait at a counter for a clerk to acknowledge your existence. Rather, it challenges you to cut a path through the obstacles to reach the information you want. Because machetes usually set off the metal detectors, you must arm yourself with more discreet tools and use subterfuge when necessary.

What you need to do

▶ Know the rules covering access to information.

Whatever state you work in, there are laws and rules governing access to court information. In Connecticut, for example, you need a copy of "Field Guide to Court Information in Connecticut." The clerks have it and have been instructed to adhere to its provisions. The guide is invoked to resolve any dispute over access to information.

▶ Introduce yourself immediately to those who control the information.

In Connecticut, that means the chief clerk for your judicial district. A good relationship with this person will set the tone for your dealings with the rest of the clerk's office, and the chief clerk often will relay information over the phone in a crisis. Meet this person before you need something. Most of Connecticut's judicial districts also have "trial court administrators" who can help you get access to people and information. Be sure to introduce yourself to them as well.

▶ Know how your court system is organized.

In Connecticut, there are 12 judicial districts, often referred to as "J.D."s. For each there is a state's attorney (chief prosecutor), chief administrative judge, presiding judge and a chief public defender. Each judicial district has a Part A courthouse, where major felony cases are tired; some judicial districts have more than one "geographic area," or G.A., court, in which minor felonies, misdemeanors and motor vehicle cases are resolved. (There are 22 such courts statewide.)

▶ Be patient.
Seldom does anything occur on time in court — unless you're late.

What you can't get
Go into court with the attitude that everything in a courthouse is open to you; most of it is. Now for the exceptions:

▶ Juveniles
Juvenile court is closed to the public. You need to know how your state defines juvenile offenders and how it processes them.

In Connecticut, juvenile offenders are those who are under the age of 16 at the time the crime is committed. Connecticut juveniles repeatedly charged with felony offenses, or with murder, may be transferred to adult court; you won't know that until they get there.

Connecticut criminal defendants who are under the age of 18 when the crime is committed may apply for youthful offender status. If granted, their hearings are held behind closed doors, their files are sealed and their penalties are limited to a maximum four years, regardless of the crime. Even the hearings on their application for youthful offender status are closed. If the case reappears on the adult docket, the status has been denied. If it doesn't, you can only assume youthful offender status has been granted. But you'll never know for sure, because no one will comment.

▶ Closed courtrooms
Under any other circumstance, if a judge attempts to close a courtroom, you should contest it. In Connecticut, we have a law — C.G.S. 51-164x — that allows for expedited appeals of court closings. Your objection must be on record to make use of it. Just stand up, raise your hand, and say you object to the courtroom's being closed and want time to appeal. Yes, it is an

uncomfortable thing to do, but it is important. Your action, by law, should halt the hearing until the newspaper's appeal can be argued before the Appellate Court. Make sure you know the proper procedure in your state for appealing courtroom closures.

▶ Sexual assaults

The identities of sexual assault victims are not public in most places, including Connecticut, but court clerks are obligated to give you all other information in that criminal file. It is their responsibility to mask the identifying information (name & address) of the victim in an affidavit. Clerks sometimes say the affidavit is not public because it involves a sexual assault. This is not the case, unless the entire file has been sealed by the court.

▶ Sealed files and warrants

One of the biggest obstacles you will face in getting access to information are files that are sealed immediately after a high-profile arrest. In Connecticut, for example, the judge presiding over the defendant's first court appearance often will seal the file for 10 days. This is a matter of judicial discretion, and one that is often abused. We have little recourse, because the file is usually unsealed before any appeal we file can be heard. Still, bring these cases to the attention of your editor immediately.

Learn the law governing search warrants in your state. In Connecticut, search warrants must be signed by a judge, and filed with the court within 10 days after police execute them. They are supposed to be open once filed in court, but often are sealed indefinitely as part of an ongoing investigation. Always ask for them, and always get a specific reason if access is denied.

▶ Hearings and arraignments

Courts are chaotic places. Don't count on being able to later piece together what you saw, or what you missed.

You may find yourself in court to cover:

▶ An arraignment, in which the state formally brings charges against a suspect, shortly after a suspect is arrested.

▶ A bond hearing at some later date.

▶ A hearing on a motion to have the defendant enter a variety of special probation or education programs that could halt the prosecution of a case.

▶ A hearing on a variety of other matters that could affect the outcome of the case.

▶ Or in civil matters, such as when the town you cover is being sued, you may find yourself at a hearing to dismiss the case, or for injunctive relief.

When you cover a hearing, be sure to get the name of the judge and the lawyers involved. If possible, read the file before the hearing starts. Once the hearing is over, it often takes hours for the file to make it back from the courtroom to the clerk's office.

▶ Plea bargains

Most criminal cases (more than 95 percent) never go to trial. In rare cases, a judge will dismiss them for lack of evidence, or a prosecutor will nolle (pronounced nolly) them, exercising the option not to prosecute.

Most cases are plea-bargained, meaning the prosecutor and defense lawyers strike a deal on the charges the defendant will plead guilty to, and on the sentence to be served. When a criminal case is plea-bargained, it often involves a reduction in charges. Be sure your information is updated and accurate.

If a judge agrees with the plea bargain, the defendant enters a plea, sometimes with some added gloss. There are pleas of no contest, in which the defendant does not contest the charge but doesn't flat-out plead guilty. There also is a plea of "guilty under the Alford doctrine," in which a defendant maintains his innocence but concedes the state has enough evidence to convict him. You frequently see this plea in sex assault cases, with the girlfriend, wife or mother of the defendant — and sometimes all three — looking on sternly.

Avoiding the confusion

If the judge finds the defendant guilty, this should be your lede. Don't confound your readers by discussing a technical plea such as "no contest" high in the story. Save the explanation for later in the story. However, don't say simply that the defendant pleaded guilty if the plea is a qualified one. It makes a difference. You might lede with: "Joe Blow was convicted Monday of XXX, after a plea agreement that reduced his charge from this to that," or "and is expected to serve only XXX years of a potential 140-year sentence."

Be sure to tell your readers what the actual sentence is. Most sentences involve some combination of the total sentence, reduced by a certain number of years, followed by a number of years on probation, sometimes with special conditions. If the judge hands down a sentence of "10 years, execution suspended after four, five years' probation conditioned on restitution, drug testing and psychological counseling as needed," boil it down to what's meaningful: "Joe Blow was found guilty of XXX and sentenced to four years in prison Friday." Save all the special conditions for later, if at all.

It is often useful, however, to inform readers of the maximum sentence the defendant faced, and let them gauge how tough the judge and prosecutor were.

Cultivating sources

Prosecutors have no obligation to show you their files or share information, but most will if cultivated as sources. They are powerful sources to have, because they pretty much control the docket and the outcome of those cases that don't go to trial. Don't snub the defense lawyers, however. They will not only balance your perspective on the case, but can give you copies of the motions they've filed or access to their clients. The sheriffs who work the courthouses know a lot of what happens behind the scenes — in the lock-up and often in the jury rooms; don't snub them, either.

Never assume an avenue of information is closed to you. Although most judges are wary of the press, some will help you on a background-only basis by explaining a decision or order they issued. Do not quote them unless you have made it explicitly clear that that is your intent before the conversation takes place, and they understand it's an on-the-record conversation. Burn a judge and you quickly become poison to most of the staff in a courthouse.

Know the jargon

You are not expected to get a law degree to cover a courthouse, but there are some terms you may need to know, and explain, on deadline. Here are some key terminology used in Connecticut. Be sure to know their counterparts in your state.

Accelerated rehabilitation is an option available to first-time offenders only. The criminal defendant must apply for A.R., which is a program that allows him to circumvent prosecution in return for a period of probation (up to two years.) If the defendant successfully completes probation, all record of his conviction is erased. (The court file remains open throughout the period of probation, however.) You cannot write that someone granted A.R. has been convicted or has pleaded guilty; neither occurs. Avoid using the term "accelerated rehabilitation" in the lede; say instead that the person has been granted or placed on a special form of probation (because A.R. really is a gift.) A.R. can be described as: "A special program whereby a criminal defendant with no past record is allowed to circumvent prosecution by agreeing to a term of probation. Anyone granted probation has his record erased if he successfully completes his probation."

Bond is what a criminal defendant posts to secure freedom pending trial. It comes in two forms, as determined by a judge. Surety bond requires the posting of some collateral — like cash or real estate — or the hiring of a bail bondsman who puts up money on the defendant's behalf. A non-surety bond requires only the defendant's signature, but the defendant is held liable for the bond amount if he flees. A third option is the "written promise to appear" — PTA — in court. It's like an IOU for the next court appearance — a nice accommodation for the otherwise law-abiding citizen, and not worth the paper it's written on for the defendant who flees.

Under the Connecticut Constitution, bond must be set in all cases except capital felonies (those murders punishable by death) or when the defendant's criminal record suggests he or she poses an immediate danger to the community.

Felony and misdemeanor. In Connecticut, a felony is a crime punishable by a year or more in jail; a misdemeanor is a crime punishable by a year or less.

Murder. There is no first- or second-degree murder in Connecticut. There is murder (punishable by 25 years to life — 60 years in prison); felony murder, which is murder committed during the course of a felony, such as robbery, even if the defendant did not do the actual killing (punishable by up to 60 years in prison); capital felony, meaning one of eight murder situations that qualify as death penalty offenses in Connecticut; and arson murder (punishable by life in prison without parole). There also is manslaughter (punishable by up to 20 years in prison).

Larceny comes in six categories in Connecticut, depending on the amount taken. They range from first-degree larceny — where the value exceeds $10,000 and is a Class B felony, to sixth-degree larceny, a Class C misdemeanor involving theft of $250 or less.

Probable-cause hearings are mandatory in Connecticut for all defendants charged with murder, unless the defendant waives the hearing. In these hearings, evidence is offered by the prosecution to sustain its charge of murder; often they are the first glimpse into the details of the case. A judge then determines if there is sufficient evidence to warrant the murder charge and the high bond that often accompanies it. The defense in these hearings has no obligation, or opportunity, to rebut the charge. The defense lawyer can only cross-examine the prosecution witness.

A probable-cause hearing amounts to a "preview of coming attractions" for the prosecution's case, and usually is worth covering. Often the detectives who processed the crime scene testify, and the autopsy report is entered into evidence. Occasionally, albeit rarely, the judge rules that the prosecution does not have enough evidence to proceed, and that's clearly newsworthy.

Access to files

It is also crucial to know when court files are open to you and when they are not. In Connecticut, if a prosecutor nolles the case, the file is open to you for 13 months after the nolle is entered (during which time the prosecutor can resurrect the charges.) The criminal file of a person granted accelerated rehabilitation is open for the duration of the probationary period set by the judge. The files of defendants who were acquitted or whose cases were dismissed are open for 20 days after that action was taken.

Eyes open

View a courthouse as a vital place, with its roots in a centuries-old constitution and its stench and pain fresh off the streets. Don't lower your head as you walk through it. Soak it up. See what you can, and come back later to see the rest. And know that everyone you encounter in that place is worth a story, if only you have the time and talent to figure out what it is.

Lynne Tuohy, whose bartending experience prepared her well for a career in journalism, landed her first reporting job with the Newburyport (Mass.) Daily News. She now specializes in criminal justice and legal issues for The Courant. Her honors include a Polk Award and an ASNE second place for deadline writing.

CHAPTER 30

It's not 'L.A. Law:' Making sense of a criminal trial

By Jack Ewing

Trials fascinate people because they deal with a fundamental question: What is truth?

But remember this: Most of the people involved are not really interested in finding the truth — at least not the whole truth.

The defense lawyer wants to get his client off. The prosecutor is hot for a conviction. The judge is trying to move the case along because the court docket is overloaded.

Perhaps the most important thing to remember as you pass through the courthouse metal detector is that old principle: innocent until proven guilty. Do not slip into the mentality that pervades even the defense bar and can be expressed in the following phrase: "If the defendant isn't guilty, why did he get arrested?"

Once in a while, somebody who didn't do anything wrong gets thrown into jail. We all want to see victims get retribution, but it only compounds the tragedy if an innocent person goes to jail. It is not an exaggeration to say that your accurate and perceptive coverage of a trial may be the only bulwark against injustice.

With this in mind, we are ready to step into the curious world of the courtroom.

Covering an anomaly

A trial is an anomaly. In our hopelessly overworked court system, where almost all cases end in plea bargains, cases that go to trial are considered failures.

If a case is being tried, it usually means there is a serious question whether the state can prove the charges beyond a reasonable doubt. Or, it may mean the defendant is extremely stupid, because judges routinely hand down stiffer sentences in cases that go to trial than in cases settled by plea bargaining. Wilmer Paradise turned down a plea bargain that would have meant a two-year sentence for his involvement in an Enfield, Conn., murder. He was convicted in a trial and sentenced to life.

Before testimony begins

Trial coverage starts before the trial. You must prepare, because once the testimony gets under way, you will be too busy to do background work.

Collect all the key background material — past clips, legal motions, arrest affidavits.

Interview the lawyers and other key players for possible use in midtrial profiles.

Visit the scene of the crime, if you can do so safely. You will be amazed at how much more clearly you are able to understand the testimony.

After jury selection is complete, request a list of jurors. Their names and towns of residence are public information. Then use phone books and reverse directories to find home phone numbers. This is a time-consuming task you will not want to face when you are scrambling for juror quotes on the day of the verdict.

During the trial, bring something to read or, better yet, a portable computer. Trials are marked by long delays.

The playbill

A trial is a form of theater: Characters play prescribed roles, and much of the action is scripted. Lawyers rarely ask a question to which they don't know the answer. Here is the cast and what each may be able to provide to you:

Lawyers

Prosecutors are an obvious source of information, and for that reason many reporters become almost wholly dependent on them. This is a mistake. Defense lawyers are the ones who file most of the legal motions and know what the defendant is thinking. For reasons of business and ego, private defense lawyers love publicity and are usually quick to return phone calls.

In dealing with all lawyers, bear in mind that their profession's Code of Professional Conduct allows them to discuss only information that is already on the record — that is, information that has already been brought before the court either orally or in writing. Lawyers often are more cooperative if you indicate that you understand this.

In addition, lawyers may be willing to tell you off the record whether you properly understood a given portion of testimony or legal argument.

Sheriffs
Sheriffs are the lifeblood of court reporting. They are well-informed and have lots of time on their hands. Get to know them.

Clerks
Court clerks, who frequently are law students or newly minted law school grads, control the file on a case. They also keep a diary of the proceedings that can help you determine which days certain witnesses appeared, when testimony began, and so on. Perhaps most important, they are responsible for cataloging and keeping track of exhibits, which you are going to need to examine.

Court reporters and monitors
Reporters transcribe hearings and trials with a steno machine. Monitors (who get paid less) use a tape recorder. A case may have either. Though they are not required to, monitors and reporters may be persuaded to replay a choice bit of testimony so you can get the quote just right.

Judges
No judge who values his job will speak about a case off the bench, but many may be willing confidentially to tip you off about an interesting witness or fill you in on the subtleties of a case. Being a judge is a lonely job, and many are eager for small talk, which in turn can lead to hard information.

Defendants
Always request an interview. You probably will be turned down, but maybe not. The results can amount to a spectacular scoop. Chances of getting an interview may improve if you agree (after consulting an editor) to avoid talking about specifics in the case. Be advised that the Connecticut Department of Correction, like most prison authorities elsewhere, will not

allow you to interview any prisoner who has pending charges unless his lawyer agrees in writing.

Libraries

Legal arguments will make a lot more sense if you look up the cases that the lawyers cite as precedent. Don't be intimidated by law books and law libraries. In Hartford, the state law library is in the Supreme Court building on Capital Avenue, and the librarians are usually willing to help you find a case.

It's not "L.A. Law"

A reporter whose courtroom training consisted of watching "L.A. Law" once remarked after a day of testimony, "This is really boring!" That may be true, at least on the surface. A few moments of pointless violence can, during a trial, lead to weeks of testimony. Every aspect of the case will be dissected by the lawyers, who are trained that thoroughness is a greater virtue than efficiency. (After all, they get paid by the hour.)

Your job is to mine the nuggets of meaning and excitement buried beneath truckloads of backfill. There is no recipe for doing this, but a few general rules may be helpful.

Focus on action, not procedure

Try to take the reader to the scene of the crime. A word picture of a lawyer grilling a witness may be dramatic, but probably not as dramatic as what witnesses say happened at the shooting scene.

Try to find out more than was revealed by testimony alone

For example, always ask the clerk to see exhibits such as photographs and reports, which often provide details — the color of the victim's hair, an ironic bumper sticker on the getaway car — that are irrelevant to the court but invaluable to you.

Look for themes

Trials proceed in fits and starts. Readers may have difficulty following the case from day to day unless you identify a central issue that unifies the testimony. In the Hartford, Conn., murder trial of Joe Lomax, the issue was race. In the Hartford mob trial, with its turncoat witnesses, the theme was the degradation of the Mafia's much-vaunted code of silence. In the Daniel Webb trial — where there was never much question that he had casually kidnapped and murdered a Hartford office worker — it was simply the nature of evil.

It's not about the lawyers

Think from the point of view of the people whose lives have been changed. Lawyers tend to dominate trial news because they do all the talking. But those whose lives are most affected are the victims, a term that can apply to the family of the defendant as well.

Don't jump to conclusions

Beware of convicting the defendant on the basis of one day's testimony. A witness whose testimony seems damning one day can be blown away the next, when he is forced under cross-examination to disclose perjury convictions dating from the 1950s. During the Lomax murder trial, "citizen eyewitnesses" who appeared to seal the prosecution's case instead proved to be a collection of junkies, thieves and paid police stoolies.

Managing your time

Covering a trial is a major commitment of time, and it may not be necessary, or possible, to be there every day. There are ways to cover a trial without attending every minute of testimony. Trials always have certain points that provide a hook for a story as well as a summary of what has happened so far.

On the first day of jury selection, the defendant formally enters a plea and the allegations against him are detailed in an "information" that is read aloud. The prosecutor also reads a list of the witnesses he expects to call. The questioning of individual jurors often provides clues to the strategy the lawyers plan to use and what the major issues will be.

Another benchmark comes after the prosecutor finishes presenting the evidence. Almost always, the defense lawyer makes a motion for judgment of acquittal, or MJOA in courtroom parlance. This is necessary in order to preserve his right to appeal later. The defense lawyer explains why he feels the evidence does not support a conviction, and the prosecutor outlines what he believes the evidence has proved. You get a nice summary of the evidence.

When both lawyers are finished calling witnesses, they present final arguments to the jury. If you don't know anything at all about a case, the dueling final arguments present a compact and balanced picture of what evidence has been presented. This is a good time to pick up on a case you may have ignored so far.

After the case goes to the jurors there is no way to know when they will return with a verdict. If the case is important enough, you simply have to wait. Otherwise, you can check with the clerk's office at the end of the day, but this is not foolproof, since jurors have a way of reaching verdicts at 4:59 Friday afternoon.

A final tip

Finally, one seemingly trivial but crucial word of advice: Dress like an adult. Lawyers and judges place an unreasonable emphasis on clothes. As unfair as it may seem, their respect for you will be affected by how you dress.

You know you're underdressed if, at the start of a case, the judge asks you to step forward and enter a plea.

Jack Ewing began as the entire sports staff at the weekly Santa Fe (N.M.) Reporter. A former court reporter for The Courant, he is now a freelance writer living in Stuttgart, Germany. His honors include the Unity Award for a series exposing racial disparity in bail imposed on defendants.

CHAPTER 31

The care and feeding of sources

By George Gombossy

To become a great science reporter, you don't have to be a scientist. To become a great court reporter, you don't have to have a law degree. To become a great investigative reporter, you didn't have to be a detective in your prior life.

What you do need are sources. Scientists, lawyers, accountants, historians, merchants, secretaries, teachers, criminals — people from all walks of life who are willing to share their time and expertise.

Sources can help you figure out why something happened, what is really going on, and who is pulling the strings. And they can tip you off to great stories.

Finding and developing sources is not that difficult. Anyone who has common sense, likes people and wants to write great stories can have good sources. If you are shy, the process of finding sources could help you get over your shyness.

Two categories

Sources fall into two general categories: public and private.

Public sources usually are people whose job includes communicating with the press: city officials, official spokesmen, heads of companies and public relations types. These people are easy to find. More often than not, they will find you. They generally are helpful if you treat them with courtesy and are fair, but they won't tell you the whole story. At best, they provide you with information intended to convey their side of the story. They might not lie to you, but chances are they will leave out inconvenient facts. They want you to think that their side of the story is the whole story. But there is always another side.

Private sources are the people who can tell you the rest of the story.

They are people who shun the limelight or do not have the power to have the lights focus on them. They may be important people. Often they have little personal power yet hold the key to the best information.

You will meet both types of people all the time. It's important to know what their roles are and what motivates them. You also need to understand that sources can shift from the public category to the private category depending on the story. For instance, the president of a computer company is a public source when he or she talks on the record about that firm's growing share of the marketplace. But the same person can become a private source when leaking information about an illicit deal involving a competitor.

How it works

Let's see how this works in practice. Say that you just started your reporting career in Willimantic, Conn., and your first assignment is to cover the appointment of a new police chief by the mayor and the common council.

After the meeting, the mayor invites the handful of reporters in attendance for a drink to chitchat about the new appointment. Most reporters will not pass on the compliment of being invited out by a powerful politician.

You take a rain check. Instead, you slip away for a drink with a private source you have cultivated — the deputy town clerk. Over a beer, the deputy clerk lets it drop that the new police chief had been involved in a fatal accident in an earlier job. You check it out with the authorities where the chief formerly worked and find out it is true. You are certainly going to have a much different story than the reporters who went out with the mayor.

Why hadn't the mayor or council members in his party been up front about the police chief's background? Maybe they didn't know or were taking the chance that reporters would not fully check out the new chief. Why didn't council members in the opposition party bring it up at the meeting? Maybe they didn't know or didn't want to rock the boat. In a small town, the minority councilmen sometimes have to go along with the majority to get the things they want, such as a favor for a relative or passage of a pet ordinance.

So why would a deputy clerk tip off the reporter? There are many possible reasons. It could be good citizenship: The source thinks the public needs to know this. It could be personal: The source has a beef with the mayor and is trying to get even. Often, it is about power. The source has no formal power of his own. His power comes, instead, from knowledge of confidential matters. He perceives himself working harder for a lot less money than his bosses, and wants to vent his frustration by letting the world know what kind of fools are running things.

Who's in the know

Sources are not limited to clerks and elected officials. There are all kinds of people who can tell you what is going on in your town or on your beat.

Some of my favorites:

▶ Lawyers, especially criminal defense lawyers. I find that they love to gossip. Lawyers and reporters have a lot in common; both are drawn to the excitement of news and the excitement of their professions.

▶ Technocrats, people who amass a great deal of data through their intimate knowledge of a company or of a political organization. They often know more than their bosses, and don't feel appreciated by them.

▶ Merchants, people who manage or work in stores and come in contact with hundreds of people. People who work in small stores or small restaurants can be the most helpful. They hear things. Have you ever just sat at the counter of a greasy spoon and just listened to the conversation? Shopping in the town you cover gives you the opportunity to meet many potential sources.

▶ Clergy. The men and women of the cloth can be especially helpful and have a different insight into problems or can turn you on to interesting success stories.

▶ Union people. Many rabble-rousers are in the union ranks. They love to rock the boat.

▶ League of Women Voters. This organization exists in many towns, and its leaders have strong ideas about how government should be run. They may know who is competent and who isn't. Typically they want change and are more than willing to talk to reporters.

▶ Retirees. They have plenty of time, have amassed a lot of knowledge, and have little to lose by talking to you.

▶ Real estate agents. They come in contact with a lot of people and they love to talk.

▶ Teachers. Just by the contact they have with children they gain a great deal of knowledge about any community.

▶ Outcasts, people who are on the outs economically, politically or socially. An engineer fired from United Technologies Corp. is certainly going to have more motive to tell you about problems at the plant than the engineers secure in their jobs.

Getting to know them

It's best to cultivate sources — to get to know them and to get them to trust you — before you need them for specific stories.

You can choose people you have already met or people that you wrote about in news stories. You can choose people in the news: a person just promoted, someone announcing a new store, someone celebrating 15 years at a company. Or you can simply find a person in the Yellow Pages.

If you need an excuse to talk, you can always do a story. For example, if you want to get to know a zoning enforcement officer who has just been given additional duties, you can call him and suggest a story about his work.

Not everyone will be receptive. That's OK. Others will be honored that a member of the fourth estate picked them as people worth getting to know.

If you are uncertain whom to approach, get input from your editor. Even if your editor was never a reporter, it is always good to have a sounding board. Chances are your editor will be pleased that you are going out to chat with potential sources instead of chatting with other reporters.

The first meeting

Whoever said first impressions are critical is right. People form impressions very quickly. The way you behave and your body language tell more about the kind of person you are than what you actually say. Sometimes a person can form an opinion of you before you even say a whole sentence. Your initial goal is to build rapport. You might be a trustworthy and caring person, but if your body language is telling your source the opposite, you will not be trusted.

Some of this advice may seem trivial. It is not. It may be crucial.

Here are some ways to help establish rapport:

▶ Where. Let the source pick the meeting spot. It does not matter whether you like the restaurant. What matters is that your source feels comfortable.

▶ Dress. If your source is a banker and picks a nice restaurant, dress up. Don't wear a suit if you sense that your source is going to wear jeans. During the Vietnam War, there were days I wore my field jacket to a college anti-war demonstration and changed to a tie and sport coat to meet the college president. A demonstrator might not feel comfortable talking to a guy in a tie, and the college president might not feel at ease talking to a young man dressed like one of the troublemakers.

▶ The handshake. Let the source guide your handshake. If your source likes to crush hands, do not put a limp fish in his vise. He might equate a weak handshake with a weak person. You do not have to match his strength, but you must return a firm handshake. If your source has a limp handshake, take some pressure off yours so you don't intimidate the person.

▶ Eye contact. If your source looks into your eyes all the time, you must maintain that eye contact or the source might think you are untrustworthy. If your source tends to look away, you might make that person uncomfortable if you continually try to lock onto the source's eyes.

▶ Listen. Your first goal is to learn about your source. The only thing you need to communicate at first is that you can be trusted and are keenly interested in learning about and from the source. But be sensitive to the needs of your source. If your source wants to know more about you, be prepared to share a little of yourself.

▶ Connect. Find areas of common interest. It can be anything: sports, children, cooking, photography or the people you know in common.

▶ Go slow. Get to know your source. If you are interviewing a banker, it might not be a good idea to ask during the first session what kinds of security systems are used at the bank. Remember, you are looking for a long-term relationship and not a quick hit.

Ground rules

When you feel you have reached a point where your source seems comfortable, start talking about ground rules. For the background material you can expect to receive at the first meeting with a new source, you can safely accept information on an off-the-record basis. As your relationship gets more involved, you will have to negotiate how you can use certain information.

Be careful that you and the source have the same understanding of the ground rules you agree on. Off the record may not mean exactly the same thing to you as it does to your source. Does off the record mean you cannot use the information at all? Does it mean you can use it as long as you don't quote your source? Can your source be quoted as an unnamed "industry specialist" or as a "court official?"

If the source believes you violated an agreement, you have probably lost that source forever. Even if there was an honest misunderstanding, it is hard to regain trust lost in this fashion. A source who feels betrayed will hold that grudge for a long time and will tell others not to trust you.

It is also important to keep in mind that there are strict limits as to what you can and cannot agree to, without having that agreement first approved by your editor.

Never accept information that is for your ears only. At the minimum, your source must permit you to print the information if other sources confirm it. Never agree to keep something out of the paper. You don't know whether some other reporter may be working on the same story or if another source will give you the same information at a later date. Never agree to put something in the paper in return for a piece of information. You have no control over your editors and cannot promise that a quote or a statement will actually appear in print.

It is OK to say you don't have the authority to negotiate a deal. It is better to say, "I need to run this by my editor," than to rush into an agreement you may be unable to keep.

You will quickly establish your reputation. If you have a reputation of a trustworthy reporter, new sources will be easier to find. Some will even call you with information. But, you may want to consider a career as a shoe salesman if there is a question in the community about your integrity.

Developing the relationship

Take a little time after the initial meeting to write some notes to yourself about your source. Write down your impressions, things you found in common, and what you believe the source's motivation is for talking to you. Write down in detail a couple of the things your source told you. If your gut instinct is that this person knows relevant information and is trustworthy, develop the relationship. If a little voice inside says there is something wrong, listen and be careful.

On a regular basis, call this source and other sources you are developing. One good way to check their reliability is to get them to repeat something they have already told you. See how the first and second versions compare.

Don't call only when you want something. Ideally, you will have found something in common with each of your sources and it will not be a chore to once in a while call them to chat.

Get close enough to your sources so you get to know them, but not so close that you feel uncomfortable writing objectively about them. This is tricky, especially if you genuinely like your sources. You have to make it clear that just because they are your sources, it does not mean you can or will protect them. If you believe you are so close to your source that it may turn out to be a problem, talk to your editor. Your editor can help you decide whether you need to put some distance between you and the source or to have some other reporter write about your source.

It is up to you to make sure that your source has a clear understanding of your function as a journalist. Your job is to tell as much of the story as you can. Your job is not to help or protect sources.

That does not mean that you are not offering anything to your sources. First of all, sources have the possibility of influencing your stories. They can enlighten you about aspects of a story (probably in ways favorable to them or their agendas) that you have never thought about. You can provide a sympathetic ear.

At times you can trade information. But never pass on confidential information without first getting permission from your original source. Sources have been known to check out reporters by giving them false information, just to see what the reporters will do with that information. With enough practice, a good reporter covering a criminal trial can talk to the prosecutor, defense lawyer and judge and be able to keep in mind at all times what is confidential and what isn't.

While it is important to develop trusting relationships with your sources, it is just as important to never totally trust your sources. Never do anything or say anything in front of a source that you would later feel ashamed testifying about in public. It is not out of the question for a cornered source to turn against a journalist. And no matter how accurate a source may have been in the past, always assume that your source might be inaccurate in the future. Sources, like everyone else, have blind spots and hidden agendas that even they might not be aware of.

Whistle-blowers

Whistle-blowers are a special category of source. They will usually call you, sometimes anonymously, to tip you off about someone else's misdeeds. They can lead you to wonderful stories, but be careful dealing with them. While some are simply honest people who are disturbed about wrongdoings, others have axes to grind.

The ones with the axes may not always tell you about their total involvement in a caper or may be so consumed with anger or hate that their versions are highly distorted. That does not mean you don't listen to these kinds of sources, it just means you should be even more careful as you check out their stories.

George Gombossy began his career covering the little town of Willimantic for The Courant. He was a bureau chief of The Courant's Avon bureau and is now business editor. His honors include the George Polk Award for local reporting.

CHAPTER 32

The art of schmoozing

By Bill Hathaway

Schmooze with everybody.

And when you schmooze, listen and file it away. It's probably the most important thing you do.

Regardless of what your editor says, you should spend 10 times more hours schmoozing than writing.

Many people are bored with their lives and jobs, flattered by your interest, and appreciative of anything you do to lighten their day with gossip and jokes. If you schmooze them, they're more likely to remember you when they have news or tips.

How it's done

Everybody likes to receive information. And everyone likes people who listen to them.

So tell people things you know. Make people co-conspirators in the drama of your story. Even bit players like to think of themselves as cast members, and may have the piece of information you need.

Always ask their opinions. Never be arrogant. Self-deprecation helps.

Ask them about themselves. Start with the obvious — clothes, family, health, their favorite baseball team. Keep going till you see the light in the eye that means they are engaged in the topic.

Then listen. And listen some more.

Seem agreeable, be skeptical

Once I was introduced to a politician's wife who told me, "Oh what a horrible job you have. You use people all the time."

She had it backward. Reporters get used all the time. People by nature sell their own version of reality. Few tell the whole truth, and some of them lie. I find sorting out competing versions of reality one of the more entertaining aspects of the job.

One time one of my town's upstanding old Yankee citizens, a

Republican, wanted me to do a story about how the town's Irish mayor, a Democrat, was denying him an easement from his land through city property simply because of politics. A friend of both, whom I had schmoozed for years, just laughed and said, "Don't you know what (the Republican) did to (the mayor) 10 years ago?"

There was a story — about how class differences and old resentments play a role in how things get done, or don't get done, in a community.

Act as if you believe the disreputable and doubt the honorable.

When talking to the disreputable, pick the part of their story most closely resembling the truth and nod earnestly in agreement. Be noncommittal during the obvious lies and self-justifications.

The disreputable, as a group, are shocked by the novelty of being believed by anyone, much less by a reporter. They may take you as an ally in their nefarious cause and confide in you. One day you can go back to them with a direct question and they may find it hard to lie to you well because you already know too much.

The opposite tack works better on those who are honorable. They generally have reams of good reasons and facts to justify their positions. The trouble is, these reasons may not be their main motivations.

Sometimes they won't tell you everything because the real reasons for their actions may not seem so nice. With these people, express skepticism often. After you have questioned all the superficial but perfectly sound reasons for their position or action, they sometimes blurt out the crucial one in the midst of righteous indignation at being doubted.

The best tactic of all is to get excited about what you are hearing. Your excitement energizes people you talk to. If it ain't fun doing the story, it ain't going to be fun to read either.

Hurrah for secretaries

Always schmooze the secretaries. Treat them with the utmost respect; you may be the only one who does.

They hear and see most everything. They know the truth. And if they respect you — and like you — they might even share a little of what they know.

Here is an example from personal experience.

You go to see the mayor. The secretary says he is not in that day. You ask why.

If you have never asked how her kids or grandkids are, if you have not shared stories or jokes, if you have not treated her with respect — she may say she doesn't know, or brusquely respond, "On city business."

But you had chatted with her many times about her family and swapped stories. Hizzoner, she confides, is meeting with a congresswoman and major executives of General Motors to save a local bearings plant.

And you've got a story.

William Hathaway got his start covering local and college sports for the Longmont (Colo.) Times-Call. He is now the housing and real estate reporter for The Courant. His honors include the National Association of Black Journalists' Award for enterprise reporting.

CHAPTER 33

The tough interview

By Jon Lender and Greg Garber

Here are a few points about interviewing. Some of this may be obvious. All of it is subjective. Everyone has to develop an interviewing style suited to his or her personality.

There are exceptions to many of the rules mentioned here; you have to judge how to play an interview subject case by case — depending on your reading of him or her, and on how the interview is going.

But here are some general points, big and small.

1. An interview is not a normal conversation, but most of the time it should sound like one.

Your job is to get the person who is being interviewed to give you the information you need to write your story. Sometimes, it is not in the interview subject's best interest to tell you what you want to know. So, you've got to make it as easy as you can for him or her to blab.

This involves a lot of management — maybe even manipulation, to put it bluntly — by you.

Be non-threatening. This applies even to heavy-duty confrontational interviews. You can be accusing someone of a felony, but you can do it calmly and politely. You don't have to come out hammering, like you're Perry Mason in the courtroom.

Be low-key yet relentless. If your guy evades, keep bringing him back to the main point. And you've got to keep the subject talking. No talk, no information.

2. Warm up your subject like a car on a cold morning.

When you first walk in, talk about anything — the weather, sports, food, the little kids in the picture on the desk. It doesn't matter. You have to establish a rapport.

Many interview subjects are wary of reporters, and they are more likely to confide in somebody who likes kids, or drives the same unusual kind of car that they do, or is a fellow fan of the Green Bay Packers.

Newspaper reporters have a luxury that broadcast journalists lack, or don't enjoy to the same extent: The public does not hear us pose our questions. That means we can hem and haw a bit, and beat around the bush until the moment is right.

It takes some of the pressure off us, and it leaves the subject a bit off balance. All the while, we know what we're looking for, but the interviewee may be a bit lost in a blizzard of unrelated questions.

Most standard advice about interviewing says you should not talk about yourself — that you should ask short questions and let the interview subject do most of the talking. We don't agree. Excellent interviewers who are naturally outgoing often spend a lot of time talking about themselves. For example, they might say how they have reacted to problems similar to those faced by the interview subject. Interview subjects are more likely to open up to a sympathetic or understanding ear.

If this works for you, and if it's natural, keep doing it. Just be aware that it does involve risk. Don't compromise yourself by confiding something real that puts you in the same boat with the interviewee, or somehow gives him some leverage over you.

For example, you ought not to say something like this: "I know these drug charges must be a tough thing for you to deal with in your role as a moral leader of thousands. I've never been a drug user, but I hate to think of the number of times I've driven away from a bar after four hours of drinking; I never would have passed one of those breathalyzer tests."

3. You've got to build your interview.

Think of it as a structure. Maybe it's a rollercoaster. Or maybe it's a gallows.

Do your homework. Try to know the answers in advance to as many questions as possible. It helps you build your case, and it prepares you better for an unexpected answer.

Ideally, you come into an interview with a wealth of research, and you may take an hour just building up to one or two tough questions that you're thinking about the whole time.

But you just can't ask those questions cold. So you meander a bit, all the while keeping your eye on the target, building the interview until it's time to ask the big questions.

Lots of times you're covering spot-news and you don't have all day. Then you've got to accelerate the pace. You have to know what kind of stuff you're going to need to make a story.

Thus, if you find yourself interviewing a millionaire lottery winner on the day of his/her good fortune, you find yourself getting through the preliminaries in 30 seconds and then going right for what you need, as delicately as you can without sounding like a jerk:

"So . . . how will this money help you?"

"Oh, I just don't know. Right now I'm so happy."

"Well, what I mean is, sometimes when people win the lottery, it turns out that somebody in their family has serious problems that the money can help solve . . ."

Quizzical look from interviewee.

". . . I mean, is there anybody in your family who has a serious illness. Or somebody in jail with kids back home? Or anybody who dropped out of high school, or anybody with a drug problem, or maybe a daughter who has a baby and is single and living at home?"

You run the risk of putting the person off — but if you've been trying for a few minutes and all you get is the usual "Even-with-a-million-bucks-I-won't-quit-my-job-at-D&L-because-I-have-so-many-good-friends-there," then you're probably better off by just going right for the goods.

4. Ask your questions in reverse order of their toughness.

In other words, ask the kind or purely informational questions first and the meanest ones last. This gets you the basic information — "How long have you worked for the state, why do you like public service?" etc. — before you reach the explosive stuff that is the reason for the story: "How long has that contractor been making those payments on your house in Vermont?"

The latter will probably bring the interview to an abrupt, noisy conclusion: "Get the hell out of my office."

5. Avoid questions that can be answered yes or no.

Rather than ask Mr. Smith whether he likes being governor, ask him how he likes being governor.

Ask as many loaded questions as you can: Have you stopped cheating on your income taxes?

Say you're assigned to cover a big philanthropist's presentation of a check for several million dollars for a new hospital wing and you heard vaguely all kinds of politicking was done by X, Y and Z hospitals to get the philanthropist to come across with the money before the philanthropist decided on giving it to X.

Rather than ask "Is it true that X, Y and Z lobbied heavily for the donation," maybe ask, "who contacted you first in hopes of getting the donation, X, Y or Z?" So what if you get laughed at? Maybe you get a more interesting story.

6. Ask the stupid question. Don't try to look smart all the time. Don't assume anything.

It's better to look stupid to the guy you interview than to thousands of readers. Sometimes you can even play possum by not seeming as smart or knowledgeable as you are; that may make your subject take you lightly and make him more willing to talk.

Here is an illustration of some of this stuff. It involves a story that depended on a guy's being willing to admit that he had falsified some city records. He knew he shouldn't have done it but seemed a little proud of his accomplishment and, when given the opportunity, blabbed about the way he was able to do it.

There was a construction inspector hired on a contract basis by a municipality for a road-paving project. Witnesses said they had seen the inspector driving construction equipment for the contractor; things seemed altogether too chummy and slipshod.

All of this became a matter of interest after the pavement began to deteriorate. There were supposed to be inspection records. This inspector was supposed to compile a daily construction diary on forms provided by the city public works department. Some city councilmen demanded the forms, more than 100 pages of forms. The public works director refused to turn them over, saying the councilmen were on a witch hunt. Finally, he relented and handed over the forms, which seemed curiously consistent in the way they were filled out. The same pen was used on all the forms.

A reporter was able to get the inspector to sit down for an interview because an intermediary who knew the inspector vouched for the reporter's fairness.

The guy was willing to come into the newspaper office. He was, of course, offered a cup of coffee. There was chit-chat about this and that for a moment.

Then, because the reporter had used an intermediary to get the guy to sit down with him, he had to make sure the inspector was not under any wrong impressions.

For example, if an intermediary speaks for the reporter and says he's a nice guy, then the person who agrees to be interviewed by that reporter might come in with the impression that he's going to get a free ride in the interview and the reporter will in effect be an instrument with which he will smite his enemies.

It's important to make sure you're not getting cooperation under false pretenses. So, just to be sure, the reporter told the inspector he was happy the guy had decided to sit down with him, and he wanted to ask him some questions about some information he had learned, and at the end: "I'm going to write what happened, period, and if it means these guys who are saying bad things about you are wrong, then that's what I'll write. But if you screwed up, then I write that, too."

Now came the moment where the guy might decide to get up and leave, and if he wanted to do that, there would have been a hurried barrage of the key questions this particular inspector had to answer about his own conduct.

But for some reason, the guy stayed put and the reporter kept talking as quickly as possible.

"There's a few things I don't understand about these construction diaries. For one thing, why do you need to fill them out, anyway? Why the paperwork?"

That gave the inspector a chance to minimize the importance of the forms, and it gave the reporter a chance to say, "Oh, I see," and nod a few times. The inspector grew more confident, seeing that he was enlightening the young man.

Reporter: "You're supposed to fill these out at the end of every work day, right? Or else you'd never be able to put in that sort of detail about linear feet paved, etc."

"Yeah, that's right. Every day."

"But you don't really do that every day, do you? I'd be surprised if every inspector on every job filled out the forms every day."

"Yeah, you're right. We're too busy for that."

"In fact in this case people tell me you had to make out all these forms at once, same pen, same everything, all of it in the past few weeks. That's pretty clear. What I don't understand is how the hell you remembered what the weather conditions were for each day (the forms had a space for a notation of each day's weather). What'd you do? Look it up in the newspaper in the library?"

The inspector smiled. "I got it from the weather bureau."

"And you filled it all in, what, in the last two weeks?"

"Yeah."

"I never would have thought of doing that. That's pretty amazing. This was your idea, huh? Nobody told you to?"

And so on.

By the end of the interview, it was only right to bring home to the inspector the point that he may have defrauded the city and this was going to be the focus of the story.

It's never good to take a damaging statement from an interview while leaving the interviewee blissfully unaware that he has just hanged himself. You should always let the person know the gravity of his statements and make it clear that the story will not be a pretty one.

For one thing, it's the right thing to do. For another, once the person realizes he's going to take a fall, he may point his finger at the boss who told him to do what he did.

Which is what happened in this example. The inspector said a public works official had handed him a pile of forms and told him to finish them within a matter of days. You'll notice that the reporter did not immediately tell the inspector that he had probably defrauded the city and was going to look bad in the newspaper. Instead, the reporter said "I never would have thought of doing that. . . . This was your idea, huh?" The reason is that by putting off the bad news until later, it gave the inspector the chance to keep talking without feeling overly threatened and to say, on his own, that his boss had told him to do it. He passed up this first opportunity but took the second, when it was made clear that he was out on a limb by himself and this was not going to look too good in the paper, etc.

The principle here is to get the interviewee to give as much information as possible willingly, before it hits home that with everything he says, he is digging a deeper hole for himself. Once he realizes this, of course, he'll be wanting to put on his coat to leave.

7. Always write down your questions.

Unless you are a super-being, you need to do this. Sure, you can go into an interview with some general impressions that you know you can instantly turn into questions without writing them down. But you should at least write down the main questions that you cannot afford to forget.

This serves two purposes. First, it keeps you from leaving something out. Second, the exercise of writing them down forces you to think about the subject in a logical, structured way — the same way you will have to deal with it when it comes time to write the story.

Write them down, and keep them on a separate sheet from the rest of your notebook so they won't disappear the first time you turn to a fresh page. You can cross them out as you ask them, if you want to. And, of course, don't let your subject see them. Some of those people can read upside down, just like us.

8. Always try to leave yourself another opening for follow-up questions at a later time. So, on your way out, make sure you preserve the opportunity to reach the person again.

No matter how we prepare, no matter how many questions we write in advance, it's inevitable that someday we will find ourselves back at the office, writing on deadline, and needing an answer that we don't have. It may be a fact, or simply a no-comment where it's absolutely necessary to have one and we can't believe we were stupid enough not to put that question to the person.

That's when we need to be able to call the person on the phone, or to call his/her lawyer. If it's a story with a long-term deadline, maybe you want to reserve or even arrange a follow-up sit-down visit.

9. Never give your subject an 'out.' Never, never, never be the one to break an awkward silence.

It's a human trait to want to start the answer for someone who is tongue-tied in reaction to an embarrassing question you've asked — but resist it at all costs. Be the winner of every staring contest.

One thing that reporters sometimes do is to ask a good question and immediately devalue it by offering two alternative responses — one damaging and the other exonerating. Gee, guess which one the guy will pick?

"Coach, three players saw you berating Rex Dunko and pinning him against the wall outside the locker room, and five minutes later one of his eyes is swollen shut.

"Did you punch him, or was it an unintentional jostle during a playful little scuffle? — because, after all, nobody actually saw you two during those five minutes. There are no witnesses, and of course Rex is too loyal to open his mouth."

Bad questioning.

There's a better way to do this. Even if Dunko isn't talking about his eye-hematoma, and even if there were no witnesses, why do you have to come out and tell the coach you've got nothing on him?

Wouldn't it be better to phrase it in a way that would allow a person with a guilty conscience to believe you know more than you know?

"Coach, Dunko's eye is swollen shut, and there are these three guys who saw you two in that angry confrontation against the wall, and — well, why don't you tell me how it happened?"

So the coach figures you're bluffing, and says: "Nothing happened. What the hell are you implying? Are you telling me that I hit him? What does HE say?"

If that's what he says, you're basically lost. But you still have one or two interview-technique tools.

A simple tool that sounds stupid but works sometimes is to take a big pause and say: "Wait, wait, wait, hold it, hold it. I just want to write that down exactly."

And then you repeat it slowly as you write it down in slightly exaggerated fashion: " 'No-thing hap-pened . . . What-the-hell-are-you-im-ply-ing' — that's what you said, right?"

The coach, thinking that you have or will get the story and that this would be his only response, might become nervous enough to say something a little closer to the truth. But, honestly, probably not.

It's OK to bluff that you know more than you do, but it's not OK to bluff and be found out. That's stupid; you'll look like a fool. If you don't have enough, back out gracefully.

10. Never let the subject turn the interview around and start asking you the questions?

Subject: "What do you think about the situation? I'm asking you. Do you think I have done anything unethical?"

Lots of power-person types try this kind of stuff. There are a number of ways to counteract this. One is to smile and pause, and then say something like, "No, really, what's the answer?"

Or, "What I think doesn't matter. What you think matters."

Or, "Oh, I guess you don't want to answer the question, huh?"

Or, "That's your answer? Let me get that exactly. 'What do YOU think about the sit-u-a-tion?' "

If the person is being a persistent jerk about it, you can't avoid being blunt and saying, "I'm sorry, but I'm interviewing you, not the other way around."

11. But on the other hand, it's good for you, in thinking of what questions you will ask, to think what your response would be.

This helps in plotting strategy for a confrontation interview. For example, you can anticipate an evasion ('What lies would be open to me, if I were asked that question, knowing that facts X, Y and Z are already on the record?') and be ready with a follow-up.

But also, if it's a softer interview and you're just trying to bring out the person's personality, it still helps to think what YOUR answer would be if somebody asked you, on the spur of the moment: "What's your favorite book?" Maybe if you ponder that, you'll think, "I wouldn't be able to come up with a quick answer on that."

Maybe it would be better to first ask: "What is the last book you've read?" (Just like in the Dewar's Profiles.) Because if you truly read books, you'll likely come up with the answer. And if you haven't read a book in years, then that's an interesting answer too.

12. Every once in a while, you can Columbo somebody.

At the end of your interview, turn the tape recorder off, or put your notebook in your pocket, and stand up as if to leave. This often will make the interviewee drop his guard. Then say, "Oh, by the way, I forgot to ask you..."

Or "I wasn't clear on what you said about . . ." It's amazing how this can work. Then take out your notebook and write down what the person said. It's fine if you didn't announce, "The interview is over."

13. Sometimes it's easier to ask the question almost through the

voice of an imaginary person, providing an imaginary distance between the two of you and the question, making it easier to answer.

For some reason, it's easier to ask: "Now, if a person were to ask you if you have always been a good husband/wife, and never cheated on your wife/husband, what would the answer be?" than to ask: "So, have you ever cheated on your spouse?"

Then follow up the hypothetical answer with: "And that's your answer, right?"

14. Both of you have to understand and agree what "off the record" means.

"Off the record" doesn't have a universal meaning.

To him it can mean the information he gives you on that basis must never see the light of day. To you it might mean you can use the information without attaching his name to it.

If the guy wants to talk off the record, you have to ask him what he means. If you are the one who offers an off-the-record opportunity to him, you have to establish what it means first.

You also should know your paper's policy on granting subjects the right to speak off the record, and on publishing information from unnamed sources.

Permitting the interview to go off the record is tricky because you don't want to tie your hands on writing information that the interviewee ought to be willing to give on the record. But lots of times, particularly with someone you have dealt with for a while, going off the record is either the best, or the only, thing you can do.

Of course, you have to preserve as many options as you can, and you have to be aware of certain important questions that you need an on-the-record answer to.

Jon Lender has been a reporter, and occasionally an editor, for 23 years. He has worked as a bureau chief covering Connecticut towns, and later was an investigative projects reporter. He has covered Connecticut politics and government for more than a decade, and now serves as The Courant's political writer.

Greg Garber began his career as the sports editor of the Dover (N.J.) Daily Advance. He is now an investigative/enterprise sports reporter for The Courant and a reporter for ESPN. His honors include three Emmy's and an Associated Press Sports Editors Award for enterprise reporting.

CHAPTER 34

Hone your phone interview

By Eric Lipton

Getting a reluctant person to give you information over the telephone isn't easy. But here are a few techniques that have worked for me.

Before you dial

Consider the obstacles you might have to overcome. The person might not want to speak with you because he/she:

1) Has done something wrong;

2) Has been told not to talk to reporters;

3) Thinks he will get in trouble if he is quoted;

4) Has a reputation of not talking to reporters and wants to live up to it;

5) Does not want to get involved.

Ask yourself whether you should call the subject at work or at home. If you are on deadline, you may not have a choice. But otherwise, you may find a reluctant source more willing to talk at home, where he or she cannot be overheard by a boss or co-workers.

Keep in mind that your first shot is your best shot. Once a person makes up his mind not to speak with you, it is easy for him or her to stick by that decision. So be prepared with your best case.

Sometimes it is best to put off the call until you have a good idea of the role the subject played in what you are writing about. Say, for example, you are calling a municipal employee who has been fired from his job. You want to know why.

Call the union president, fellow workers and the employee's supervisor first. Some might talk on the record and others on background, but the information they give you can help you find ways to get the fired employee to talk.

Make sure you have thought about what you have learned and can retell it concisely. Use it to prepare a list of questions, and place them in order with the most innocuous first and the most confrontational last.

Making the call

Typically, the subject answers the phone, listens as you tell him/her who you are, and then says, "no comment."

Try to keep the subject on the phone.

Say, "Before you hang up, I understand you are not ready to comment, but I would at least like to tell you what I know about what happened. You should know what we might be putting in the paper. I don't want to get it wrong and you are the one that knows best what happened."

If the person hangs up before you can get the words out, consider calling back again right away (or even going to the subject's house unannounced).

If your subject gives you any opening, immediately launch into your concise account of what you know. Do it in a way that raises questions that beg for reaction.

Mention names of people you have spoken with, if you can do so without betraying anyone's trust. That might make the subject feel more comfortable speaking. It can also show him or her that you know what you are talking about. Tell him you are close to writing a story, and that story will not have his point of view if he does not cooperate.

This, of course, may be a bluff.

You may not be able to write the story without the subject's cooperation, or you may not be as sure of the facts as you are pretending to be. But your bluff may make the subject conclude that it is in his or her interest to cooperate.

Watch your tone

Your tone of voice is essential. Don't lecture. Don't sound like a prosecutor. Don't talk too loudly. You want the subject to conclude that you are fair and open-minded; that you are truly interested in his point of view.

If the subject does not respond as you relate your brief account of the events, you can conclude the account by asking, "Does that sound right?"

If the subject is still unwilling to talk, you might offer him/her a chance to clear up things off the record. (Make sure, of course, that you know your newspaper's policy concerning taking information off the record.)

"I won't quote you, but at least tell me what is wrong so I can eliminate it from the story."

It is important not to sound threatening at any point, but you can gradually get more direct, using more pressure as you go along. At this point you might specifically list the allegations you have heard, taking a harder line than before.

Make the subject realize that if he or she does not respond, these allegations may appear in the paper without the context, corrections or point of view he can provide.

If you mention the allegations at the beginning of the call, the subject is likely to get angry and hang up. But you must mention them at some point to give the subject a chance to respond.

Last resort

If the subject is about to hang up, you might say, "OK, then you just want me to say you have no comment?"

This makes it clear that this is the subject's last chance to give his side of the story and sometimes it will loosen him up. If he still hangs up, you can always go to his house and try again. Take along the bullet-proof vest.

Eric Lipton got his start covering local government at the Valley News in Lebanon, N.H., before becoming city hall reporter at The Courant. He now covers politics and government in Fairfax County, Va., for The Washington Post. While at The Courant, he won a Pulitzer Prize for explanatory journalism.

CHAPTER 35

Beating deadline
(before it beats you)

By Ken Davis

Deadline writing.

An editor must have thought of that fatalistic term to describe the process that brings so much of our news to the newspaper. No respectable reporter would have inflicted that added pressure on an entire profession.

Dead-line. Come on, isn't that a little harsh? What's wrong with "Beat the Clock" or "Send Your Story Now Please." Those are gentler ways of saying the same thing.

Unfortunately, deadline writing is here to stay. And if you work at a newspaper with multiple editions, like The Courant, you sometimes may face four or five deadlines before the night is over.

I came to The Courant in 1985 to cover the University of Connecticut basketball team. During my job interview, the sports editor repeatedly asked me how I functioned on deadline. I guess he was concerned because I came to The Courant from the Baltimore News-American, an afternoon paper. At the News-American, you could cover a night game, be the last reporter to leave the clubhouse, drive home, grab a sandwich, transcribe your tapes, outline your story, change your lead 20 times, lose your story in the computer, write until 4 a.m., and still not push deadline.

"I've worked at AM papers before," I told the sports editor. "And I wrote on deadline for the Sunday News-American."

But my experience usually involved one deadline and it was midnight or later. I had never written about a game before it was over — while I was still watching it. I had never been faced with making first deadline, plugging in quotes for the next deadline, then turning my thoughts to a write-through and another deadline an hour later.

One of my early assignments at The Courant was the day before a Celtics-Lakers exhibition game at the Civic Center. I was assigned a feature from the Lakers' practice session at the University of Hartford.

When I returned from practice that afternoon, I started to write the story. About 30 minutes later, the sports editor walked up to my computer terminal and asked if I was done yet.

"I just got back," I said.

"This is an AM paper, Kenny," he said. "We don't have all day."

As the editor walked away, he looked back and smiled. He had been kidding, but he also made a point I have never forgotten. Deadline writing is a discipline that requires practice. If deadline writing is a part of your job description, there's only one way to get used to it. You've got to do it over and over. Next time you have a few hours to write a story, impose your own deadline. Restrict yourself enough to get a good feel for the push of deadline.

In "Pond Scum and Vultures," a book about sportswriters by Gene Wojciechowski of the Los Angeles Times, the chapter on deadlines is titled "God's Curse."

Wojciechowski tells the story of one writer whose spirit was broken by the combination of deadline and a malfunctioning computer. He threw the computer out the press box window.

I've never gone to that extreme, but I have slammed several telephones and a few tables on deadline. I also find the closer I get to deadline, the more limited my vocabulary becomes. In those final five minutes, I usually find myself reduced to four-letter words that are unprintable in a family newspaper.

"You can always tell which writers are facing impending deadlines," Wojciechowski writes in his book. "They're the ones who groan with every walked batter, every pitching change, every pinch-hitter, every seventh-inning stretch. At game's end, they stand outside the locked clubhouse, staring at their watches, shuffling about as if they need to use the restroom."

I have developed a simple philosophy: Beat the deadline; don't let the deadline beat you.

In addition to practicing, there are other ways to survive the stress of deadline writing. You may discover your own along the way. What works for one person may not work for another. Which brings us to deadline philosophy No. 2: Whatever gets you through the night.

For now, here are a few points to consider:

Organization and preparation

This is so important. What you do early in the day may save you when time is running out.

The better you know your subject, the easier it will be to function on deadline. Go in prepared for anything and you reduce the possibility of confusion or surprise.

I do most of my writing away from the office. When I go to a stadium or a press conference and I know I am filing by portable computer, I get there early to check everything out. I want to know where my work area will be and what the telephone situation will be. No phone means no story. If I'm sharing the phone with a lot of people, a self-imposed earlier deadline may be necessary just to make sure I'm not waiting in line as deadline passes.

You aren't the only one

Take into account that you aren't the only one on deadline. The copy editors who handle your story are working under their own restrictions. Give them time to do their jobs. Since you are working quickly, the chance of error increases. Give them enough time to catch your mistakes. You'll respect them more the next morning — as long as they haven't rushed and made their own mistakes.

Know your limitations

A major part of deadline writing involves gathering your information and reporting under the restriction of time. You must stick to the basics. Know when you have enough information and leave. Have confidence in your decisions. Move quickly from source to source.

If someone thinks you are abrupt or rude, just explain your circumstances. It is an unsettling feeling to leave a source with other reporters. But if you have everything you need, you must take that chance. Your competitors may not face the same restrictions.

Chances are they won't uncover anything new or better in another 15 minutes of interviews. I know; I used to be the last one out of the clubhouse.

Pace yourself

After working on deadline a few times, you will know how much time you need to write a 20-inch mainbar or a 15-inch sidebar. Sometimes circumstances will get in the way, but always allow enough time to write after you've done your reporting. When you write, stay focused on the news but touch on all the important facts. Remember, there will be another paper tomorrow if additional questions must be answered. That's the purpose of a follow story.

Be flexible

Things don't always go according to plan. A game may go into overtime, election results may not come in on time, a concert might be delayed — but deadlines aren't going to be adjusted for you. When you are writing on deadline, you must be prepared to adjust. Have background information ready that you could use to enhance your early stories, buying time until your final deadline when you can report the news. It all goes back to preparation and familiarity with your subject.

Don't fight the clock

You must, of course, keep track of what time it is. But don't look at the clock every two minutes. You lose valuable time and create additional stress. You've got enough pressure as it is. And if you are on the road, covering an event in a different time zone, don't forget to take that into consideration. I usually keep my watch on Hartford time in honor of my good buddy, Mr. Deadline.

Write ahead of time

On a lot of deadline stories, what happens on deadline is only the final element — the city council vote, the jury's verdict, etc. — in a story that has developed over days or weeks. Write as much background ahead of time as you can.

Even if events take an unexpected turn, it's faster and easier to rewrite than to write from scratch. Just a couple of paragraphs written in advance can save valuable time on deadline, especially if they explain a complex issue clearly. On a running story, such as a court case, put a few tight sentences of background on a save-get key of your computer.

I won't tell you that deadline writing is fun. I'd rather watch Lawrence Welk reruns.

But there is a lot of satisfaction in writing a good story on deadline. It actually happens once in a while. And once you get used to it, you may find your writing is clearer and more concise than it was when you had all that time to organize your story.

And face it, you didn't need that late-night sandwich either.

Ken Davis, who began his career at the St. Joseph (Mo.) News-Press and Gazette, has covered college basketball for The Hartford Courant since 1985. He has received three awards from the Associated Press Sports Editors, including a first place for enterprise reporting in 1993.

CHAPTER 36

The art of
meaningful detail

By Bruce DeSilva

Look inside most reporters' notebooks and you probably will find little but quotes and paraphrases of what people said.

But how were those words said? There is a big difference between, say, a conspiratorial whisper as the eyes shift about the room, and a snarl as the corners of the mouth turn up in a smirk.

For that matter, where were the words said? There is a big difference between, say, a gleaming glass desktop with not a scrap of paper in sight, and an old wooden desk so covered with paperwork that you can barely see the cigarette burns.

If details about people and place are not in the notebook, they are not likely to show up in the story. Maybe that's why so many newspaper stories are devoid of details that make the people being written about seem real. Maybe that's why most newspaper stories fail to put readers at the scene of the action so that, in a fire story, for example, they can smell the smoke and feel the heat.

Remember the five Ws? When did "who" become just a name? When did "where" become just an address? Become adept at reporting detail and you can get your stories closer to the truth and set yourself apart from many of your colleagues.

Why I hate "color"

When writers and editors talk about getting detail into stories, they often use the word "color." I hate that term. To me, it suggests that details merely decorate stories the way a child's crayoning decorates a coloring book.

Think "color" and you are apt to fill your stories with sentences such as: "He leaned back in his chair and looked out the window." Who cares?

That doesn't reveal anything about either person or place. Don't report that a person leaned back in his chair unless someone has sawed halfway through the chair legs and the chair is about to crash to the floor. Don't report that someone looked out the window unless his wife is being murdered out there.

What you need to report is not "color" but meaningful detail — detail that conveys telling information about character, place or action. Such details don't decorate the facts; they are facts, vital ones that add meaning and depth to your story.

The lesson

I learned this lesson years ago in a discussion with Don Murray, the first newspaper writing coach. As we talked, I was smoking a cigar, and by the time the conversation wound down, the cigar had burned down so far that it almost set my mustache on fire. You know, Murray said, if I were writing a story about you, I might write about how you smoked that cigar. And then again, he said, I might not.

You see, he went on, it depends on whether it means anything. It might mean that you are so absent-minded that you could almost set your mustache on fire and not realize it. It might mean that you are so cheap that you can't bear to waste any tobacco. Perhaps it was your last one and you are so addicted to tobacco that you had to inhale every last puff. Or maybe it was something that had never happened before and didn't mean anything.

How would you know what it meant? I asked.

Well for one thing, he said, I could ask you.

All the senses

Reporting meaningful detail means using your senses, just as Murray used his eyes to notice how I smoked the cigar. And you need to use all your senses.

When reporters do report detail, it is usually only what they see. They take note of the way the body was sprawled on the floor of a tenement hallway next to a graffiti-covered wall. But what does the hallway smell like? Is the stench of urine blending with cooking smells from the apartments, or are the other smells overwhelmed by the metallic scent of blood? What does the hallway sound like? Do you hear the muffled cries of children from behind closed doors or music blaring from passing cars? What does the hallway feel like? Can you sense the grit of a dirty floor under your shoes?

Finding the words

Observing alone is not enough. You must also find the words to convey what you hear, smell, touch and see.

Suppose, for example, you cover a meeting at which the mayor gets up and leaves after being booed by the crowd. You can write that he walked out, but that is not detail. I can't see "walked." It's too generic, too abstract. How the mayor walked may tell a lot about his character and his mood. Did he stalk out? Or did he stride out? Or maybe march, traipse, strut, saunter, lope, bolt, amble, tramp, stroll, skip, shuffle, totter, stagger, shamble, hobble, slouch, scuttle, prance, flounce or swagger? Each word conveys a distinct word-picture of the mayor.

Sometimes, of course, you aren't at the scene of the action to report detail first hand. Instead, you are interviewing someone — a cop, perhaps — about an event that has already taken place. In that case, you can ask what he saw, smelled, heard and felt. What was the victim wearing? What color was it? Was it hot in the hallway? Did you light a cigarette to keep the smell of death out of your nostrils?

Get meaningful detail in your stories, and readers will love them because they will feel more real. That's because you will be giving readers information in a way that approximates the way in which they get information in the real world — through the senses.

How much description?

Once you decide to put meaningful detail in your stories, the big question becomes: How much detail is enough? Look around the room you are sitting in now and think about how many items you can see, how many sounds you can hear, all the things you can smell and touch. Try to write them all down in your pad and you won't have time to do any other kind of reporting. Put them all in your story and you will fill columns.

A few years ago, when I first met Gregory McDonald, the author of the "Fletch" detective novels, I was in my "descriptive period" as a writer. My magazine-style national news features for The Courant usually began with elaborate descriptions of sights, sounds and smells. I figured I was showing readers places they had never seen. I thought it was pretty hot stuff.

So McDonald's books troubled me. The fast-paced novels are 95 percent dialogue with very little description. Yet, as a reader, I always had a mental picture of his characters and of the places where the action unfolded.

How, I asked McDonald, did he do that?

Well, he said, it's like this:

Back when Sir Walter Scott was writing, readers were people who had never been more than 50 miles from their homes. So, if he set some action on a street in Paris, he had to describe the street, the buildings, the carriages, what was in the shop windows, what the people were wearing. Descriptions went on for pages.

Today, McDonald said, readers have millions of images stored in their heads from photographs, movies, television, and the varied experiences of their busy lives. A description doesn't have to go on and on anymore; all it has to do is trigger a memory. Want to transport your readers to a dentist's office? Mention the whine of the drill or the smells of antiseptic and blood and the reader fills in the rest of the picture himself. You don't have to mention the white porcelain spitting bowl — readers already picture it in their minds. The 3,000-word descriptive passage Scott would have written can now be reduced to a paragraph, or maybe even a sentence, McDonald said.

This can't be, I said. (I could not give up my wondrous descriptive passages so easily.) I had just returned from a reporting trip to northern Maine potato country, I said, and had to describe it in detail because my southern New England readers didn't know what it looked like. After all, few of them had ever been to this remote area, and they were not apt to have seen any pictures of it.

Well, McDonald said, why don't you tell me what it is like there?

Um. Well. Let's see. It has what the geologists call "hill and swale" terrain. Uh, that means, um, well . . . it means the land rolls and swells like the sea. And the towns don't look like New England towns at all. They have wide main streets with cars parked diagonally at the parking meters like horses tied to hitching posts. They have two-story, false-front buildings with outdoor staircases roofed with corrugated metal running up the sides. The towns look like . . . uh . . . well, they look like the movie set from that great old Alan Ladd Western, "Shane."

Thank you, McDonald said, for proving my point by describing something as looking like a movie we have all seen.

This jolt from McDonald helped me better understand what detail is for. Detail, like every element in a piece, should add meaning to your story. It should never be there for decoration. It should never be there because you are showing off how good you are at description. And you should never use more words than you need to trigger that mental image that readers already have in their heads.

Eiffel Tower!

Get the picture?

Two examples

To understand this better, it is helpful to examine examples from newspaper writers who are masters of meaningful detail. First, the lede on a series about Chicago schools from The Chicago Tribune:

Third-grade teacher Mary Leahu is standing in the middle of Room 312, one shoe resting on a crumpled candy wrapper and her glasses slightly askew. Her face is pressed close to a page in the teachers' manual that suggests how to conduct the reading lesson for the day. The room smells like corn chips. The pencil sharpener is grinding.

This passage does not tell you what color the blackboard is, what the teacher is wearing or how the room is lit. Still, you pictured a generic classroom, didn't you? That picture is plenty good enough for the writer's purpose, which is to tell you how this classroom is different from many other classrooms you may have been in.

This is a classroom where the teacher has lost control. How does the reader know this? The same way he or she would have known if present in the room: by what you can see, hear and smell. Candy wrappers are not supposed to be on a classroom floor, nor is the room supposed to smell of corn chips. Teachers who have a handle on things do not have their heads stuck in teachers' manuals during class.

Now, let's examine an excerpt from a story about a typical day in a Hartford courthouse by Ed Mahony of The Courant:

Across the lobby from Arraign Court B, members of a street gang sprawl over a bench. They look like a hedge of trees toppled in a big wind; some are seated, some lie down, one is perched on a seat back, others sit on armrests with their feet on the benches. Their mouths sparkle as they laugh and snarl. Many have capped their front teeth with gold.

A young woman in bleached denim pants and matching jacket walks across the lobby.

"Tsst. Tsst. Miss. Tsssssst. Excuse me, miss," a young man hisses. He is tall, wears a black jacket with a yellowish Day-Glo stripe. His skinny legs end at an enormous pair of red and black sneakers.

"Man," he says, "I'm getting me the finest lady in the courthouse today. Tsst. Tsst. Beautiful lady? Excuse me."

The young woman takes a seat at the other end of the lobby. She tries not to notice. But Day-Glow stripe has started something.

"Tsst. Tsst. Tsst."

The bench of young men in sneakers is hissing.

"Tsssssst."

Notice what Mahony does not describe. He does not tell you the color of the hallway walls, what the bench is made of or how the hallway is lit. Yet, you pictured a courthouse hallway, and that is sufficient for the writer's purpose. It doesn't matter whether the walls are painted buff or institutional green.

But Mahony does want the readers to experience that hallway. To achieve that end, he selects telling detail from the many things he saw and heard. The sprawled young men, the sparkle of their capped teeth, the way they hissed.

Bruce DeSilva's first job was covering Warren, R.I., for The Providence Journal. He was The Courant's writing and editing coach and now is enterprise editor for the Associated Press. His honors include The New England Master Reporter Award, given in recognition of excellence in a body of work over a career.

CHAPTER 37

A way of thinking:
The gestalt of numbers

By Dan Haar

Virtually any local or state budget story, and most commercial finance stories, can be done with mastery of nothing more than sixth-grade arithmetic and a bit of simple algebra.

A news story may contain raw numbers, such as the number of pigs and cows on a farm. The raw numbers can be compared with one another: three pigs for every cow; which leads to percentages: Among the animals, 25 percent are cows and 75 percent are pigs.

The raw numbers can change in increments measured by percent: Enlarging his herd of 10 cows, the farmer added two Holsteins, for an increase of 20 percent.

Whenever numbers are compared, it is possible to establish a rate; that is, the rate of one figure per another. With a herd of 12 cows, and property tax payments of $1,800 a year, farmer Bob pays taxes at a rate of $150 a cow per year.

Percentages are one form of rate; they are rates per 100, thus the name, perCENT. So, if Bob has three pigs for every cow, his herd is 75 percent pigs because he owns pigs at a rate of 75 per 100.

Working with rates allows a reporter to make all kinds of analyses with ease:

Bob told the board he needs a tax break or he'll have to sell to developers. For each cow, he pays about 50 cents a day in local property taxes. But the cows give only 10 gallons of milk a day, and Bob sells each gallon for 40 cents, so the taxes consume 12.5 percent of Bob's revenue.

Bob says farmers in other towns pay taxes totaling about 6 percent of revenues.

The key is to report on numbers the way you were trained to report all stories: by deciding what you think is important, not just what the board of finance says is important.

So, why all the difficulty? In a word, formulas. A mathematical formula can be a shortcut to an answer. It can also cause errors if the reporter uses it incorrectly but doesn't recognize the problem as a problem.

Only by understanding the logic and reasoning behind a formula can you safely use the formula to write a story. Usually, that just means taking a simple, step-by-step approach.

If Mike Wonder edits 145 stories in 87 days, and Patricia McNeely edits 214 stories in 63 days, how many stories is each editing in a week, or a year? To arrive at the formula (see below), think about the first factoid you will need: the number of stories they edit in a day. Then, it's easy to get to the number of stories they edit in a week, or a year.

Or, if reporter Sandy Beach knew the middle school has 1,500 students, and 30 dropped out, how could she figure out how many dropouts there are for every 100 students? (The percentage dropout rate.)

What is a percentage?

A percentage is a rate per 100. The formula for calculating a percentage is: A divided by B, times 100, equals the percentage of A to B.

In the dropout example, that means:

$30/1500 = .02 * 100 = 2$

Therefore, 2 percent of the students, or 2 for every 100, have dropped out.

Now, forget the formula. You must find a way from your starting point, 30, to the missing number. For every 100 students, there are a missing number — X — dropouts.

The problem is, basically, an analogy just like a word analogy: X is to 100 as 30 is to 1,500.

The relationship between any two numbers — the ratio — is found by dividing one into the other. 30/1500 (30 divided into 1500 parts) equals .02, or 1/50.

So, if the ratio of 30 to 1,500 is .02, then the ratio of X to 100 is also .02. You are looking for a number which, when divided by 100, equals .02. You multiply .02 by 100 and get 2.

Calculating rates

The problem is no more complex if the numbers are not round, or if the figure you want is not a rate per 100 (percent). Let's return to Mike Wonder's 145 stories in 87 days. You want to know how many stories he edits in a week. The analogy is, 145 is to 87 as some number, X, is to 7.

First, you get the ratio of 145 to 87:

145/87 = 1.67

So, you know that X/7 = 1.67. Multiply 7 * 1.67 = 11.69.

In plain English: 147 stories in 87 days comes out to 1.67 stories a day. So, in a week, that is just under 12 stories.

The formula is the same as percentages: A divided by B, times C, equals the rate per C.

In the case of McNeely, who edits 214 stories in 63 days:

214/63 = 3.4, multiplied by 20 (working days in a month) = 68.

So, we know that McNeely edits at a rate of 68 stories a month.

BE CAREFUL! In the above examples, Wonder's weekly rate was based on a seven-day week; but McNeely's rate was calculated based on business days. So, they shouldn't be compared unless a new calculation were made. The world of numbers is full of pitfalls of that sort, most having nothing to do with mathematics.

Calculating percentage changes

To figure out how much something has gone up or down in percentage terms, remember that what you are measuring is the difference between two numbers, and that your key figure in that calculation is the first number, the starting point before the rise or fall.

Say you want to determine percentage increase over the past year in the gasoline price, which rose from 78 cents a gallon to $1.19. Your starting point is 78 cents. What you are measuring is the difference, 41 cents. So divide the difference, 41 cents, by the starting point, 78 cents, and you get 0.526, a 52.6 percent increase.

Suppose the price falls from $1.19 back to 78 cents. That is not a 52.6 percent decline because the starting point is different. The starting point would be $1.19 a gallon; you would subtract 78 cents from $1.19 and get a difference of 41 cents. Divide the difference by the starting point and the answer is 0.3445, a 34.5 percent decrease.

When something doubles, it goes up 100 percent (not 200 percent), if it triples, it goes up 200 percent, and so on. Say spending increases from $222 million to $444 million. It is true that $444 million is 200 percent of $222 million, but remember that we're measuring a difference against a starting point, so in this case we'd be dividing $222 million (the difference) by $222 million (the starting point) and end up with a 100 percent increase.

Guidelines and common problems

▶ If your newspaper has a stylebook, there is probably a comprehensive entry on how to describe and write numbers. Look up the numbers entry, and read it.

▶ A well-written number-based story may have — in fact, should have — very few numbers, so as not to confuse the readers and, especially, the editors. Of course, it is just as bad to leave a gap by omitting a key number. With number-based stories, it's very important to step back and take a last, detached look before sending.

▶ It is helpful to spread numbers out within a story, leaving the reader plenty of text to help explain things. You should never have more than three numbers, including dates, in one paragraph.

▶ Percent increases from one year to another cannot be added together to form a total increase.

The teachers signed a contract Tuesday that gives them pay raises totaling 9 percent over three years. A common construct, but it's probably incorrect. If the teachers signed a deal giving them raises of 2 percent, 3 percent and 4 percent in successive years they do not have a raise of 9 percent. It is close, but it is wrong.

Percent increases must be compounded to form a total. Avoid getting into compounded totals simply by saying, The teachers signed a contract Tuesday giving them pay raises of 2 percent, 3 percent and 4 percent in successive years. (Notice that the word percent is repeated after each number, a style point designed for clarity.)

▶ Proposed spending plans are just that, proposals, until they are sealed by the final budget authority (by which time they are outdated, of course). So, when the school superintendent offers a proposed budget, and the board of education adopts it and sends it to the selectmen or the council, it is still a proposed budget. The board has not adopted a budget.

▶ There is a little game that some bureaucrats like to play, in which last year's spending level is compared with this year's approved budget — even though this year's budget has been amended. Always compare actual spending to actual spending. Example: Cashtown's schools were given a $43 million budget on July 1, 1991. Two months later, $1.2 million was added. School officials continued to say their budget was a decrease from the prior year's $44 million spending. In fact, it was a slight increase. The reporter had to recalculate figures on several documents to convey the correct idea.

▶ Decimals should in most cases be rounded off to one digit after the point. It's easier to read The landfill budget would rise from $4.2 million to $6.1 million, than The landfill budget would rise from $4.18 million to $6.13 million. It may be helpful to use more digits if the numbers are close together, or if the story hinges on the fate of a few dollars.

▶ This from the stylebook, directly: Note the difference between percent and percentage point. If unemployment rises from 4 percent to 5.2 percent, it rises 1.2 percentage points — in this case 30 percent. This frequently comes up in polls; some gauge margin of error in percentages, most use percentage points.

▶ There is seldom a good reason to use the word mills in a town budget story, unless you're talking about those old buildings down by the river. The amount of money property owners pay is based on the town's tax rate, which is measured in mills — thousandths of a dollar. And most readers do not know what a mill is. The tax rate (not mill rate) is measured in dollars per thousand: If the council adopts Moonshine's plan, the tax rate would rise by 3.4 percent, to $45.60 for every $1,000 of assessed value.

▶ Remember, once you have a firm grasp of numbers, you decide which figures are most important to the readers. Often, they are not the same figures the officials play up in their debates.

Dan Haar got his start as a photographer for the Milford (Conn.) Citizen. He now covers manufacturing, emerging technology and the state's economy for The Courant. A former president of the Connecticut News Photographers, he has won awards as both a photographer and reporter.

CHAPTER 38

What is computer-assisted reporting?

By Kenton Robinson and John Moran

This chapter will not teach you how to do computer-assisted reporting. No mere chapter can do that. This chapter is intended simply to tell you why computer-assisted reporting must become an integral part of your job.

The sermon

It is curious that even as we stand on the eve of the 21st century, America's newsrooms are still so thick with Luddites.

Luddites? you ask.

At the beginning of the 19th century, the Luddites were the English textile workers who smashed labor-saving machinery because it threatened their jobs. At the end of the 20th century, the Luddites are the reporters who refuse to learn how to use computers to do their jobs.

Imagine where journalism would be today if, when the telephone came into common usage, reporters had refused to learn how to use it. Absurd, you say?

And yet, while business and government have long since moved into the 20th century — putting virtually all their records on computer — most journalists are still using 19th-century reporting techniques.

Most information in the world is now available on computer disk or tape, where it can be retrieved in an instant and manipulated to give new insights into the subject. But most reporters persist in seeking the information on paper, which can take hours to slog through and can tell them nothing more than what they see on the page.

The result: They are missing stories, because they have handicapped themselves. Worse, they have surrendered control of the information to the businessmen and bureaucrats, the experts, officials and authorities.

Every good journalist knows the control of information is power.

And yet, all too often journalists are content to leave that power in the hands of officials. And while they are outraged when those officials try to block their access to information, they are surprisingly docile if only those officials will dole it out to them — preprocessed — on paper.

A couple of stories we've done in the past few years illustrate the risk of giving them that power: If you let them control the information, you can end up publishing lies.

The stories also illustrate that when you wrest control of the information from the experts and bureaucrats, you can expose incompetence and deceit.

First example:

In the past, we, like most newspapers, waited for the Connecticut Department of Environmental Protection to release its annual list of the state's top polluters, those companies that released the largest amounts of toxic chemicals into our air and water. We had no way of knowing whether the list was right or wrong; we simply waited for the list and dutifully reported it to our readers.

In the first year of our computer-assisted reporting project, we didn't wait. We took a laptop computer over to the agency, entered the data the agency had collected from state industries, and analyzed it.

This enabled us to:

▶ Publish the list of the state's top toxic polluters four months ahead of the agency's annual report.

▶ Reveal that the agency had no idea who was or was not complying with the law.

▶ Reveal that because the state never cross-checked its data against federal databases (we did), one of the state's biggest polluters had managed to stay off the state's annual list. (In other words, the lists we had published in previous years had been wrong.)

Then, when the state finally published its "official" list, we used that same database to show that the state was not reporting so-called "off-site" emissions because, state officials said, they weren't sure where the emissions ended up.

We showed that about half of them, several millions pounds of toxic crap, were being dumped in town landfills or otherwise disposed of in state.

Second example:

This also involved using federal data, in this case a magnetic tape containing all prime defense contracts in Connecticut. We dumped this tape into a PC and analyzed it to do a story about the true depth of the state economy's dependency on defense spending.

Our story revealed that the defense monkey on Connecticut's back was much larger than ever reported by the state or federal governments, and that neither state nor federal government officials whose business it was to monitor these things had any idea of its scope.

Furthermore, our own state Department of Economic Development had failed to comply with a state law requiring it to issue a report on the state's defense dependency each year.

When we told this agency's commissioner we were working on this story, he tried to undercut us by whipping out a "report" the Friday before our story ran.

The commissioner's "report" was a confused mass of computer printouts shoved into a shiny blue cover. It failed to include more than $600 million in prime defense contracts.

Back in the old days, before we began doing our own analyses of computer data, we probably would have published the commissioner's report, and no one would have been the wiser.

But those days are gone. (And so, by the way, is that commissioner.)

These are just two examples. The list of the stories you can do with computers is endless. We have used them to reveal violations of contribution limits to political campaigns, to show the vast amount of food, drink and gifts lobbyists pump into our state legislators and to analyze census data to reveal population trends.

We assembled a database of unsolved murders in the Hartford area that pointed to the existence of a serial killer and led to the formation of a special task force to track him down.

We analyzed more than 2.5 million attendance records to show that state employees take incredible amounts of time off from work.

You can even use computers on deadline. One newspaper, doing a deadline story on a fatal school bus accident, simply ran the driver's name through the computerized moter vehicle records it had previously obtained from the state. In minutes, the reporters knew the driver had a history of drunken-driving arrests.

And if you think this is all irrelevant to you because you cover town news, think again.

When a Simsbury businessman and his wife died in a suspicious plane crash late one afternoon, I got a frantic call from a reporter who wanted to know whether there was any way for us to check the courts to verify (or discredit) rumors that he was in financial and marital trouble.

There was. I was able to check civil, family and bankruptcy courts in the state in a matter of minutes (and without leaving the newsroom), because we're plugged into them on-line.

And on dozens of occasions when a local reporter was trying to track down someone who had left town several years before, we have used an on-line service to search him out.

Meanwhile, paper documents are fast becoming an endangered species.

More than 90 percent of all federal documents are already on nine-track tape, and the federal government plans to have eliminated all paper documents by the year 2000. Much of the census information now being released, for example, is available only on tape, disc or CD-ROM. The government will not be publishing it on paper. The state and town governments are following suit.

All of these facts add up to one simple conclusion: If you want to be a reporter, you must use computers. Computers are neither an exotic toy nor a frivolous luxury; they are an essential tool.

What computers can do

Computers do essentially what good investigative reporters have been doing for years: They sift, sort and match information.

Where they differ from investigative reporters is that they can sift, sort and match hundreds, thousands, even millions of pieces of information and they can do it in minutes.

Computers never forget. So, where a reporter may spend hours going through thousands of pages of documents to find a name he is sure he remembers seeing somewhere, a computer can find the name in a nanosecond.

For example, say your governor awards a big contract or important position to somebody you've never heard of before. You wonder whether that person was a big contributor to the governor's campaign. Campaign finance records, which in Connecticut are still on paper only, make the job of answering that question one that could take an hour or more.

But if you've entered the campaign reports into a database, the computer can answer that question in an eye-blink.

It is in this sense that computers are like file cabinets, and databases are like sets of files. Such a set of files is our campaign contributions database, which can supply us with names, addresses, dates and amounts of contributions to our gubernatorial candidates.

For example, we used that database to discover that a man named John Lepore, appointed deputy comptroller after Gov. Lowell P. Weicker Jr.'s election, and every member of his large extended family, gave tens of thousands of dollars to Weicker and Comptroller William E. Curry Jr.

We discovered this when we asked our computer to tell us everyone who maxed out, that is, gave $2,500 to the governor's campaign. We noticed an awful lot of Lepores turning up on that list, so we then asked the computer to give us everyone named Lepore who contributed. All of this took only a couple of minutes.

Then, of course, there was still the reporting to do. We had to make sure these people were related. We also had to determine how old they were. Some very young Lepores were very big contributors. As a result of those stories, John Lepore was investigated and indicted.

But computers can do a lot more than just look things up. In addition to telling you who contributed to your local congressman, for example, with a few simple commands, your computer can tell you who gave him the most money, how much of the money he got was from PACs, what kind of PAC gave the most, and how much of his money came from out of state.

And that's just for starters. Then you can look at how many people, like the Lepores, got around campaign contribution limits by having their wives and children give the maximum amounts, or you can look at how, at contribution time, employees of certain companies that do business with the government exhibit surprising wealth.

These are all things you could do without a computer, if you had nothing else to do for several weeks at a time. With a computer, you can do them in minutes.

In other words, computers allow you to do stories you simply never could do before.

And computers help you to see patterns you never could see before.

As a result, when you get to the interview you can ask questions that are harder hitting and more on point, questions you never could ask before.

In other words, computers can make you smart.

What computers can't do

Computers, on the other hand, are not smart.

Computers are, in fact, exceedingly stupid. It may help you to think of them as electrical file cabinets with primitive saurian brains.

They are, after all, machines, and like all machines they are strictly literal-minded.

This is a great strength, as it means they always do exactly what you tell them to do and they don't make mistakes.

It is also a great weakness. If you make a mistake in programming, the computer won't tell you about it; it will simply run the program.

Because they are not smart, computers do not "think." They will not tell you how to analyze the data; they cannot tell you when the information is flawed.

This last point is particularly important. The first rule of computer-assisted reporting is the same as the first rule of reporting: Verify, verify, verify.

You must cross-check your information both internally and externally, by looking at it in as many ways as possible inside the machine and by comparing it with data from other sources outside the machine.

This is because the source of all computerized data is human, and humans screw up.

Computers will not explain the data; they cannot supply meaning. For that, you still have to interview humans. For example, our computer showed us that the state had failed to include off-site emissions; we had to talk to state officials to find out why.

Gee, you make it all sound so easy

At first, it's a bitch.

At first, you can't find the switch to turn the damn thing on.

To make matters worse, there are people who will tell you, repeatedly, until it makes you crazy, "It's simple." The maddening thing about this is they're right. It is simple, once you understand it.

Brant Houston, former database editor at The Courant, and now managing director of the National Institute for Computer Assisted Reporting, calls this the phenomenon of the dark room: You have to go into a dark room and turn on the lights. The expert says, "It's simple. Just go in and flick the switch." But the room is dark, and you don't know where the switch is. Sure, once you've found it, it's simple. But until then, you're going to be doing a lot of fumbling around.

The truth is computers really are simple. Teaching yourself how to use them is a lot like teaching yourself Russian; you don't really learn the new language until you understand the grammatical rules that govern it. There is one difference: learning to use computers is a lot easier because, unlike Russian, the rules that govern them are at least semilogical.

It is for this reason that your learning curve will be steep. When Brant and I started implementing the computer-assisted reporting project more than four years ago, we knew almost nothing about computers.

Since then, we have learned to make use of more than a dozen different softwares, how to link our machines together, how to do sorts on our mainframe and how to access a variety of on-line databases.

And we've taught a lot of reporters and editors how to make use of computers to do their jobs.

Going on line

If you have never gone on-line, never explored the Internet or the world of bulletin boards, no short essay can explain all you're missing. But here are some examples of the stories others got by finding information on-line — often right on deadline.

▶ Projects reporter Lyn Bixby used the Internet to find sources and reams of information while researching a story about the mysterious Unabomber. Internet e-mail was also the only way he could reach some world-class researchers who had been threatened by the bomber.

▶ Federal court reporter Mark Pazniokas used on-line access to the federal court docket to discover that a tough sentence was being readied for a convicted swindler. The resulting story led the paper the next day.

▶ Data downloaded from an obscure federal bulletin board system led to an exhaustive examination of hospital quality by reporter Bob Capers.

It would be impossible to detail the myriad other ways that knowledge of on-line services has contributed to news stories. For many reporters, a trip to the computer has become standard operating procedure, whether they are investigating an individual, researching a business or preparing background for a feature story.

As more and more of the public goes on-line, it also becomes vastly easier to find people who are otherwise impossible to identify.

Say you're looking for fans of the TV show Mystery Science Theater 2000. Reporter Bill Keveney was. He could have gone down to the mall and started tapping people on the shoulder at random. It would have been a long day. Instead, he tapped into the Internet and came up with half a dozen MST fans — including Connecticut residents going to college in other states. Try locating those people by conventional means.

On-line data gathering is still the newcomer in computer-assisted reporting. But as the tidal wave known as the Internet has made clear, it's here to stay and likely to grow.

The bottom line is that using on-line resources can be a great reporting tool. It's no substitute for all the other qualities that make a good reporter: determination, intelligence, writing skill and street savvy, to name a few. But it can be a helluva big help.

Kenton Robinson began his career as a correspondent in The Courant's Groton bureau. As the paper's projects and investigations editor, he was instrumental in establishing the newspaper's Computer-Assisted Reporting Project. His is now writing a book for Rodale Press in Pennsylvania.

John M. Moran, who began his career as a reporter for the Westfield (Mass.) Evening News, is now a member of the Courant's projects desk covering computers, technology and on-line services. He has received an Associated Press award for business coverage.

CHAPTER 39

Using the Freedom
of Information Laws

By Lyn Bixby

Freedom of information laws are among our most important reporting tools. We can use them to find out how well public officials are doing their jobs, whether they're wasting money, whether they're abusing their positions.

The laws can also be used to dig up information kept by the government on private companies and individuals.

By understanding and using the laws, we learn what information is available, where it is kept and how to get it.

Wherever you work, you can benefit from the federal freedom of information law. Many states also have their own freedom of information laws, which usually apply not only to state agencies but to county and local governments as well.

The federal law

Many reporters are reluctant to use the federal Freedom of Information Act, having heard horror stories about how long it takes and how many exemptions it has. The federal law can be frustrating, but it is also a potentially valuable tool.

Several years ago, I filed a federal FOIA request for the racial composition, by job level, of the work force at Pratt & Whitney, a major Connecticut defense contractor. The company refused to give me the information, but the government had it.

My request languished for weeks before it was denied. I appealed, and about two years later I got a letter asking whether I wanted to continue with the appeal. I checked the "yes" box, sent it back, and I haven't heard anything further.

But some of my other federal requests have been successful. When I wrote a three-day series on fraudulent tactics used by military recruiters, the stories were based largely on information obtained through simultaneous FOIA requests to the four military services. Getting the information on recruiting took about four months, but it was worth it. Fraud had been increasing for 10 years and had reached record levels.

Many federal officials do not like the freedom of information law, grumbling that it is time-consuming and a hindrance to their agencies. But many agencies have FOIA officers who take their jobs seriously. My request for information on recruiting involved a lot of work for the FOIA officers, putting together 10 years worth of statistical information. We got to know each other well.

It is best to do some research before writing FOIA letters. Determine exactly what information you want, find out where it is and craft the letter carefully.

Be very precise. Requests can be denied because they are unclear or too broad. Some agencies require fees for processing FOIA requests, but the federal law provides for fee waivers if the information benefits the public. Ask for a waiver in your letter.

None of the military services ever brought up the issue of charging me for my FOIA request on recruiting, though answering it required a considerable effort on their part.

I had low expectations when I faxed the letters to each of the services because I was asking for potentially damaging information. So I was shocked that most of my questions were answered, even by the Marines. I had done a database search of recruiting stories from around the country and had seen the Marines time and again refuse to release the kind of information they provided in response to our request.

The state laws

If your state has a freedom of information law, get a copy of it, read it, and if you don't understand it, get an editor or a lawyer to explain it to you.

Whenever you want to see a government document, assume it is public. If you are denied access by a public official, make the official provide a reason, citing a specific exemption in the law.

Next, check the official's explanation with an expert. In Connecticut, for example, call a staff lawyer at the state Freedom of Information

Commission, which interprets the law and rules on complaints. If the lawyer agrees with your position, you've gained some serious leverage to get that document without having to go through the process of filing a formal complaint.

Go back to the official who denied your request and try reasoning with the person. Don't threaten. Explain that you have researched the law, which shows the document cannot be withheld. If the answer is still no, go higher. Talk to the official's boss. Go to the top of the organization if necessary.

If the answer is still no, explain that you are going to write a letter, formally requesting the document, and that you expect their response to cite the specific section of the law on which they base their refusal to grant your access.

If the official still won't budge, write your letter, laying out all the steps you have taken to that point. You might want to include a copy of past commission decisions that support your position. Personally deliver the letter. Now the public official knows you are serious.

Under Connecticut law, the official must respond to your letter within four business days. If case law is on your side, you will probably get what you want. But if the written answer is still no, some serious decisions have to be made. It's time to consult editors about your next step.

In states that have freedom of information laws, the types of records that are open to public inspection change constantly as the law is challenged and interpreted. Connecticut's freedom of information law (Section 1-15 through 1-21 of the General Statutes) took effect in 1975 and says essentially that anyone has a right to obtain records and attend meetings of all state and local public agencies with certain limited exceptions.

For example, an agency may meet behind closed doors in an executive session, but only after a two-thirds vote of members present and only for certain reasons, such as debating strategy over a lawsuit. The FOI law also exempts certain kinds of records from public disclosure, such as personal financial data required by a licensing agency.

Whenever a public agency goes into executive session, you should make sure the required vote was taken and a valid reason was given.

Many of the FOI exceptions in the Connecticut law are broad, complex and open to a range of interpretations. One of the most contentious is a provision that exempts certain records of law enforcement agencies from public disclosure.

Exactly which records are exempt is determined in Connecticut by the state Freedom of Information Commission. If your state has a freedom of information law, it probably has a similar agency. The commission's decisions can be, and sometimes are, appealed to the courts.

In some states, including Connecticut, the FOI commission hearing process is designed for plain folks like us. But getting a ruling can take months or — if the decision is appealed — years. So it is much faster and more effective to use your knowledge of the law to persuade public officials to comply with it.

The Courant has a policy that the managing editor must approve the filing of any complaint with the commission. Before you file a complaint, make sure you know the policy at your newspaper. The Courant doesn't file many complaints, but it usually wins. In recent years Courant reporters have filed complaints over illegal meetings and access to a range of different kinds of records.

The commission is most valuable to reporters for its knowledge of the changing FOI landscape. It has a staff of lawyers available to answer questions about what is and is not considered public information. If you have a question about interpretation of the law, the commission's lawyers can frequently provide guidance from memory. But they will also research an issue and send you copies of commission rulings or court decisions.

When you do get what you want and you find yourself in a drab room reading a lot of similar documents, one handy tip is to make a form for recording information.

A number of years ago Courant reporter Larry Williams and I did a project assessing how well the state Commission on Human Rights and Opportunities was doing its primary job of investigating civil rights complaints. We had a lot of anecdotal information, but we needed evidence. Using the FOI law, we reviewed more than 1,000 case files.

To ensure that we got consistent and complete information from each file, Larry suggested creating a form with separate labeled blocks: date filed; investigator; type of complaint; type of resolution; date of resolution; and so on. After reviewing the cases, we were able to quickly divide our forms into separate piles to analyze the cases and select examples to document the agency's dreadful enforcement record.

Now, that same type of form can be created on a laptop computer, and the information can be used to build a database. A computer can analyze information a lot faster than Larry and I did.

Computers and FOI

The newest FOI frontier is electronic information, and The Courant has been in the forefront of the fight to tap into it. The newspaper was the first in the state to get public information on computer discs and tapes and the first to gain online computer access to civil court cases. But reporters and editors had to overcome tremendous resistance by state officials.

Due in part to the efforts, Connecticut's FOI law was amended in 1992 to leave no doubt that public information stored on computers is the same as public information on paper. The landmark computer-access amendment says, "Any public agency which maintains public records in a computer storage system shall provide to any person making a request . . . a copy of any non-exempt data contained in such records, properly identified, on paper, disk, tape or any other electronic storage device or medium requested by the person, if the agency can reasonably make such copy or have such copy made."

Find out the status of the law regarding computerized information in your state.

Obtaining electronic information may require tough negotiating over price. Some public officials have tried to demand outrageous fees for copying computer information to discs and tapes. In most cases the process is simple, quick and inexpensive.

Lyn Bixby began his career as a copy boy/librarian/obituary writer for the Journal Inquirer of Manchester, Conn. He is now on the government desk specializing in gaming coverage and investigative work. His honors include the Unity Award for public affairs reporting from Lincoln University in Missouri.

A sample FOI letter

Here is a copy of the FOIA letter Lyn Bixby sent to the Marine Corps when he was researching his story on fraud in military recruiting:

July 7, 1989

Commandant of the Marine Corps (Code PAM)
Headquarters U.S. Marine Corps
Attn: Major Ron Stokes
Washington, D.C. 20380-0001

Dear Major Stokes,

We talked today by telephone about my request under the Freedom of Information Act for information relating to recruiting activities over the last 10 years, including the 1979 year.

Regarding recruiting violations, I would like annual statistics from 1979 to the present on:

1. The number of allegations of violations, broken down by type of allegation, such as the use of ringers on exams, fake diplomas and transcripts, concealing criminal records. Also of interest to me are any allegations that recruiters sought sexual favors from female applicants or sought kickbacks of enlistment bonuses.

2. The number of investigations conducted.

3. The number of investigations where violations were substantiated and the locations where the violations took place.

4. The number of investigations that led to disciplinary action.

5. The number of recruiters who were disciplined or punished, broken down by the type of action taken, such as whether it was reassignment to other duty, fine, demotion. I would also like to know the locations and how many of these actions were taken as a result of court-martial.

6. The number of recruits discharged as a result of these investigations and the types of discharges they received. I understand there are discharges for defective or erroneous enlistment and fraudulent enlistment.

7. All the above statistics broken out separately for the recruiting district which covers Connecticut. (I would also like to review written reports of any investigations conducted in this recruiting district.)

Regarding quotas and costs, I would like annual statistics from 1979 to the present on:

1. Total annual quotas and numbers of recruits signed up.
2. Total amount of enlistment bonuses paid out.
3. The percentage of recruits with high school diplomas.
4. The percentage of recruits with college degrees.
5. The job categories where the Marine Corps fell short of its quotas, if quotas are set by job category.
6. The ranking of the recruiting districts, based on meeting their quotas.
7. The total number of people on active duty.
8. The total number of recruiters.
9. The total budget for recruiting, broken down into spending categories.
10. The cost per recruit.

Regarding recruiters, I am requesting annual statistics from 1979 to the present on:

1. The percentage of recruiters who volunteered for that duty as compared to the percentage who were assigned to it.
2. The number of recruiters discharged prematurely and the types of discharges involved.
3. The number of recruiters reported AWOL.
4. The number of recruiters reported to have had stress-related problems, such as medical, alcohol, drug or family-related problems with a breakdown by category.
5. The divorce rate for recruiters, if possible, as compared to other job categories.

And regarding recruits, I am requesting annual statistics from 1979 to the present on:

1. The number of recruits discharged prematurely, broken down by those discharged before the end of basic training, those discharged before the end of advanced training, those discharged before the end of their first

year. I would also like to know the types of discharges received.

I understand this is a large request for information, but I expect that most of it has been compiled in some form. Thank you for your cooperation. I look forward to hearing from you.

Sincerely,

Lyn Bixby
Staff Writer
The Hartford Courant
285 Broad St.
Hartford, CT 06115

CHAPTER 40

Who owns what: Using land records

By Lyn Bixby and Thomas D. Williams

A lawyer representing a developer was approached by the chairman of the local planning and zoning commission who wanted a bribe.

The lawyer's client was trying to build a large subdivision. In exchange for a few of the lots, the chairman said, he wouldn't make any trouble for the developer.

Instead of dealing with the chairman, the lawyer decided to investigate him. He reviewed the minutes of past commission meetings, charting all the applications that came before the commission, whether the chairman voted on them and how he voted. Then he moved to the land records, looking for anything on the chairman and his family.

BINGO.

The lawyer found that the chairman's son recently had bought a new house. The developer who built the house had put up two nearly identical houses on either side of it. But the prices paid to the developer were not the same. The chairman's son got his house for $30,000 less than his two new neighbors.

The lawyer continued digging and discovered more evidence in the land records that the commission chairman was corrupt.

The lawyer turned his research over to the police department. At the same time, the lawyer suggested to a reporter that he follow the same trail through the land records. The combination of the local police investigation and the newspaper stories led to a grand jury investigation and eventually to the conviction of the commission chairman and two other town officials.

Not every crooked official is as easy to expose. But the longer you are in this business, the more you will see the arrogance of corruption. When these people get away with something once or twice, they begin to believe they are untouchable. And some of them get sloppy.

Keeping an eye on it

Any public official who deals with land use issues ought to be checked because of the potential for payoffs. Keeping an eye on the land records is one way to try to identify careless corrupt officials. It doesn't take long. If you have free time, even a half-hour, stop by the town clerk's office. Get familiar with the indexes and the records, deeds, mortgages, options to buy, leases, liens, attachments. Don't be reluctant to ask questions. The clerks can be very helpful. They see all the records that pass through their offices and they notice trends or unusual filings and they make some interesting observations.

Last year I was searching records on the state's purchase of a private house as a group home for retarded people. While I was in the assessor's office looking at the card for the property, the assistant assessor asked me if I was an appraiser. No, I said. "Well," she said, "if you were, you'd be the first appraiser to look at it. It's disgusting what the state paid for it."

Land records preserve history. They also show you what is happening in town today. Search the names of prominent people and businesses to find out whether their fortunes are rising or falling.

Land records also provide clues about what may happen in town next week or next month. It is a good practice to visit the clerk's office regularly to review all the filings. Depending on the size of the town and how often you stop by, it can be done in a matter of minutes. A number of options to buy land in the same area could indicate that somebody or some corporation is trying to assemble a large piece of property, possibly for a new industry or a shopping center or a hazardous waste dump.

Most documents filed in the land records are written by lawyers, and some are deliberately difficult to decipher. But the more familiar with them you become, the easier they are to understand. You can learn a surprising amount of information about a business or an individual from the land records.

Getting started

Getting started is easy.

If you are checking the ownership of a specific property, go to the assessor's office and ask for a copy of the assessment card for the property. The card gives the market value as of the last assessment and describes the property in detail. If the owner has a swimming pool or a jacuzzi, it will probably show up. The card has information on present and previous own-ers, showing dates that the property changed hands and giving volume and page numbers, showing where copies of the deeds are stored in the town clerk's office.

If you want to know how many properties an individual or a company owns in town, the assessor can tell you and give you the cards for each one.

In the town clerk's office, copies of land records are stored in books. If you know the volume and page, documents can be found in seconds.

If you want to search the records for a specific name, such as the mayor, the place to start is the grantor and grantee indexes. In a land sale, the grantor is the seller and the grantee is the buyer. The indexes are set up alphabetically for a given period. Start with the most recent grantor and grantee indexes, and you can move back in time from there. Look up the mayor. For every record under the mayor's name, you will find information describing the document as well as the volume and page number where it can be found. It might be a tax lien or an attachment indicating a lawsuit.

Once you have gone through the grantor and grantee indexes and noted all the records you want to see, look them up in the books. It may be easi-est to understand the progression of the documents, particularly mort-gages, if you begin with the oldest one and work up to the most recent.

On deeds, the first and last pages are important. The first page lists the buyer, the seller, and price and the conveyance tax. If the price is listed as "$1 and other considerations" or some other misleading figure, check the conveyance tax. The real price can be calculated from the tax. The last page of a deed lists lawyers and witnesses to the signing. Make a note of the names. They could reveal interesting connections.

On mortgages, pay attention to the amount of money financed compared to the value of the property. Also be sure to check the interest rate. If the amount of money seems high or the interest rates low, or both, that person may be getting favored treatment. It could also signal violations of banking laws. When we were doing stories on bank failures in the late 1980s, we found one bank president who was borrowing heavily from his own bank at interest rates lower than other customers could get — a breach of federal regulations. The information was sitting in the town hall where anyone could find it.

When dealing with deeds and mortgages and liens and such, it is useful to go back to your computer, create a file and build a chronology of events. It is especially helpful when comparing the private dealings of town officials to their public actions. Merge the public and private events together. Connections can emerge by seeing them sequentially.

The corrupt chairman of the planning and zoning commission is one example. Before and after his son got the $30,000 discount on his house, the developer who sold it to him had applications pending before the planning and zoning commission. The chairman voted favorably on them.

Lyn Bixby began his career as a copy boy/librarian/obituary writer for the Journal Inquirer of Manchester, Conn. He is now on the government desk specializing in gaming coverage and investigative work. His honors include the Unity Award for public affairs reporting from Lincoln University in Missouri.

Thomas D. "Dennie" Williams got his start covering local news for The North Kingstown (R.I.) Standard. He is now an investigative and courts reporter for The Courant. His honors include The International Platform Association's Jack Anderson Award for investigative reporting.

CHAPTER 41

Backgrounding an individual

By Lyn Bixby

Fragments of people's lives are recorded in public documents, ranging from the name, address and date of birth on a driver's license to the extensive personal and financial information that sometimes can be found in a lawsuit.

Those pieces of paper are parts of a puzzle that can lead to relatives, neighbors, employees, business associates, government officials, friends, enemies and more pieces of paper.

Most documents are factual accounts of something that happened at a certain time. Few of them explain why something happened the way it did. You need people to bring those pieces of paper to life. Records produce names of potential sources. And records should be used to check information from sources.

Putting yourself in the place of the person you are backgrounding is one way to begin looking for documents and sources. Consider the person's lifestyle, job, friends, hangouts. Find out where that person's name would most likely appear in the public domain.

A developer would leave a trail of paper at the zoning commission and in the building inspector's office listing names of lawyers, engineers, subcontractors.

A fund-raiser should file reports with state charities regulators, and copies of federal tax returns should be available if the person's organization is tax-exempt.

A plumber or electrician should be licensed with the state, might be in a union or could be involved in a government-sponsored program, such as one training apprentices.

A landlord's record can be found in housing and fire code inspection files or in housing court. Maybe the landlord is receiving some kind of government financing, generating still more public records.

Court files can be especially valuable. If the person has ever been convicted of a crime or sued or divorced or declared bankruptcy, the records should be available. Check both state and federal courts. Some lawsuits are settled by agreements of confidentiality, but don't be deterred. A lawyer may talk or refer you to sources who can talk or point you in the direction of other public documents that will shed light on the outcome of a lawsuit.

When you think you've reached the end of the line with little to show, step back, study what you've done, look for oversights and new angles, and you'll find more possibilities.

If you encounter resistance in obtaining documents, you can try using state and federal freedom of information laws. Writing a letter takes only a few minutes. Even if it takes weeks or months to get a document, the wait can be worthwhile.

Be cautious. Don't spread stories when talking to sources or suggest that someone is a crook. If you are in an adversarial situation, the target may use any opening to try to discredit you or block you with a lawsuit. Be sure documents relate to the person you are backgrounding and not to someone with the same name. Check addresses. Note dates and names on documents. Look for inconsistencies and connections. I find it very helpful to build chronologies of events.

Don't assume a document is accurate just because it comes from a court or a government agency. Some are erroneous. Many are incomplete. Make copies of records when you find them, because they can disappear. Also, you may overlook some detail or not appreciate its significance until much later. Have certified copies made if the documents are particularly important or sensitive.

Here is a checklist of steps you can consider when backgrounding someone:

Getting the basics quickly (Name, date of birth, address, occupation, property ownership)

1. The newspaper's news library (often overlooked); computer database searches of other newspapers, magazines and trade publications.
2. Telephone books, street and cross-reference directories.

3. Motor vehicle department licensing and registration records; voter registration records.

4. Assessment records and grantor and grantee indexes of land records for property ownership; mortgage information; business or tax liens; partnership and trade name filings at town hall.

5. Tax collector for delinquencies.

Fleshing out the picture

1. Classmates, teachers, coaches, principals can be located through high school and college yearbooks. Find out what the person did after graduation through alumni associations.

2. Contact neighbors by knocking on doors or by getting phone numbers through street directories. Be careful what you say. Get information. Don't give it.

3. Police, courts. Look for criminal cases, civil lawsuits, divorces. Estate settlements can be found in probate court, housing cases in housing court. If the person ever declared bankruptcy, extensive financial information with names of creditors may be found in U.S. Bankruptcy Court. If the person ever had a serious dispute with the IRS, records in U.S. Tax Court in Washington are public.

4. If the individual was ever investigated, even if no action was taken, look for records; make contact with investigators. They may talk, sometimes out of frustration.

5. Building and zoning permits can be helpful. Was the cost estimated properly, did the application accurately describe what was done, was the approval process expedited, who did the work? Look for political connections.

6. Check family members and relatives and lawyers for political or other connections.

7. Contact state tax officials to check the registration of the individual, or the individual's business. Ask for delinquencies or other enforcement actions.

8. Military service and Veterans Administration records.

9. Firearms permit files. These can contain a surprising amount of information, including arrest records, past addresses and jobs, letters of reference and the reason for wanting a gun permit.

10. Campaign contribution records.

11. Birth, marriage, death certificates.

12. Yacht and airplane registration records from state and federal officials.

13. Uniform Commercial Code filings, usually in the Secretary of the State's Office, contain liens, give information on collateral used to secure loans and occasionally disclose much more. UCC filings are sometimes used by people who want protection on loans and at the same time want to keep the relationships somewhat concealed. A UCC filing is not something most people look for.

Occupational information

1. If a job is licensed by the government, check professional and occupational licensing boards for records of registration and complaints of misconduct. The list is long. Some examples are plumbers, electricians, private investigators, accountants, architects, engineers, real estate agents, stockbrokers, lawyers and doctors.

Industry regulatory agencies should also be contacted. If you don't know whether an occupation is licensed or regulated, find out. These records can provide valuable information.

2. If the person operates a business, check corporation, partnership and trade name records for registration and annual filings on officers and ownership. Trade name and some partnership filings can be found in town halls. Depending on the type of partnership, records may also be found at the secretary of the state's office, which is responsible for corporation filings.

Also check the Better Business Bureau and consumer protection officials. If the business is regulated by the state, such as a nursing home, look over regulatory records.

3. If the business is tax-exempt, check state charity officials for registration information and financial disclosure. Contact the IRS for copies of 990 tax returns — public for tax-exempt organizations. Check the state agency first to find out if copies of 990s are on file there. It will save a lot of time.

4. If the person does business with the government (consulting, providing supplies, leasing buildings, obtaining government guarantees for financing), ask the agency involved for all pertinent records. Look for political connections.

5. For lawyers, get lists of their clients from a court computer. Check the

grievance committee for complaints and disciplinary action.

6. Records of professional associations should be checked to determine membership and find business associates and sources.

7. Talk to people in the same profession or business. Many of them know what the competition is doing.

8. Co-workers may be contacted through labor unions. Another possibility is the state unemployment office, where documents are filed by company name. If the company fought payment of benefits to workers and hearings were held, records should be available listing names and other information.

For public employees and officials

1. Financial disclosure reports with ethics officials.

2. Telephone, expense and travel records on file at the agency he or she works for.

3. Personnel records.

4. Grievance records.

If the individual is elusive (Changing business names or moving out of town):

1. Check postal officials for changes of address or changing company names on post office boxes. If a box is used for business purposes, the information is public.

2. Check with the telephone company. Its records can tell you if someone changed telephone numbers or if an old number has been switched to a new location.

3. Talk to landlords. They may allow you to see rental applications and lists of references.

The tangled story of an elusive Hartford attorney shows the value of pursuing the paper trail.

I had just started working on a project on bankruptcy when I found out that the attorney had been removed from his job as a trustee appointed by the government to convert the assets of bankrupt businesses and people into cash to pay off creditors. The U.S. Department of Justice had discovered he was taking money from some of his cases to pay himself without court approval.

That much was laid out in a written motion on file in Bankruptcy Court in one of the attorney's many cases. The motion also said $8,400 was missing from one of the attorney's cases.

But that was all I could get out of the Justice Department, which was supposed to have been supervising the attorney's work as a trustee. Nobody in Justice would talk about the matter on or off the record. Nor would court officials. And we had nothing in our clip files on him.

Who was he and what had he been doing?

When I first heard about the attorney, I had already contacted congressional committees and obtained two federal reports that criticized the Justice Department's supervision of private bankruptcy trustees, warning that the system was vulnerable to fraud.

I had also obtained Bankruptcy Court computer records of all fees paid to lawyers and accountants and others during the previous two years in Connecticut. The computer information included the names of cases from which the attorney had been paid during that time. We also had an on-line computer link with the Bankruptcy Court for case information.

I used the computers to get names of debtors and creditors and lawyers involved in some of the cases in which this attorney served as a trustee. I got names of lawyers who had worked for this attorney from the Martindale-Hubbell Law Directory.

I checked the Statewide Grievance Committee and found that four grievances had been filed against the attorney in the past few years. Then I got on the phone.

Almost every call produced names of more people to call and more documents to check. A tantalizing picture started taking shape of a burned-out attorney who didn't allow his associate lawyers or staff to get involved in the money aspects of his cases.

But nobody I interviewed had heard anything from the Justice Department or the FBI about how much money was missing from the attorney's cases. I went to the court and looked through some of his case files.

Lawyers representing a bank had recently filed appearances in a number of cases. The bank's lawyers, it turned out, had vague indications from the FBI that the situation involving the attorney was serious. The bank's lawyers had obtained a list from the Justice Department of all the cases the attorney had when he was removed as a trustee. There were 250 of them.

Using our computer link, I checked recent docket entries for every case and found one that indicated missing money. Sure enough, documents filed recently in the court showed that at least $150,000 was missing from the estate's bank account. Lawyers in the case were willing to talk on background. A week earlier they had been told by Justice Department officials that as much as $1 million was missing overall from the attorney's cases. Other sources confirmed the figure.

Though the Justice Department didn't want it out, the story had taken shape, a profile of an attorney that raised serious questions about the government's supervision of private bankruptcy trustees. We had only a few people talking on the record, but we had documents to back up.

During the early stages of reporting the story, I took the basic step of getting information from the attorney's driver's license, finding out that he had moved 10 months earlier from Meriden to Windsor in Connecticut. That little piece of information served me well during later reporting.

One of the lawyers I interviewed wanted to serve the attorney with notice of an eviction proceeding, but did not know where he went after he left Meriden. I helped him out with an address (a matter of public record, after all), and he helped me out in several important ways on the story.

Though I had cruised by the attorney's house to see if he was still living there, I didn't try to interview him until the reporting was complete. I wanted to be well prepared with solid information before I approached him. When I did knock on his door, he answered, but wouldn't talk.

However, in many cases when backgrounding someone, it may be worthwhile to try for an interview early on. Don't assume the person won't talk to you, even if an investigation is under way. You may be surprised. You can try to put the person on the record early and go back later as you develop more information. You may discover inconsistencies.

Lyn Bixby began his career as a copy boy/librarian/obituary writer for the Journal Inquirer of Manchester, Conn. He is now on the government desk specializing in gaming coverage and investigative work. His honors include the Unity Award for public affairs reporting from Lincoln University in Missouri.

CHAPTER 42

AtenSHUN! Getting information from the military

By Lyn Bixby and Thomas D. Williams

A local Army Reserve unit is called to active duty to help fight a war in the Middle East.

A political candidate's claims of an exemplary military record are disputed.

A Vietnam veteran commits suicide after being turned away from a Veterans Administration hospital.

The submarine fleet that has called the local Navy base home for decades looks like it will be redeployed elsewhere.

An engine made by a local company is blamed for the crash of an Air Force jet fighter.

A former high school football star, now in the Marines, is seriously injured during war games, possibly because of defective equipment.

Reporting any of those stories requires that you deal with the military, which can be intimidating for someone who has never been in uniform and doesn't know the difference between a sergeant and a captain.

Don't let it bother you. You'll learn.

Get ready to talk with public affairs officers who call you "ma'am" and "sir" and who don't deviate from the orders they get from their superiors because they don't want to get court-martialed. If they are willing to go off the record, you can bet it's on instructions from above.

The military can be frustrating because it is highly ordered and compartmentalized, and you sometimes think you're not getting anywhere. But the military can also be good at efficiently responding to concise, concrete questions. Be patient, but persistent. Think "orders" and "chain of command."

When a public affairs officer gives you a statement, find out what military divisions are involved and where the divisions are located. That way you can contact the divisions directly.

If a public affairs officer sends you to another public affairs officer at a different military division, find out where you are being sent. There are lots of divisions within the military. For example, if you are looking into something involving Army weapons and ammunition, the information you are seeking may be at any one of a number of locations: the Army Material and Munitions Command in Rock Island, Ill.; the Army Research and Development Command in Dover, N.J.; or the Army Engineering Corps and the Army Explosive Ordinance Corps, which have offices in Washington D.C.

Sometimes when looking for information from the military, you may be asked to file a federal Freedom of Information Act request. Don't fight it. Fax it. The military services have people assigned to process FOI requests, and they generally do a good job. Phone back regularly to check on the progress of your request and to remind them that you are serious about it.

One place where you will almost surely have to file a written request to get anything beyond a few basic facts is the National Personnel Records Center in St. Louis (314-263-3901), a division of the National Archives and Records Administration.

The center, which is divided into civilian and military sections, is the custodian of veterans' service records. But its officials are stingy about what they give out. Unless you have permission from the person you are researching, you will probably not get much beyond dates of service, duty assignments and decorations.

All requests for information to the center should cite the federal Freedom of Information Act and should ideally contain the following information: the veteran's full name, correctly spelled; his or her Social Security number, date of birth or both; approximate dates of military service; and branch of service.

Dealing with the records center is pretty straightforward. Digging up information on active military issues is not so easy.

For a reporter trying to navigate the military maze, the top of the chain of command is the Pentagon press office: 703-697-5131 for military matters; 703-695-0192 for Department of Defense matters.

If you need information from one of the four major services — the Army, Navy, Air Force or Marines — you can start at the Pentagon and work your way down if you don't know exactly where you want to go.

Public affairs officers are very good at issuing prepared statements or directing you to more public affairs officers. But they are not very good at putting reporters in touch with people directly involved in an issue. In most cases you are going to have to do that yourself.

If you have names of officers or servicemen you want to reach, you can call them directly. If you have a name, but don't know where that person is stationed, a public affairs officer can find out and provide an address.

You may be able to find the kind of people you need through retired officers' organizations and through database searches. When you are running a search for published material, make sure you check military specialty magazines and newspapers. Among the best publications for in-depth stories are the Army Times and the Armed Forces Journal International.

Remember that the armed services are answerable to Congress through a number of committees, most prominently the armed services and appropriations committees. Congressional committee staffers never talk for attribution, but they can help by directing you to published information or leading you to potential sources.

The investigative arm of Congress, the General Accounting Office, produces dozens of reports every year on military matters that can be an invaluable source of information for a story. If you're writing about a military issue, chances are the GAO has produced a report on it. Another congressional arm that produces timely, informative reports, some involving military matters, is the Office of Technology Assessment.

Private watchdog organizations are also good sources on military and defense issues. There are many watchdog groups, most based in and around Washington. A few are the Government Accountability Project, the Defense Budget Project and Greenpeace International. Get in touch with one, and it will lead you to more.

Lyn Bixby began his career as a copy boy/librarian/obituary writer for the Journal Inquirer of Manchester, Conn. He is now on the government desk specializing in gaming coverage and investigative work. His honors include the Unity Award for public affairs reporting from Lincoln University in Missouri.

Thomas D. "Dennie" Williams got his start covering local news for The North Kingstown (R.I.) Standard. He is now general assignment and courts reporter for The Courant. His honors include The International Platform Association's Jack Anderson Award for investigative reporting.

CHAPTER 43

Sniffing out corruption, conflict of interest, mismanagement

By Thomas D. Williams

Here are some typical ways in which corruption and conflict of interest seep into municipal government, and some tips on how to sniff it out.

These cases, based on actual events in Connecticut cities and towns, should alert you to what to look for to keep your town honest. Looking out for the public interest is one of the most important jobs you have as a reporter.

Alarming alarms

The police department makes up confidential daily burglary reports so it can see patterns of burglary in the city and assign officers to high-crime districts.

A police captain, who has access to the information, operates a burglar alarm company on the side. Is he using the confidential burglary reports to locate potential customers?

How to proceed

Start with police burglary records, including the daily burglary reports. Double-check their accuracy with the police dispatcher. Check the state police, the local police department, the Better Business Bureau and government consumer protection agencies for data on the captain's business. Then call as many burglary victims as possible to ask them if the captain or someone representing his company has solicited them. It may show a pattern. They may even tell you someone representing the captain showed them the confidential reports to convince them that their neighborhood is at high risk for burglary.

Interview police officers and burglary victims to see what the captain does in both his off-duty and on-duty jobs. (Is he working at his private business on city time?) Finally, interview the captain and then check with his supervisor or the police chief for reaction.

A vote for self-interest

A developer wants to create a new condo or office units in town.

Before he can begin construction, the developer must get an easement across town land to allow runoff to flow from the development into the storm sewer. Town regulations require that an easement be voted on by the board of selectmen.

One of the selectmen has a real estate business. He votes to approve the easement.

Might the selectman have a conflict of interest?

How to proceed

You should be wary of a selectman/Realtor voting on matters involving real estate. You check him out with a variety of sources including the state real estate commission, which licenses Realtors and has files on them; rival Realtors in town; records of the planning and zoning commission; the zoning enforcement officer; other selectmen; and developers. In this case, one of them tells you the selectman is involved in selling property owned by the developer.

The selectman has a definite conflict of interest. Check your town's ethics code (as you would in all of the cases cited below as well) to determine if it is a legal violation. Even if it slips through a legal loophole, you can still write about it; and with a little checking, you could point out that it would be illegal in many neighboring communities.

Land-use abuse

A school board member, who also is a member of the planning and zoning board, buys a piece of land across from the school. Then he calls for a confidential meeting of the school board and offers to lease his property to the school. The board rejects the offer. Subsequently, the official casts a vote on the planning and zoning board to approve "office zone" as a new category of land use in the town. Then he applies to have his property across from the school rezoned for office use.

You should spot three ethical violations. The official's call for a confidential meeting of the school board; his offer to lease the property to the board he serves on; and his application for a change of zone after voting on the planning board for the new office zone.

How to proceed

Check records in the town clerk's office to determine when the official bought the property and what he paid for it. Verify the mortgage. Get copies of the planning and zoning minutes for the office-zone approval and for the official's zone change application. Also ask for the minutes from the closed school committee meeting. If you are denied them, file a Freedom of Information request. Interview planning and zoning board and school board members as well as the zoning enforcement officer. Get land-use experts or Realtors to estimate how much the value of the official's land was increased by the rezoning. Check the town ethics code, if any; finally, interview the official himself.

Engineering a deal

A developer is intent on creating a huge, single-family housing project around a man-made pond. A controversy develops over the proximity of the pond to the new septic system.

The town sanitarian is an engineer who is also in business as part of an engineering partnership.

Without the sanitarian's knowledge, one of her partners is retained by the developer to give him advice on how to engineer the pond so it will not be affected by the septic system.

The partner gives an expert opinion that despite the clay-like nature of the soil, the project will not need an elaborate pipe septic drain-away system. The developer presents the plan to the town.

The sanitarian, who has since learned of her partner's involvement with the project, continues her oversight, giving the town planning and zoning board advice on the septic engineering plan presented by the developer.

This is a problem for the sanitarian because profits of the partnership are shared by the partners. Thus, the sanitarian stands to gain financially from her own supervision of a large development project in town, and her decision to minimize the drainage system can save the developer money and hurt the town in the event of flooding.

How to proceed

This is the kind of conflict of interest that insiders talk about, and, if you are paying attention, you will hear about.

And if you really know your town, you may already know that the sanitarian and the engineer for the developer are partners.

Check ownership of the land and its initial sale price to the seller as well as to the developer; check town planning and zoning records. You need to know the size of the deal to see how big the story is, and you want to find out if the sanitarian favored the developer in any way. Under many town ethics codes, even if the sanitarian did not favor the developer, she should have disclosed her partnership with the engineer working for the developer.

Interview town health officials, planning officials and the sanitarian's engineering partner before final interviews with the sanitarian and the developer. Here you want to talk to first-hand sources to see what they think about the sanitarian's judgments on the project in light of her partnership with the developer's engineering firm. And, you need to interview the sanitarian and her partner at length to see what their perspectives are on the conflict of interest.

Self-serving opinion

A developer wants to build a nursing home on a site that drains into a wetland. On the other side of town, another developer wants to put a carwash not far from a pristine stream loaded with stocked trout.

The town attorney, who has a private practice in another town where she represents developers and vendors before town land-use boards, is asked to interpret whether wetland regulations apply to the carwash project. The attorney issues a written opinion that the wetland regulations do not prevent the carwash from being developed.

As it turns out, these regulations are the same ones that are at issue regarding the proposed nursing home.

An environmental group gets wind of the opinion and protests it to the board of selectmen. The group says the lawyers for the nursing home now plan to use the town attorney's opinion to support its development across town.

How to proceed

Find out the names of all of the private clients the town attorney has represented in court. In some communities, checking this means a lot of work slogging through court files. But in many places, it is easy because records are computerized. In Connecticut, for example, the information is available from the state judicial department's computer in Hartford for a $25 fee.

In this case, you find that the town attorney has done work for the nursing home developer in other towns. That means that her opinion on wetland regulation represents a conflict of interest. (Check further and you may find the attorney has also represented other vendors and developers who do business in your town, suggesting a bigger story.)

Read the town's ethics code, if any, the state lawyers' ethics code and American Bar Association ethics code for lawyers.

Get the applicable wetland regulations. Interview officials at the state Department of Environmental Protection and town planning and zoning commission members. Finally, interview the town attorney, a representative of the nursing home and any developers and vendors involved.

A judge's judgment

The judge not only rules on cases but administers the court, supervising both the chief clerk and the sheriff's office.

The chief clerk hires the judge's daughter as a secretary to an assistant clerk. The sheriff appoints the judge's son as a deputy.

Is it a story? Definitely! Even though the clerk and the sheriff did the hiring, the judge supervises them. He may have influenced their decisions or they may have been currying favor by hiring his children. So, it's either nepotism or favoritism.

How to proceed

Use state judicial and state auditors' records to confirm the names and salaries of the judge's relatives employed in court. Check the Judicial Canons of Ethics for what the judge has violated. Interview clerks, sheriffs and judges supervising the judge in question. Finally, confront the judge.

Other things to watch for

Here are some other commonplace forms of corruption, conflict of interest and mismanagement.

▶ The fire chief or fire marshal or building inspector overlooks safety or fire code violations for his friends, relatives or business partners. Or the chief ignores fire code violations for other agencies of government, mainly because of political or governmental pressure.

▶ The building inspector or his aides have their own construction or development business in town.

▶ Officials use municipal vehicles for their personal trips, or frequently leave work early to work other jobs or play golf.

▶ A public works director uses town equipment for private work or sells town-owned sand, gravel or road salt and pockets the proceeds.

▶ Check the tax rolls once a year for the biggest delinquents; some of them may be officials.

▶ Find out where the town has invested its money. Is it secure? Town checking accounts should be kept at a minimum because town money is best held in interest-bearing accounts.

▶ Does the local agency that regulates wetlands ignore its provisions to the benefit of developers?

▶ Check the file of your community's state legislator at the state ethics commission. The files contain financial statements filed by the legislator. They might show or hint that lawyers or businesses lobbying for certain legislation are also doing business with your legislator.

▶ Bidding specifications can be written to favor certain town contractors. Check to see if the same contractors are always getting the bids. If they are, look at the specifications and talk to losing bidders to find out why this happens.

▶ Town insurance contracts are frequently in the hands of one agent and one insurance company. Is the agent connected politically or personally to officials who vote on the contract? Do other agents and insurers offer the same coverage for less money?

▶ Check political contributions at least annually so you know who is bankrolling your local politicians. Do these major contributors get favored treatment in town?

▶ Where are the municipal pension funds invested. In the usual places such as solid mutual funds, or in unusual places such as local real estate partnerships. If the latter, who controls these businesses and what is their relationship to the people who control the pension money?

▶ Nepotism. Take a check around city hall once in a while to see if supervisors are hiring friends and relatives.

A word of caution

In pursuing any story, be careful not to repeat unsubstantiated rumor in your questioning. Such information has a way of getting around town quickly and could come back to haunt you.

It is absolutely necessary in any story, but especially in accusatory stories, to double-check every single fact, to make sure you contact all sides of a dispute and to treat everyone involved fairly.

When the going gets tougher

The cases cited above are common and not overly difficult to report. If you run into more complex corruption, there are places you can go for help.

First, turn to the reporters and editors on your newspaper who are most experienced in investigative reporting.

You should also contact Investigative Reporters and Editors (IRE), 100 Neff Hall, School of Journalism, University of Missouri, Columbia, MO 65211. The telephone number is 314-882-2042.

This organization, which you can join for a reasonable fee, has a library of investigative stories written or broadcast around the country. Perhaps someone has already done a story like the one you are working on. IRE will send it to you, and then you can contact the reporters and editors who did the work for their advice.

A list of all of the stories in the IRE's Journalists' Morgue is available from the organization for a small fee.

IRE also produces The Reporter's Handbook, written by experienced reporters around the country. The handbook goes into more detail than there is room for here on methods of investigating private, public and business corruption.

Thomas D. "Dennie" Williams began his career covering local news for The North Kingstown (R.I.) Standard. He is now an investigative and courts reporter for The Courant. His honors include the International Platform Association's Jack Anderson Award for investigative reporting.

CHAPTER 44

Working with your editor

By Steve Grant and Bob Capers

Communication with your editor is important at every stage of the reporting and writing process.

This means informing your editor about what you know, how you're thinking of approaching a story, and when it will be done.

It also involves listening to the editor's thoughts on all these issues and more.

This can't be stressed enough; taking the time to discuss a story is always worthwhile. Five minutes now can save hours of re-reporting, reorganizing and/or rewriting later.

Disagreements between editors and reporters almost always result from a failure to communicate. Disagreements mean the editor and reporter have a different idea of what the story is, how it should be approached, how long it should be or when it should be done.

When communication breaks down, the relationship between writers and editors becomes combative. When it works, the relationship is collaborative. As the person with most of the information about a story, it is incumbent upon the reporter to keep the editor informed every step of the way.

Editors are busy. Do what you can to help them. It's your job as a reporter to get the facts right and spell words correctly. That shouldn't have to be an editor's job.

And keep in mind that the reporter who never needs editing hasn't been born yet. Editors can improve your stories, and they will do that if you give them a chance. That is not to say every suggestion from every editor is on the mark, but they almost invariably have a point. Maybe the editor's idea can be improved if the two of you talk about it.

A colleague of ours says: "Some editors are like land mines: Step near them with an idea they don't like or a story that is complicated and takes you away from daily news hits and they explode with contrary opinions. 'Forget it! It will take far too long!' Or, 'That's too complicated. No one will ever understand it. Why is it important, anyway?' "

Yes, that can happen. But the greater likelihood is that the editor wants the complicated, time-consuming-but-important story as much as you do and will work with you to help you find the time to do it.

Discussions about a story should begin before the reporting. A conference, even a brief one, is useful whether the story is breaking news or a feature.

Reporter and editor need to discuss what the story is. Is it breaking news or a feature? Is it a daily story or something that may take a few days to finish? Is a photographer needed?

The editor and reporter both need to know what the other expects.

They should confer again before the writing begins. Has reporting turned up information that changed the original idea? Did the news break so long ago that a second-day lead is needed? How will the story be organized? What will the lead be? Is it a straight news story, or is an analysis needed? Is more reporting needed? When will the story be done? How long will it be?

These discussions can save enormous amounts of aggravation later. Your editor is not going to be happy with you if he's expecting a 15-inch analysis at 5 p.m. and you give him a 30-inch straight news story at 7. And you aren't going to be happy when he tells you to rewrite it. You'll like it even less if he rewrites it himself.

Reporters also should touch base with editors on procedural questions — questions, for instance, about what kind of agreements can be made with anonymous sources — or questions about libel law.

All relationships between editors and reporters are different. Some reporters are testy about the slightest changes in their copy, however much it needs changing. Some reporters are mellow about editing. The same is true about editors. Some are fussier or harder to work with than others.

But as a rule, when an editor says you have written a clunky lead, it's a clunky lead. And when an editor tells you he can't understand one of your sentences, it isn' clear.

Remember this: If an editor doesn't understand a sentence or a paragraph, there undoubtedly will be readers who won't understand it either. It doesn't matter if you, the writer, like it.

Reporters also should be enterprising in suggesting story ideas. On any beat, there are undoubtedly a thousand stories that could be done at any time. The smart reporter combs the beat and selects the best of them.

The reporter who does not is forcing his editor to do the selecting for him.

Keep in mind, though, that an editor who is one step back from the beat sometimes has valuable perspective and may see an important story the reporter doesn't.

Bob Capers began his career by doing everything from reporting to paste-up for a small Massachusetts weekly. Now he is a full-time botany student at the University of Connecticut. As a general assignment reporter for The Courant, he won the Pulitzer Prize for explanatory journalism.

Steve Grant began as a local reporter for the Journal Inquirer of Manchester, Conn. A former politics editor for The Courant, he now writes about nature for the paper. His first-person accounts of long-distance hiking and canoeing have revived the 19th-century American tradition of adventure journalism.

CHAPTER 45

Dealing with the copy desk

By Harvey "Flash" Remer

This isn't the lead I had on this piece.

I wrote a crisp, creative and daring lead. I pushed the envelope. This lead is limp, predictable and safe.

Every time I try to do something different, the copy desk shoots it down. Why? Why can't they give me the benefit of the doubt?

Of course that sounds familiar. You're a reporter, and that makes you a writer, and that makes you someone who has an editor, and that makes you someone who has known the desire to kill and the relief of having your butt saved.

You want the benefit of the doubt. You want respect. You want copy editors to have so much confidence in you as a reporter and writer that they never touch your work. Know what copy editors want? They want you to be so thorough and accurate that they never have to.

Enough with the absolutes. Your copy is going to get changed. It's going to need changing sometimes. Some of the changes are going to tick you off. By sharpening your reporting and writing skills, you can head off a lot of those changes and earn the benefit of the doubt.

Copy editors aren't there to do your work; they're there to check it, polish it a little. But it's your story, and you're supposed to care about even the smallest detail. If copy editors see patterns of mistakes or inconsistencies in your work, why should they trust you? Why should they believe that you've been any more careful about anything else?

When you leave something wrong in your story, you force a copy editor into action. The more you have wrong, the more the copy editor has to change. When there's a lot wrong, two pretty lousy things can happen:

1. The copy editor takes ownership of the story. Why? Human nature. When copy editors have to make a lot of changes, they get angry at, and

frustrated with, you and your copy. They figure that if they have to make a lot of changes to fix sloppy work, they might as well make a few more changes and substitute a word they like better or recast the sentence that's just a little bit awkward or switch the placement of those two paragraphs. (It was OK the way you had it, but this is just a little better, yeah, might as well do it.) Pretty soon it's not your story anymore. Your voice is gone. You no longer matter.

2. The copy editor stops paying attention to content, meaning and clarity in your story and starts looking only for errors. Copy editors have only so much time for each story, and if they believe they have to use it to track down and fix little problems, they won't have time to catch and fix big ones. I hear you out there now saying, "Well, there won't be any big ones to catch." C'mon. Wanna buy a bridge? Everybody makes a big mistake once in a while. Don't you want a copy editor to have a chance to catch it? The best way to ensure that your major gaffe gets by the copy desk is to keep copy editors busy on all the following "little stuff."

Spelling

Thought you left this one behind in grammar school? Not so. If you don't know how to spell something, look it up. At The Courant, look it up in Webster's New World Dictionary, Third College Edition. Throw away your copy of "Just Sound It Out" and your copy of "Alturnative Inglish Spelings" and your copy of "Let's Be Inconsistent." Use the first spelling listed in Webster's. Don't use variants, such as "grey." If you look up "grey," you won't see a definition there. It's under "gray," so that's the spelling you should use.

Grammar

You hated it in high school, and now it's back to haunt your every sentence. A couple of tips: Grammar books disagree on a lot of things, but not on the basics. Any grammar book can help you, so take your pick. Look at it once in a while. Leave it in the bathroom. Don't try to use it the way you would a dictionary. You can't be looking up every grammatical point or you'll never get the story over.

Write yourself out of grammatical corners. Say you're not sure whether you should use "who" or "whom" in a sentence. You look up the grammar rule, and it says to use "whom." But that sounds awful to you. Pompous and uninviting. So why not rephrase it to make it more conversational?

But maybe you decide the heck with grammar, you're going to leave it "who." Now you've put the copy desk in a corner. If the copy editor has time, she might recast your evil sentence. If not, she will make it "whom," and your story will end up with that cumbersome, egg-headed feel. Fix it yourself.

Usage

Remember that words not only have dictionary meanings but carry tones and shades of meaning the way tourists carry baggage. Make sure the words you use do exactly what you want them to do.

Suppose you are writing about the mayor's trying to persuade someone to do something for him. You might use the word "coax." But you could also use "cajole," or "blandish" or "wheedle." All involve persuasion, yet they differ in important ways. "Coax" suggests gentle persuasion. "Cajole" suggests deceit or false flattery. "Wheedle" suggests artful flattery. And "blandish" suggests clumsy and obvious use of flattery and charm.

You can do this with any set of synonyms. The rarest thing in English is a pair of words that mean exactly the same thing. You should respect words and use them precisely.

Dictionaries can help. Books by wordsmiths can help. An even better idea is to ask another writer or an editor about the word in question.

Why not ask a copy editor? It's a good way to introduce yourself, make a friend and show that you are interested in using words correctly. A good copy editor will be eager to help and can't help but be impressed by the effort you've taken.

What about new words? Why can't a writer use words that everyone is saying on the street? Why can't writers just make up words to get across their ideas?

Sometimes, they can. That's one way language and usage change. But you have to decide whether you really need that new word or need to make one up. If there is an established word that would be perfect for you, and you use something else, a good copy editor will rein you in a bit. But if your single word can't be replaced by any other, you have a good case for using it. Will it get by the copy desk? Maybe.

Using "contact" as a verb comes to mind. If the town clerk wants people to contact her for information, they might call her, send a letter or drop by town hall. If she specifies that she wants people to use the telephone, then write "call" rather than "contact." Some copy editors will change "contact" to "get in touch with." But that's four words. Contact has clearly entered the language as a verb. It is spoken and written all the time. But that doesn't mean the copy desk has to accept it. Many English teachers consider this usage a barbarism.

If you have questions, don't be afraid to talk to the people on the copy desk who are in charge of making style and changing it. They care about the language as much as you do.

Style

Many newspapers, such as The Courant, have their own stylebooks (in book form or on computer). Others use standard references such as the Associated Press Stylebook. Whatever stylebook your newspaper uses, get a copy. Use it.

No one expects you to know style the way a copy editor must, but you should know some basic style rules. At The Courant, for example:

1. Use numerals for ages of living things: She is 3 months old, the dog is 2 years old, a 3-month-old baby (notice the hyphens).

2. Spell out numbers under 10 for other measurements of time: six months ago, three years from now, it took five weeks.

3. Use numerals in other cases for dimensions, weights and measures: 2 miles long, 5 feet high, 3 ounces of heroin, 6 cups of flour.

4. For addresses, use the abbreviations St., Ave. and Blvd. only when the address contains the street number: 6 Main St., 9 Columbus Blvd. But: He lives on Main Street. She works on Capitol Avenue.

5. The names of town or city boards and commissions are lowercase unless the name of the town or city is used: the board of selectmen, the Coventry Board of Selectmen; the board of education, the Hartford Board of Education.

If you at least know your newspaper's style for these few things, you're on your way to making lots of friends on the copy desk. But what's most important for you to know is that style matters. It is a manifestation of the newspaper's insistence on consistency. That's how readers know the paper cares about details.

Style is there to make your job easier, but you have to learn to make it work for you. You have the choice. You can, and should, take command of the basics. You can, and probably should, leave the tortuous style deci-sions, such as which courtesy title to use in a minister's obituary, to the copy desk.

Here are some other ways you can take command of your stories.

Facts

Double-check all numbers and all of your math. If you're not sure how to figure percentages, ask someone.

When you come across something with an unusual spelling, or some-thing that is so unusual or incredible that a copy editor is likely to question it, write "cq" (in notes mode at The Courant) next to the item after you have double-checked it. Use "cq" to show that you've double-checked math. And whether spellings are unusual or not, double-check names of people, places and things. Spell them the same way all the way through. Don't think that you can put a "cq" on the first reference and then use two or three variations the rest of the way. That's sloppy, and the copy desk will have to call you. For people, are all the first references where they ought to be? Have you told the readers who they are?

Copy editors are valued for their doubting minds. They read the story from a reader's point of view. Have you answered the questions a reader is likely to have based on what you have written? If not, you have more work to do. If you can't or won't do that work, don't be surprised if the copy desk wakes you that night.

Be the double-checker

Before you can say you're finished writing, check that lead one more time. Make sure it's the best it can be. Is the story structured logically? Do the transitions work? If you haven't given these points the consideration they deserve, you shouldn't be satisfied with your story. No one else, including the copy desk, will be.

Rebellion

You want to push that envelope. You want to go where no writer has gone before. So remember, when you were little, you crawled before you walked. When you have mastered the art of clear writing without flaws in grammar, usage, style and spelling, then you can throw away the rule book. Meanwhile, learn the rules, and they shall set you free.

Harvey "Flash" Remer's first newspaper job was covering the little towns of Willington and Union, Conn., for The Courant. He is now a copy chief for The Courant. A decade ago, he switched careers from library work to newspapers and is glad he did.

ABOUT THE EDITORS

Bruce DeSilva's first job in journalism was covering Warren, R.I., for The Providence Journal. He came to The Courant in 1983 as Boston bureau chief. In 1988 he became the paper's writing coach and frequently served as a writing consultant to other newspapers. He is now enterprise editor for the Associated Press. His honors include The New England Master Reporter Award, given in recognition of excellence in a body of work over a career.

John Mura began at The Courant as a community news reporter. He has been the paper's transportation reporter, special projects editor and eastern Connecticut bureau chief. He now is assistant managing editor/content at The News Journal in Wilmington, Del.

ABOUT THE COURANT

The Courant is the oldest continuously published newspaper in America. It was started as a weekly in 1764 by a printer named Thomas Green, who at first helped keep it afloat by selling clothing, stationery, hardware and spices out of a store in front of the newspaper's office. He sold the newspaper to his assistant, Ebenezer Watson, who ran it until he died of smallpox in 1777. Watson's widow, Hannah, inherited the paper, thus establishing her legend as one of America's first woman publishers. During the Revolutionary War, The Courant had circulation as large as any paper in the colonies and was an influential backer of the rebel cause. The Courant was considered so important to the war effort that, when its paper mill was burned down — perhaps by Tories — the Connecticut legislature authorized a lottery to raise money to build a new one. In the meantime, The Courant printed a few issues on wrapping paper.

The Courant's owners also ran a thriving book publishing business, printing Noah Webster's famous "Blue-Backed Speller" in 1783. In the mid-1800s, when the country was dividing over the issue of slavery, The Courant was inspired by a visit Abraham Lincoln made to Hartford. The paper became a leading supporter of the new Republican Party and Lincoln's presidential campaign.

Soon after the Civil War, a series of business deals and deaths left The Courant in the control of two men who would become its most illustrious editors. One was Joseph Hawley, a war hero who served four terms as Connecticut's U.S. senator. The other was Charles Dudley Warner, whose collected essays, first published in The Courant, found a national audience. At one point, Warner was regarded as a greater writer than his friend and collaborator, Mark Twain. The two wrote "The Gilded Age" together and lived near each other in Hartford's famed Nook Farm. Both Warner and Hawley still held ownership in The Courant when they died in the first decade of the 20th century.

The Courant has been a daily paper since 1837, but kept publishing a weekly edition until after it started a Sunday paper in 1913.

In 1979 The Courant was purchased by Times Mirror, a media and information company based in Los Angeles. The Courant won the 1992 Pulitzer Prize for explanatory journalism for a series of stories on the flaws that plagued the Hubble space telescope. The Courant has a circulation of more than 200,000 daily and 300,000 Sunday.

To purchase additional copies of this book

Fill out a copy of the coupon below and send it to:

The Company Store
The Hartford Courant
285 Broad St.
Hartford, CT 06115
(860) 241-3912

The price is $13.95 plus $4 shipping and handling per copy. Credit card orders may be faxed to (860) 520-3000.

FIRST EDITION

The Straight Scoop

An Expert Guide to Great Community Journalism

By the staff of
The Hartford Courant

O R D E R   F O R M

Name _____ Number of copies _____

Organization _____

Street _____

City _____ State _____ Zip Code _____

Daytime telephone (Required for credit card orders) _____

Credit card (circle one)   VISA   MasterCard   American Express

Card number _____

Expiration date _____